CONUNDRUM

CONUNDRUM

Why Every Government Gets Things Wrong
– And What We Can Do About It

Richard Bacon
Christopher Hope

Biteback Publishing

First published in Great Britain in 2013 by
Biteback Publishing Ltd
Westminster Tower
3 Albert Embankment
London SE1 7SP
Copyright © Richard Bacon and Christopher Hope 2013

ISBN 978-1-84954-552-5

10 9 8 7 6 5 4 3 2

A CIP catalogue record for this book is available from the British Library.

Set in Sabon

Printed and bound in Great Britain by
CPI Group (UK) Ltd, Croydon CR0 4YY

For Victoria, Rollo and Ranulph
and for Sarah, Barnaby, Sapphire and Pollyanna

The tendency to overlook implementation issues is not surprising, given how difficult, and unglamorous, it is to figure out the nuts and bolts of real programs – and how much more enticing it is for politicians and policy analysts to bandy about big ideas. The implementation of policy is less visible and less dramatic than the framing of policy – and, often, frankly, more arcane. The neglect of implementation issues is more than a simple intellectual mistake: it may be a rational response to the fact that our political system confers more rewards for the shrewd deployment of symbols and generalised arguments than it does for detailed realistic analysis and forecasting.
Theodore Marmor

A man who neglects what is actually done for what should be done learns the way to self-destruction rather than self-preservation.
Niccolo Machiavelli, *The Prince*

CONTENTS

ACKNOWLEDGEMENTS

We have incurred many debts in writing this book. We are grateful to the staff at the National Audit Office (NAO) who produced the value-for-money reports on which much of our book is based. We are especially indebted to those NAO officials who read and provided comments on some of the chapters, undoubtedly saving us from various blunders: Geraldine Barker, Philip Gibby, Angela Hands, Aileen Murphie, Lee Summerfield and Paul Wright-Anderson. We also received invaluable advice from Steve Baker, Michael Gove, Sir Leigh Lewis, Robert Matthews, Sir Richard Mottram and Peter Riddell, each of whom commented on early drafts or portions of the book. We are very grateful to them all, although we alone are responsible for what follows.

Richard would also like to record his particular gratitude to the staff in the Public Accounts Committee (PAC) office, Adrian Jenner, Sonia Draper, Ian Blair and James McQuade; to the Comptroller and Auditor General, Amyas Morse, for his professionalism and wise counsel; and to many other NAO officials who have provided tremendous assistance over the last decade, notably Sir John Bourn and Tim Burr, as well as Tim Banfield, Laura Brackwell, Gabrielle Cohen, Mark Davies, Keith Davis, David Finlay, David Goldsworthy, Peter Gray, Keith Hawkswell, Sally Howes, Ed Humpherson, Jeff Jones, Alex Kidner, Barry Lester, Elaine Lewis, Professor Sir Andrew Likierman, Jim Rickleton, Nick Sloan, Max Tse and Michael Whitehouse. Richard is also grateful to Graham Coster, for originally suggesting that he should write the book; to Tony Collins, for a decade of stimulating conversation about the issues examined in the book; to the staff in the House of Commons Library, who were immensely helpful at all times; and to past and present parliamentary colleagues including

PAC members with whom he has informally discussed themes in the book, notably David Davis, Nick Gibb, Helen Goodman, Margaret Hodge, Edward Leigh, Peter Lilley and Alan Williams. He would especially like to thank his own office staff for their patience and good humour during the writing of the book: his senior researcher Mike Rigby, who has a rare ability to coax the most recherché of facts from the electronic ether; Tracy Reeve and Michele Savage, who have kept the busy constituency office running smoothly; and Malcolm Venning for help at Westminster.

Richard is enormously grateful to Christopher for agreeing to become co-author and provide some narrative discipline. The book has become a thoroughgoing collaboration, with all parts influenced by both authors. We would like to thank the team at Biteback, notably Iain Dale, Sam Carter and Hollie Teague, whose excellent advice improved the book significantly. One helper must remain publicly unacknowledged but he knows who he is and how valuable his contribution has been.

Above all, we would like to thank our long-suffering families – Victoria Bacon, and children Rollo and Ranulph; and Sarah Hope, and children Barnaby, Sapphire and Pollyanna – and to apologise to them all for the time we didn't spend with them while writing this book. We hope they think the result was worth it.

Richard would like to thank the constituents of South Norfolk for sending him to the House of Commons as their MP to keep an eye on how the government of the day is looking after their money; and Christopher would like to thank the *Daily Telegraph* for employing him to work in the House of Commons, with a fine vantage point from which to monitor the work of the politicians and civil servants who run Britain. We would also like to thank our respective Jack Russell terriers – Zephyr and Queenie – who are the only creatures we know who have watched the writing of this book with complete detachment.

INTRODUCTION

*Even in the scarcest times, public money may always be found to
be employed foolishly.*
Alessandro Manzoni, *The Betrothed*

It is always sensible to make the most of what you have. This
simple principle is honoured by most of the world's major
religions. It is the basis of economics, the study of matching
scarce resources with competing and potentially limitless wants.
And it should be the foundation stone for governments, which
spend other people's money rather than their own.

Yet our governments do not make the most of what they
have. They often spend precious taxpayers' money wastefully
and even stupidly. They hire as civil servants some of the brightest people in the country and then employ them in ways that
stifle their creativity and inhibit them from taking personal
responsibility for what they do at work. And they often change
the ministers who are the temporary political heads of government departments with such bewildering speed that it is all but
impossible for those ministers, even the highly talented ones, to
obtain a sufficient grasp of what they are doing before being
moved on.

One of the central features of our government is how much
money it spends. Currently this is around £673 billion per year.
Such a number defies our sense of scale but it amounts to nearly
£11,000 each year for every single person in the UK. There
is a further £18,000 per person of accumulated national debt.
The national finances are unsustainable and public spending
is now being curtailed in many areas, although total government spending will still be higher at the end of the current
spending period in 2015 – at around £744 billion – than at
the beginning; in effect, it is the *rate* of growth that is being

slowed. The money pays for schools and teachers; for hospitals, doctors, nurses and prescription drugs to treat patients; for pensions; for welfare benefits for those who don't have a job; for building and maintaining our roads; for tax collectors to keep the money coming in; for social workers to help people in difficulty; for police officers to catch criminals, courts to prosecute them and prisons to incarcerate them; for our armed forces and their equipment, from frigates and helicopters to missiles and body armour; for collecting the rubbish; for public libraries; for meals on wheels; for firefighters and ambulance drivers; for the planning system; and much, much more, including the huge interest payments on our debts.

In this book we examine a wide variety of cases where many hundreds of millions of pounds of taxpayers' money – and in some cases many billions – were spent on projects and programmes that went wrong and, in particular, those cases where individual members of the public suffered as a result. By doing this we hope to learn more about why things go wrong and how they should be done instead. Our study draws deeply on the work of Britain's public spending watchdog, the National Audit Office – often known simply as the NAO – and also the Public Accounts Committee, through which the NAO reports to Parliament. We also make use of the work of other commentators and other parliamentary select committees. The Public Accounts Committee or PAC, as it is commonly called, was set up by William Gladstone in 1861 after agitation by the Treasury, which had failed for years to get a proper handle on inflated bills for running the Royal Navy. The main work of the committee was to examine the accounts of government departments and then report to Parliament. In the last 150 years there have been numerous changes to the system of auditing and scrutinising public money, most notably the replacement of the Treasury's internal Exchequer and Audit Department in 1983 by the National Audit Office. Over the last thirty years, the NAO has established a reputation as one of the leading supreme audit institutions in the world. Better resourced and more independent than its predecessor, it is now the auditor for all central government departments and agencies, as well as a wide range of other public bodies. In addition to auditing the financial accounts, the NAO also produces a wide range of value-for-money studies, reporting to Parliament independently on how wisely the government is spending public money. It is mainly these value-for-money studies that interest us.

Using the NAO's value-for-money report as the basis for its inquiry, the Public Accounts Committee holds public hearings in the House of Commons – always chaired by an MP from the main opposition party – where it takes evidence from officials who are responsible for particular areas of spending. Unlike most select committees, the PAC does not normally take evidence from ministers. Instead, the chief witness is usually the most senior civil servant in the relevant government department, the Permanent Secretary. This very senior official, who will be familiar to many readers as Sir Humphrey Appleby from the television series *Yes Minister*, is also known as the Accounting Officer for the department. He or she is legally responsible for the stewardship of public money and is expected to be able to account to Parliament for its use and to ensure that money is only spent for the purposes which Parliament has intended. Upon appointment, an Accounting Officer is issued by HM Treasury with a little-known but exceptionally important Whitehall 'bible' called 'Managing Public Money'. This guidance document sets out the responsibilities and duties of accounting officers in considerable detail. It provides the central reference point for their actions and the basis for discerning whether or not any proposed expenditure is right and proper. If the Accounting Officer believes that a proposal would involve spending public money improperly, he or she can refuse to support the expenditure unless the minister issues a formal 'Direction'. The mere threat of asking for a Direction is often enough to dissuade a minister from a particular course of action. If a minister insists on going ahead and issues a Direction to an Accounting Officer, the matter will then be formally drawn to the attention of the NAO and the Accounting Officer will be exonerated from any subsequent blame. At PAC hearings, MPs question the Permanent Secretary and other witnesses on the NAO's value-for-money report and then the committee produces a separate report containing its own conclusions and recommendations.

There is a particular focus on the big beasts of public spending – the National Health Service, the Department for Work and Pensions, the Ministry of Defence, HM Revenue and Customs, the Department for Education, the Ministry of Justice – although useful lessons can be drawn from what goes on in the smallest organisations and so many other bodies attract the committee's attention; indeed, the NAO's value-for-money studies may cover any area where public money is spent. The work of the NAO and the PAC is therefore a lexicon of the public sector, covering everything from agricultural payments and animal health to Arts Council funding and accommodation for asylum seekers; from battleship helicopters and cigarette smuggling to coal miners' compensation, the disposal of nuclear waste and European Union finances; from fishery protection and further education to the sale of gold reserves and gritting the highways; from hospital-acquired infection to Jobcentres and the operations of the armed forces in Kosovo; from the Land Registry and the magistrates' courts to the Millennium Dome, the national programme for IT in the health service and the London 2012 Olympics; a wide range of individual Private Finance Initiative projects; pension regulation; prisoners' food; queue relocation in Dunstable (really!); transport for the Royal Family; Sure Start children's centres; urban development corporations; VAT carousel fraud; the BBC World Service; the refurbishment of Wembley stadium; youth offending; and much more. As a result, in addition to hearing from permanent secretaries, the PAC also takes evidence from a whole array of other senior officials and managers, from hospital chief executives and doctors to veterinary surgeons and highway engineers, from sports administrators and trading standards officers to the heads of regulatory bodies covering energy, water and telecoms, university vice-chancellors, senior military officers, the head of HM Revenue and Customs, the head of the Prison Service, the director general of the BBC, the chief executive of the NHS, and many others.

Consequently the PAC is an excellent place from which to observe the British government's spending habits. Nearly all government activity involves spending public money – and thus nearly all government activity is subject to the committee's scrutiny. Despite its name of 'Accounts' Committee, the PAC only rarely looks at the financial accounts of government bodies, holding occasional hearings into fraud or irregularity. This work would have occupied most of the committee's time in years gone by – and the PAC should almost certainly devote more time to this than it now does, since these documents can be illuminating as well as entertaining. For example, when HM Revenue and Customs hived off its prosecutions division into a separate body, the financial accounts of the new Revenue and Customs Prosecutions Office showed that the first act of the new chief operating officer hired to run the organisation was to award £100,000 worth of HR consultancy to his wife; when a consignment of satellite phones were stolen in Iraq, the financial accounts showed that the Foreign Office continued paying for the stolen phones even as they were being used to run up a £600,000 bill on betting lines and sex chat lines; and when the administration of the Home Office collapsed and the NAO pressed the auditor's nuclear button by 'disclaiming' the accounts – meaning the NAO literally had 'no information' with which to form an opinion – it followed an earlier warning from the NAO to the Home Office that the gross transaction value of debits and credits on its accounting system was, at £26.5 *trillion*, almost 2,000 times higher than the Home Office's gross expenditure for 2004–05 and approximately one and a half times higher than the estimated gross domestic product of the entire planet. 'This suggests something has gone seriously awry,' the NAO noted dryly in a memo to the Home Office's audit committee.

However, the main thrust of the PAC's work is now to take evidence on the value-for-money reports published by the NAO. These are not actually about the financial accounts but consist of detailed examinations of specific spending programmes within the relevant department in order to weigh up how efficiently, effectively and economically the government has used public money to achieve its aims. None of this is about the policies the government *should* be pursuing. Rather, it is an ongoing study of what the actual government is spending now to achieve its policies and whether it is delivering value for money. In some ways it is profoundly non-political; indeed, the NAO is statutorily prohibited from questioning the merits of government policy. Accordingly, and following the example of the NAO, the PAC does not ask questions about government policy – which is a matter for government, other parliamentary select committees, the official opposition, other competing political parties, think tanks and so on – but rather a different set of questions, about how wisely the government has used public money to achieve its aims, whatever those aims are. Thus the committee would not consider *whether* the government should spend more on roads rather than railways, or whether a limited pot of money should be put into pre-schooling for children aged three to five years old rather than into adult education, but rather *how* the government spent the money it allocated to those policies and, in particular, how well it was spent. Did the government achieve its stated aims? Was the expenditure effective? Could the same aims have been achieved more quickly or using less money? In short, did the government deliver value for money? The PAC's examination is not about the government's policies *per se* but about how the government implements them.

Sir Michael Barber once observed that the 'How?' question is relatively neglected in the writing of history and politics – a history textbook would say of some medieval king that 'he gathered an army and hastened north' without pausing to consider just how difficult that was to do. And most of the conversation in politics is about how things *should* be, rather than the mechanics of getting there. Should Britain have more nuclear power stations? Should we increase foreign aid? Should we spend more money on improving the road network? Should students pay university tuition fees? Should Britain send troops into a foreign country? Should abortion be more or less freely available? Should taxpayers support adult education? Should pensions be increased in line with earnings? Should healthcare be free at the point of use? And if so, should taxpayers still pay for the removal of a tattoo? And indeed, should government be spending more of our money, or less? Such questions are quite rightly at the heart of politics.

Yet so much of the business of government is not like this. Much of the work of government consists in spending money on things which have already been decided. On one estimate, over 95 per cent of current expenditure is already determined by past commitments. This is one of the chief differences between politics and government: the hard toil of making sure that benefits are paid correctly and on time using computer systems that work – or that hospitals are always cleaned properly, or that, when it snows, there are enough gritting lorries in the right place so that the roads remain passable – is a very different arena from the wordsmithing that takes place in television and radio studios, at party conferences or standing next to a battle bus during an election campaign. The former Governor of New York, Mario Cuomo, summed up this difference neatly when he said: 'You campaign in poetry. You govern in prose.' And it is in the prose of government where things go wrong. It is here one finds what the journalist Andrew Marr has called 'the seven-eighths of the iceberg that doesn't gleam brightly but tends to sink the ship'. It is not just in cleaning hospitals – or paying benefits, or gritting roads – where problems arise. Even a casual glance at the newspapers shows that a vast amount of taxpayers' money is not well spent. In just one single issue of one newspaper there were the following stories: a nuclear submarine suffered £5 million worth of damage after it crashed into rocks on the seabed because trainee commanders covered

vital charts with tracing paper; a new computer system installed
as part of a Department for Transport efficiency drive incurred
extra costs of £112 million instead of planned savings of £120
million, while causing unrest among staff when it took to issuing
messages in German and denying them annual leave to which
they were entitled; hundreds of thousands of immigrants were
excluded from official statistics by a counting system which is
so unreliable that it is not even possible to know the true population of Britain; and more than 8,000 patients died in hospital
after contracting superbugs such as MRSA and *Clostridium
difficile*. And that was just one day's headlines. In recent years
we have seen a renegotiation of the NHS dental contract which
left large numbers of people without a dentist; a new system for
marking school tests where up to three quarters of the marking
was wrong; a pension regulatory body which had no objectives; an urban regeneration project which had no budget; a
military radio communications project where no one was in
charge; a computer system for the probation service which had
seven programme directors in seven years, five of whom knew
nothing about project management; and much more.

In large areas of public administration, especially when the
government decides to embark on anything new, it is quite
normal for things not to turn out as planned. We don't mean
the cases where a government makes a promise and then breaks
its word; we mean those many cases where the government
had a plan, and then tried to implement that plan, but failed
to deliver it even remotely adequately, resulting in enormous
costs in terms of taxpayers' money, time and inconvenience
to the public. Given the track record, one might expect the
quality of government spending and the quality of management in government to be the subject of national attention.
And so they are, temporarily at least, when individual citizens
are directly affected, but what generally happens is that each
time something goes wrong there is a brief stir of interest from
parliamentarians and the media – or even a 'major row' where
someone's head may be on the block, often based on evidence

of failure from an authoritative source such as the NAO – and then life carries on until the next time, when similar problems are exposed again elsewhere in government. We seem to be very bad at learning from our mistakes.

In their book, *Implementation* – which examined a federally funded economic stimulus programme in California which failed to deliver its objectives – the authors Jeffrey L. Pressman and Aaron Wildavsky deliberately chose case material in which dramatic elements were ruled out, where there was no great conflict, where everyone agreed, where essential funds were available at the right time. The problems that subsequently afflicted the programme were of a prosaic and everyday character: agreements had to be maintained after they were reached; approvals and clearances had to be obtained from a variety of participants. As Pressman and Wildavsky noted, these 'perfectly ordinary circumstances' proved to be serious obstacles to implementation and, furthermore, the failure to recognise this fact also inhibited the possibility of learning from failure. The central message of these writers is that to make the ordinary happen is far from easy. Indeed, as they put it, 'implementation, under the best of circumstances, is exceedingly difficult'. Kate Jenkins, a former senior Whitehall official who helped create the Next Steps programme, which led to the setting up of executive agencies in the 1990s, emphasised this point while giving evidence to the Public Administration Committee, a sister select committee of the PAC. As she put it:

> The public, the group we ought to be thinking about all the time, have two problems. One is they are promised things that are not delivered by organisations that in large measure cannot deliver many of those things. Secondly, the core functions of government, the absolute basics, are constantly failed ... People spend a great deal of time talking about things that are at the margin, or, indeed, a great deal of time in indulging in elaborate programmes of change, reorganisation and restructuring, when what is needed is to get the basic task done properly.

One former PAC member, Stella Creasy MP, was no less emphatic when she told the Commons: 'Governments should not just start projects or policies – the public expect them to be able to finish them too. Essentially, implementation is as important as ideology in politics.'

We examine a range of examples in this book where things turn out badly. Sometimes the problems creep up slowly, sometimes a particular cherished policy objective is allowed to trump common sense, sometimes the apparent ineptitude is quite staggering. There is usually an explanation somewhere: the lack of enough people with the right experience, a key person moved on at the wrong time, a batch of computer testing that didn't quite happen in order to save time, a sudden change in government priorities or plans or legislation. But why don't people learn the lessons of past failure? It is not as if anyone actually *wants* these repeated failures. The short timescale given to ministers anxious to make a quick impact doesn't help, nor does the fact that the recruiting process for civil servants puts a premium on pure brain power rather than the ability to get things done. When the veteran Whitehall watcher David Hencke, in a highly perceptive article in *The Guardian* entitled 'Blair doesn't do boring', criticised the former Prime Minister's fondness for announcing grandiose projects with the associated headlines, he was also offering a critique of the entire system. The truth is that many politicians, senior civil servants and the media are less interested in knowing about and learning from past mistakes than in getting on with the next policy initiative, the next project or the next story.

The coalition government formed in 2010 took office brimming with ideas and proposing sweeping changes in many areas of national life, in the NHS, in schools, in welfare, in the criminal justice system and in local government. Control of most NHS budgets was to be devolved to GPs; more schools were to be turned into academies with full autonomy over their hiring practices and admissions; there would be a radical overhaul of the benefits system and the launch of a new 'universal credit' involving yet more dramatic changes to IT systems; local police authorities would be replaced by elected police commissioners; criminals would spend less time in prison and more time repaying their debt to society in the community; local councils were to be free from swathes of targets and would instead set their own priorities. Will these ideas be implemented successfully? The country is in a financial hole and there will be a very small audience for any suggestion that 'reform' requires more resources. On the contrary, it is to be done with less money, not more. Nick Boles, an MP and one of the thinkers behind recent Conservative policy, is explicit in his book, *Which Way's Up?*, a survey of prospects for the coalition, that reducing the deficit must be used to drive radical reform. Boles points out that delivering successful reform while saving money is what successful private sector firms have done for years. Indeed, on the 'burning platforms' so beloved of management writers it is only in a full-blown crisis that people will accept the radical reforms that are required – because the alternatives are worse. But as we show in this book, reforms and changes of all kinds – always started with the very best of intentions – do have a frequent habit of going horribly wrong. What are the lessons from the failures of recent years? And will they be heeded? Might something get lost along the way? Are there pitfalls which should be really obvious but which might get missed in the headlong rush for change? Have ministers paid sufficient attention to why it is that things go wrong quite so often?

The format of the book is as follows. First, we look at examples of failure which illustrate the recurring problems facing any government seeking to make things happen on its watch. Most of the cases have been the subject of a detailed study by the NAO and the PAC and sometimes by others too, and we have also paid close attention to the work of the Public Administration Committee, whose reports are a treasure trove on many of the broader themes of government. We draw heavily on all these reports. Our chief focus is on cases where members of the public have suffered directly because of government failure: the student who started the university term with no money for food, rent or books because the Student Loans Company couldn't process his loan on time; the pensioner wanting to do a computer course who discovered that money held by the government in a special account to pay for her training had been stolen before she could use it; the single mum who worked as a part-time cleaning lady who was worried sick by a tax credit demand from HM Revenue and Customs to 'repay' thousands of pounds she had never received; the families whose holidays were ruined because the Passport Office couldn't issue passports in time; the nurseries and schools that couldn't open at the start of term because background checks on new staff members were being done by an organisation in meltdown; the bizarre new system for selecting junior doctors which caused talented British medics to emigrate to Australia in a frantic search for work; the students who lost out because further education colleges planning to expand were suddenly told that money vouchsafed for their building works had also been promised elsewhere; and the Kafkaesque system for administering single farm payments which led some farmers to bankruptcy and even suicide. We also look at cases affecting all members of the public, such as the flawed national programme for IT in the NHS – the world's largest civilian computer project – which was supposed to create electronic patient records for the whole country; the fiasco of the InterCity West Coast franchise competition, which has thrown the whole rail franchising system into turmoil; and the case of the foreign nationals who served prison terms for very serious crimes – including murder, rape, arson and kidnap – and who were then released into the community even though they were known to be failed asylum applicants without any legal basis to remain in this country at all.

After looking at specific cases we then examine the role of IT, which not only plays such a crucial role in most organisations but also figures prominently in many of the big failures we have examined. Is there something about the public sector which makes it uniquely inept in running computer projects? What it is about software engineering that makes it different from other kinds of engineering? Why can ambition make things worse? We explore the paradox that IT projects continue to go wrong even though, after decades of international experience of such failures, we now know why they go wrong and also how to stop them going wrong. We ask how it can be that – even with this knowledge readily available – senior managers responsible for commissioning IT projects will often ask for functions that are difficult or impossible to deliver, without the slightest notion that they are doing so.

We then look at the role of ministers, who are supposed to set the strategy and direction for government departments. New initiatives and reorganisations are standard fare for a new minister. Would things work better if ministers stopped interfering? They are surrounded by impatient and disillusioned voters and naturally want their plans to show quick results but will they be around to see them? The length of time ministers stay in one job makes it unlikely. Will new ministers always prefer form to substance? Is there an unavoidable tendency to want to turn the world upside down? Do ministers have the right experience and skills before they are appointed? Is it really true that quietly digging in for years never got anyone anywhere? The pressures of office, the need to be seen to be acting quickly, the glare of constant media scrutiny, the fear of being seen to drift, all these make it difficult to reach well-considered decisions for the long term. There is often a fundamental conflict between the constraints of managing large-scale organisations successfully and the timescales of elected ministers. Can the requirements of government co-exist with the needs of politics? Would the radical changes suggested by think tanks on both left and right make all the difference? Why haven't such changes been made already?

Next, we look at the position of civil servants, whose job it is to help elected governments deliver their policies. How does

Whitehall manage to take some of the most intellectually capable people in the whole country and yet produce such dramatic failures? Do we recruit the right people? Are civil servants up to the job? Do they have the right career formation and training? Civil servants are sometimes moved around to new jobs more quickly than ministers. Who is in charge? Why are there so few good managers? Why isn't there enough of the right information in Whitehall? Why does no one seem to know how much things cost? Or is that now an outdated caricature? The risks and rewards for civil servants encourage behaviour that makes success more difficult. But could this change? And should it?

Then we look at efforts to improve things. What has changed already? People have talked about changing our system of governing the country for fifty years and there have been plenty of attempted reforms. Has each attempt been consciously thwarted by mandarins who prefer the old ways? Or are we in the middle of a quiet and largely unnoticed revolution that is changing the face of the civil service for ever?

Finally we look at human behaviour and what this may tell us about our predicament. It is a deep irony that even though the origins of economics lie in studying the behaviour of human beings, after the arrival of psychology – with its strange new rites and rhythms – economists quickly fled towards the respectability and internal logic of mathematics, becoming less interesting and less useful as a result. Yet while economics has now recovered some of its earliest insights about how humans actually behave, the question of what government and politics could glean from studying behaviour remains largely unanswered. Why is it that the same old problems crop up decade after decade, from a lack of financial skills to jaw-dropping ignorance about risk? Do we spend too much time on incessant proposals for reform and not enough on examining how we behave?

One big omission from our book is defence procurement, which would have made a book in itself. The NAO and the PAC do examine defence issues, which involve the spending of many billions of pounds of public money, and the dreadful procurement record of the Ministry of Defence amply supports Ernest Fitzgerald's maxim that 'there are only two phases of a weapons programme: "too early to tell"' and '"too late to stop"'. However, we have avoided the subject here partly because the failings of defence procurement are covered elsewhere in such books as Lewis Page's *Lions, Donkeys and Dinosaurs*, and also because we wanted to keep the focus on areas of public spending where failures by government have direct consequences on individual taxpayers, the consumers of public services. Sadly, this means passing swiftly over many amazing stories of the spectacular misuse of public money which the Ministry of Defence has generated over the years, including boots that melt in hot weather, body armour for troops which remains unused because the army don't know where it is, helicopters that can't fly in the rain, radios that won't fit into battle tanks, military transport aircraft that can't fly into war zones, naval frigates with no weapons and aircraft carriers with no fighter jets.

Another very substantial but necessary omission from the book is the Private Finance Initiative or PFI, originally developed in the mid-1990s under John Major's Conservative government, then massively expanded when Gordon Brown was Chancellor of the Exchequer in the succeeding Labour administration, and now worth some £233 billion of cash payments to contractors spread over the next few decades. Private sector suppliers to government are nothing new, of course, but PFI is different because contractors supply an entire service, for example the designing, building and then running of a large acute hospital, which they finance with private loans. The government doesn't pay anything up front but only starts paying the contractor – including, crucially, enough to repay the private loans – when the hospital is fully up and running with patients coming through the doors. PFI has been used for developing schools, hospitals, prisons, government buildings, roads, sewers and much more besides. It has been controversial, attracting many critics as well as supporters. At its height PFI became such a publicly financed bonanza that a leading

City investment banker was moved to tell one of us: 'I like PFI. It's a good source of income. It's good for the business. But as a taxpayer it really pisses me off.' PFI has been a significant area of government expenditure and we would like to have included it here, together with its close cousin Public Private Partnership or PPP where, in the egregious example of London Underground, project managers spent £29 million on advice from just one law firm while only spending £6 million on consulting engineers assessing the condition of the rail track. However, to have examined PFI and PPP in any depth would have made for a different and much longer book. There are also some signs that such financing methods are fading from fashion as the long-term costs become more visible and the financial crunch further increases their pricing – although the temptation for governments to pay for projects with the equivalent of an expensive credit card is never far away. And in December 2012, the coalition government did set out plans for a new improved PFI – imaginatively called 'PF2' – which was said to be quicker and more transparent, avoiding the drawbacks of the original PFI schemes.

Some may think we are promoting a desiccated and managerial view of the world, empty of political conviction or passion. We don't think so. On the contrary, one would have every reason to be very passionate or angry about the failures we describe. We are simply saying that whatever a government's political convictions, and whatever its plans, they will work better if there is a budget, if there is someone in charge, if there are objectives, if everyone understands why projects are so often dragged down by failing IT, and that anyone who cares about making government work needs to care about these things. Governments need to perform well. Far too often they don't. Politics does not place a sufficient premium on implementation in the way that governments need it to, and this has to change – even though it isn't easy – because if governments can't get better they won't be able to meet the expectations of the people who pay the bills.

It is not all bad. And it is certainly true that the good parts rarely get attention. Sir Leigh Lewis, who was a Permanent Secretary in Whitehall for ten years – variously in the Benefits Agency, the Home Office and the Department for Work and Pensions – tells of one occasion when a departmental press office persuaded him, somewhat against his better judgement, to meet a journalist and discuss a project which the department had just delivered with considerable success. The journalist listened with increasing dismay as he heard the details and finally said: 'You mean to tell me that this project was delivered on time?' Lewis confirmed that it was. 'And it was delivered on budget?' 'Yes, indeed it was,' said Lewis. 'And it is working exactly as it was supposed to do?' Once again Lewis answered in the affirmative. 'There's no story there,' said the journalist and left the building.

Indeed, in terms of international comparisons our governments stand reasonably well. When the Institute for Government conducted a comparative international review of the civil services in a range of developed countries it concluded that 'Whitehall is firmly within the global government premier league'. Although Whitehall was consistently outscored by a group of Scandinavian, northern European and Commonwealth countries such as Australia, New Zealand and Canada, our system of government still came out as one of the better performers in the world. However, the capability reviews of Whitehall departments led by the Cabinet Office paint a much less flattering picture, with two thirds of government departments 'less than well placed' to deliver their goals. It is true that most of the time the rubbish bins are emptied and that when you turn on the tap clean water comes out. Not everything is failing, but far too much is. And those who use the public services have every right to expect better because it is their government and they are paying for it.

1

CHILD SUPPORT AGENCY

It ranks among the worst public administration scandals in modern times. The facts almost beggar belief.
Edward Leigh MP, chairman, Public Accounts Committee

'No father should be able to escape from his responsibility.' It was these words from Prime Minister Margaret Thatcher that helped to fire the starting gun on one of the most notorious, expensive and error-prone government agencies ever to be created. In a speech on 18 July 1990 at the Savoy Hotel in central London – near the end of her premiership – she said:

> Even though marriages may break down, parenthood is for life. Legislation cannot make irresponsible parents responsible. But it can and must ensure that absent parents pay maintenance for their children. It is not fair for them to expect other families to foot their bills too.

Mrs Thatcher recognised that the government had to do something to help the two in three children who, though entitled to receive maintenance, were not receiving anything. Simply, she said, absent parents had to be stopped from 'just walking away from their duty to maintain their children'. The Prime Minister added: 'We have decided that we must have a simpler system of maintenance, available to all. The present one is too inconsistent, too slow and too complicated.'

A new organisation would be set up called the Child Support Agency (CSA), which would have access to the information necessary to trace absent parents and make them accept their financial obligations. This was a major risk. The government was diving feet first into the vexed and emotionally charged world of broken relationships, while trying to hold to account errant parents who simply were not paying their fair share with regards to their offspring.

The government had signalled its intentions some months earlier, when Social Security Secretary Tony Newton highlighted in the House of Commons the very limited extent to which absent parents paid anything towards the costs of their children. In January 1990, Newton told MPs that only a quarter of single parents who were on benefits received any maintenance payments from an absent partner. The minister was blunt:

> That is fairly widely regarded as unfair to the taxpayer. Just as important, it is clearly unfair to the children in the family and, not least, to the lone parent because maintenance income provides a good foundation on which to build for a lone parent seeking to move from claiming benefits to work.

Mr Newton's plans did not arrive in a vacuum. The government was attempting to tackle the thorny social problem of absentee parents who had turned their backs on their child-rearing responsibilities. The issue had been moving into the centre of the political stage in Britain since the mid-1970s. The Divorce Act 1969 had made it easier to get a divorce by removing the concept of fault and replacing it with 'irretrievable breakdown' of marriage as the sole grounds for divorce, while the Family Reform Act 1987 took out most of the remaining differences between children of married parents and of those who were not. Critics said it was no coincidence that the number of lone parents had more than doubled during the 1970s and 1980s to 1.3 million by 1991, and that the number of absentee parents had risen correspondingly. Something had to be done.

By April 1990 it became clear that Newton favoured an agency modelled on approaches used in Australia and the USA for retrieving the correct amount of owed childcare maintenance. The American model, specifically one introduced in Wisconsin in the 1980s, was a state-wide formula for calculating child maintenance and collection by the immediate deduction of the relevant sum of wages from the absentee parent. The Australian model was similar, but it allowed the agency to collect payments through the tax system.

Mrs Thatcher's speech in July gave the nascent project another boost. She said that in future the government would 'move to assessing maintenance through a standard administrative formula which will take account of the parents' ability to pay, of the cost of bringing up a child – and the right of that child to share in their parents' rising living standards'. This formula would provide some certainty to separated parents when settling custody disputes, rather than the unpredictable, hit and miss nature of settlements agreed through the courts. 'The whole process will be easier, more consistent and fairer,' she said, ending on an optimistic note that she hoped the CSA would help 'to give the lone parent back her morale and her confidence. Then she will be able the better to use and develop her own abilities for the benefit of her children and herself. She can then break out of the cycle of loneliness.'

The new agency brought together the hotchpotch of procedures which were then used to ensure that errant parents paid their fair share. Tony Newton set out the existing system's weaknesses when he published a new White Paper – titled 'Children Come First' – detailing how the government would establish the Child Support Agency, on 29 October 1990. He told MPs in the House of Commons: 'The present arrangements are by common consent deficient', adding that they were clearly 'fragmented, inconsistent, and too often subject to uncertainty and delay'. Even when a maintenance obligation had been established by the Department for Social Security (DSS), he said, 'it can be difficult to enforce and the caring parent may face great additional difficulties and pressures in protecting the children's rights'.

The figures were shocking. A study by the DSS found that only 39 per cent of lone parents had received any maintenance payments, and as few as 29 per cent were currently receiving payments. Of those not receiving payments, 20 per cent said that they did not want any money from their

ex-partner and 28 per cent thought their former partner
could not afford the payments. The DSS survey estimated that
49 per cent of those who were then paying nothing could actually pay something, while 69 per cent of those paying less than
£10 a week to the single parent could afford to pay more. Just
30 per cent of single mothers and only 3 per cent of single
fathers received regular maintenance for their children.

The current situation was in the interests of neither parents
nor children, placing 'a large burden on those who pay tax, many
of whom are themselves bringing up children on perhaps quite
modest incomes'. Little wonder that the cost of income-related
benefits for lone parents had doubled to £3 billion between
1981/82 and 1988/89. The new agency, Newton said, would
remedy all this. The first words of the White Paper setting out
the plans for the CSA were a form of mission statement for the
new agency. It said simply: 'Every child has a right to care from
his or her parents.'

The work of the CSA comprised three main elements: the
first was a new clear formula for the assessment of maintenance
payments to be used by staff at the agency to calculate how
much a parent owed. The aim was 'to establish a single system
available to all, giving consistent and predictable decisions with
a realistic relationship to the costs of providing for the care
of a child'.

The second element was the new-style agency itself, a form
of 'one stop shop' for getting parents to pay for the welfare of
their children, wherever they were. The CSA would administer
the new system, as well as collect the payments and carry out
'enforcement where necessary'. The third plank in the reforms
were separate measures 'to enhance the payment of maintenance as a foundation on which lone parents can build greater
independence for themselves and their children', through
changes to the benefit rules which would help parents combine
work with their responsibilities to care for their children.

The system would work like this: the CSA would calculate a
maintenance bill which the absent parent would be expected to

pay if he could afford to do so, based on income support rates and including the personal allowance of the parent with care. Once that bill was calculated, the CSA would work out how much the absent parent should keep from his net salary 'for his own necessary expenses'. This 'exempt income' included the absent parent's own 'reasonable housing costs and the costs of any other children he is liable to support', Mr Newton said. The amount to be paid in maintenance was then calculated by working out the basis for sharing the remaining income – what is left after the 'necessary' income – 'equally with the children, up to a point at which the maintenance bill is met'. This complex calculation, Mr Newton explained, would ensure that 'children will share in the standard of living of their parents'.

Not all parents had to use the services of the CSA, but they would have to follow its rules. Some were able to make their own arrangements 'using if they wish the published formula'. If the parent with care were receiving income support she would be 'obliged to use the agency's services'. With some reservations, MPs from all parties backed the essential notion that absentee parents should accept financial responsibility for their children. Speaking in the Commons, Archy Kirkwood, a Liberal Democrat MP, said: 'The concept behind the Bill – which is that parents should be responsible for their children's maintenance – is entirely unexceptional.' Joan Lestor, a Labour MP, added: 'Nobody has objected to the principle, which is wherever possible, to make parents financially responsible for their children.'

The role of the CSA, which was to be run at arm's length from the Department for Social Security, would advise people on how to make a claim for child maintenance. The agency – not the courts – would be the first port of call for a parent seeking maintenance for a child. It would also identify and trace liable people if their whereabouts were unknown, as well as finding information on the incomes and circumstances of the parents of the child for whom maintenance was claimed. The agency was also tasked with taking 'appropriate enforcement action at an early date when payments are not made'.

In theory, it appeared to be a case of 'so far, so good'. The CSA was enacted into law through the Child Support Act 1991 and finally started work on 5 April 1993. Its very presence was a highly public way for the government to underline the principle that biological parents were financially responsible for their children – regardless of whether they had ever lived together, and whether or not they were still together. The rights of the child to a decent upbringing were paramount. The work of the CSA was to be phased in over four years – by April 1997 it was intended to take over the role of the courts in setting child support maintenance.

It is hard to imagine another government agency having as big an impact on such a large proportion of the population as the CSA. Demographers estimated that around half of the children born since 1980 were likely to spend some time growing up in a family that did not comprise two biological parents. The net was being thrown very wide indeed. Not for nothing were the changes dubbed by MPs on a Commons committee 'the most far-reaching social reforms to be made for forty years'.

But almost immediately the agency ran into a headwind of trouble. Billed as an organisation that would be the knight in shining armour for single mothers who had been abandoned by feckless fathers, one newspaper soon described it as 'about as popular as the poll tax'. By the end of September – just six months after its launch – 527,000 'assessment forms' had been sent out. Fathers were in open revolt. One MP referred to the CSA as the 'CIA'. A report from an independent case examiner in September 1993 found that parents had been 'grossly inconvenienced' by the CSA. She upheld 98 per cent of complaints in 150 cases she examined. One problem was that the agency was given very little discretion in the way it ran its operations, such as what information it could disclose about parents and the way in which it determined the date from which maintenance was due.

The CSA was behind its targets virtually from day one. In August – only four months after it opened its doors – a 'closing the gap' initiative was started. A leak of a memo further damaged confidence. Sent from a divisional manager for Wales and Merseyside, it said that staff should focus on the cases where maintenance would be high – adding: 'The name of the game is maximising the maintenance yield – don't waste a lot of time on non-profitable stuff!'

In July 1994, the first major report into the agency's first year found that it had fallen £112 million short of its £530 million collection target. The letters of complaint started to flood in. In the first year of its operation, complaints against the CSA totalled 28,000. High-profile court cases hit the headlines. There was no doubt that the CSA represented a rude awakening for some absent parents to be held to account for paying the living costs of their biological children. But the impression it was treating people unfairly was damaging. The government started to tinker. Alistair Burt, a social security minister, announced a series of changes which served to cut the amount of maintenance that some absent parents had to pay.

The changes failed to staunch the flow of complaints. MPs were soon asking, rhetorically: how did such an unpopular agency ever come into being? Most of the complaints came from absent parents, a group whom critics said the government had barely considered when plans for the CSA were being drawn up because it had far greater worries about helping lone parents. The criticisms covered both the operation of the CSA and the policies that it was implementing. The CSA's regimented formula for calculating maintenance payments often did not fit with the somewhat chaotic lives of many of its clients: one size did not fit all. As newspaper articles pointed out, the formula ignored a whole range of other outgoings such as the cost of travelling to work, visiting children, having them to stay, or the costs of looking after stepchildren who were not subject to an agency order. 'Successful' divorce settlements with a clean break – perhaps when a father had given the mother some property in lieu of settlement payments – were not allowed for. Fathers felt victimised. Frank Field MP, the chairman of the social security select committee, said: 'We unanimously support the principles behind the Child Support Act ... But if the agency is to win public support it must be seen to be fair. And under the present formula it cannot be fair because the formula is flawed.'

The CSA's own shoddy performance hardly helped matters. A report from the Chief Child Support Officer published in October 1994 found that at least four in ten maintenance payments ordered by the CSA were wrong. Only 37 per cent of cases were dealt with within forty days in the five months from April. By late August 1994, some 350,000 cases were judged to have been left outstanding for more than six months. By the end of the year the CSA's first chief executive, Ros Hepplewhite, had left the organisation and the agency had hired another 700 staff.

Some of the settlements seemed baffling and smacked of rough justice. In one report, a businessman with a £300,000 home in Buckinghamshire was told by the CSA to pay only £23 a month for two teenage children from a previous marriage, despite an earlier court agreement that he should pay £300 a month. He told a newspaper he had simply ignored the CSA and continued to pay the higher figure, saying: 'I have no idea how the CSA reached the figure. I submitted my accounts and told them how much I earned.'

Soon more legislation was on its way – the Child Support Bill, which built on a second White Paper titled 'Improving Child Support', was published in April 1995. It introduced a small element of discretion into the rigid formula which calculated how much money an absentee parent owed. A new right of appeal to the system was also introduced. This was expected to increase the sums paid out by £10 million a year in 1996/97, although it cost slightly more every year just to administer the change. In addition, the CSA would for the first time be allowed to use DNA testing to resolve paternity cases, further increasing the feeling of 'Big Brother' around the agency's work.

The error rate failed to improve. A report from the National Audit Office in June 1995 suggested that half of all maintenance demands from the CSA were wrong. An estimated £525 million was owed to mothers and the problems were blamed on a rising number of parents refusing to pay. The CSA's new chief executive, Ann Chant, admitted that much of it would never be repaid.

Civil servants seemed surprised by the level of hostility. Sir Michael Partridge, a senior civil servant at the DSS, said that his department had not anticipated 'this level of non-cooperation and wilful obstruction of the agency. It is quite unprecedented in anything I have come across in public service.' The agency was rivalling the poll tax for its levels of non-compliance. Robert Sheldon MP, who chaired the Public Accounts Committee, said: 'This amounts to an object lesson on how not to set up an agency.' Errors were even being made when staff had enough information to work out the correct level of maintenance. Hundreds of complaints were logged with the Data Protection Registrar. An editorial in the *Daily Mirror* in December 1995, prompted by another report from the PAC in which the MPs said they were 'gravely concerned' at the CSA's failings, summed it up: 'The Child Support Agency has been a total disaster ... Nothing in recent history has roused such fury and led to so many complaints to MPs.'

In the twelve months to March 1996, the amount of unpaid maintenance owed to the CSA had jumped by 70 per cent to nearly £900 million. In February 1997 the agency's 'victims' – the parents it was pursuing for payment – held a mass lobby of Parliament to protest. More than nine out of ten complaints to the Ombudsman against the CSA were being upheld. The agency opened its call centres from 7 a.m. to 9 p.m., six days a week, in a forlorn attempt to clear its backlog.

Yet the problems continued, passing seamlessly from the Conservative administration to the new Labour government. Faith Boardman replaced Ann Chant as chief executive of the unloved CSA in April 1997. That coincided with the news that the CSA would scrap its existing £600 million computer system, designed by America's Electronic Data Systems, known as EDS, and try to find a new way forward. In July it emerged that staff at the CSA had made errors in 85 per cent of the maintenance bills of absent parents. One in six of the errors was worth over £1,000. An NAO report blamed a 'legacy of error'.

By March 1998, 575,000 cases still had not been assessed. More than half of these people had waited for more than a year. Of the £1.1 billion owed by fathers, it was estimated that nearly 80 per cent or £869 million would never be repaid. The CSA's Faith Boardman told MPs on the PAC that the agency simply did not have the resources to put the errors right. The committee said it was 'appalled'. The CSA said that it wanted to ensure that 85 per cent of new cases were assessed correctly. The MPs replied: 'This is an unacceptable standard of service in a modern society.' They added: 'The agency is failing the children and families the child support system was designed to protect.' That same day *The Guardian* published an article by the father of a little girl who raged at the injustice of the agency's work. It was headlined: 'Kill the CSA now.'

Harriet Harman, the new Social Security Secretary, attempted to get to grips with the agency's problems in July 1998 when she published proposals to force seven out of ten fathers to pay maintenance, and make three quarters of mothers better off. The plans were formally published by Ms Harman's successor, Alistair Darling, in 1999, when he announced that the complicated formula would be replaced by a flat-rate levy. For the first time the government appeared to be getting to grips with the complexity of the system used to calculate maintenance. It noted: 'With hindsight, we can see that the problem lies with the way that the child support system is designed. The complex rules do not fit either with the lives of separated families or with other systems that provide support for families.' More than 100 pieces of information were needed to be collected together in one place to make a full assessment. Seven years after its introduction, the system was so complex that it was undeliverable. The CSA was now spending millions of pounds of public money on private debt collectors, yet parents were four times more likely to be overcharged than undercharged for owed maintenance money. Another study in 1999 from the

NAO found that the CSA had demanded millions of pounds more than it should from errant fathers. David Davis MP, the PAC's new chairman, warned that the legacy of error in current assessments could clog up the new system for years to come:

> These errors are not notional accounting issues, they represent injustice. For every person who gains from an error there is a loser, and where the recipient of child support is on benefit the loser can often be the taxpayer. Unless this is addressed as a matter of urgency the Agency will be beset by problems for a generation.

The Child Support, Pensions and Social Security Act 2000 attempted to put right what the two previous Acts of Parliament had failed to do. It established a new child support scheme, based on a simple percentage of the non-resident parent's net income. For one child, the rate was 15 per cent, for two children it was 20 per cent. Maintenance was cut if the absentee parent had a second family, or was on a low income, or shared overnight caring responsibilities for the child. Tougher penalties for non-payment were introduced. To sugar the pill, a new child maintenance premium was announced, worth £10 a week for parents with children. In September 2000 the government signed another multi-million deal with computer contractor EDS, which surprisingly had been given a chance to deliver another new IT system for the scheme.

The DSS said the new system would be introduced by the end of 2001. But the flow of cases coming through the CSA's front door continued unabated. And there were still so many errors in maintenance assessments that in July 2003 the head of the NAO, Sir John Bourn, issued a black mark against the accounts for the ninth successive year. Bourn did this yet again in July 2004. By now, newspapers were so familiar with cock-ups at the CSA that this highly embarrassing news only merited a 51-word report in the *Daily Telegraph*.

The new EDS computer system had finally started work – albeit for new cases only – in March 2003. It launched under a cloud – costing £456 million, some £56 million over budget, and two years late. Older cases were due to be moved onto the new system when it was working properly. However, far from improving the situation, the new system actually exacerbated the problem markedly. The two systems were tasked with working alongside one another. By October 2004, the agency was estimated to be handling 1.2 million cases – 711,000 'old' cases on the previous system, and 478,000 'new' ones. A further 200,000 'old' cases were dealt with on the new system. A damning review by MPs blamed the computer supplier, EDS. Doug Smith, the chief executive of the CSA, did not mince his words. 'If you wanted a summary of how I feel, it is that I am seriously disappointed over the last eighteen months,' he said. Mr Smith had hoped that the new IT system as well as the simpler policy changes would 'herald a new future for the agency'. It didn't.

The cause was the expensive new computer system. Mr Smith added:

> At the heart of the issues on implementation of the policy have been the difficulties we have faced over eighteen months with the computer system – it is not possible to operate a large, complex business in today's world without having a sophisticated level of computer support, both for the processing activity, the client contact activity, and the management information needed to run the business.

The MPs heard of the numbing experience of 'clients' or parents who had the misfortune of having regularly to phone staff at the hapless CSA. One single parent told them: 'I rang twice a week for fourteen months, each phone call being maybe twenty minutes or half an hour … no one will ever ring you back, but you are always encouraged to ring back later which increases your phone bill again.' She said that she was not entitled to any maintenance because her partner was a student. When she said that he also earned £30,000 a year, the CSA operator replied: 'Actually, you are right – maybe you can apply for a variation.'

She added: 'So I was lucky that I managed to speak to one person who knew, whereas I had spoken to ten people who had told me I wasn't entitled to anything.' The mother said that she never spoke to the same person for more than two or three weeks. One time the CSA triggered panic when it told her that her partner had refused to pay; but then the operator said: 'Oh, actually, no, it's a problem with the computer. He has paid and it's here.' This happened twice.

This mother's experience was not an isolated example. Other case studies collected by the MPs included examples of poor communication, inaccurate information supplied to parents, inaccurate maintenance calculations, a failure to chase up payments and a lack of enforcement activity. The MPs reported: 'The CSA continues to make up a considerable proportion of members' mailbags and constituency case work.' Citizens Advice reported that in just one year (2003/04) it had received 37,000 child support enquiries – more than 100 a day. Little wonder that the Independent Case Examiner – an independent watchdog set up in 1997 which reviews complaints from parents against the CSA – saw its caseload increase by 30 per cent in 2003/04 compared with the previous year. Half of the complaints were about the new system.

The CSA was set key ministerial targets for that year, to increase the proportion of applications resulting in maintenance calculations, achieve an accuracy rate of over 90 per cent and improve its arrears collection rate. It missed them all. The MPs on the work and pensions committee described this performance as 'shocking', 'totally unacceptable' and 'nothing less than a severe breach of trust'. They added: 'This failure means that millions of pounds owed to children from separated families has not been transferred and has detrimental implications for the government's child poverty targets.' The unmet targets were shifted onto the following year.

The main problem was the expensive EDS computers, which had been brought in to cope with the caseload. The MPs found that 'it would be difficult to find a situation further from straightforward than that which has applied' to the new system. The MPs suggested that if the computer system were not fully operational by 1 December 2004 – eighteen months after it was introduced – it should be junked. They were bemused about why the IT had gone so wrong:

> It would appear however from all the evidence that has become available since that the department wholly failed to comprehend the scale of the business transformation that was required to achieve a successful outcome of the proposed reform before any new IT considerations came into play.

They blamed the department for using the discredited Private Finance Initiative method of procurement to

> shift the risk of development of the new system away from itself entirely onto the shoulders of the contractor. Priority appears to have been given to avoiding culpability instead of establishing an effective partnership to achieve the extent of change needed to turn a decentralised, paper-based business model into a centralised system, working in an entirely new screen-based environment with all communications based on phones, not paper.

The government had failed to grasp – 'incredibly', the MPs said – that EDS could have simply walked away and pulled out of the deal, leaving the department high and dry. It was to be the last time that huge IT projects would be let under the PFI rules in this way. In future, such ambitious contracts would be broken up into bite-sized chunks. The CSA, for its part, was withholding payments to EDS. Ministers admitted that the agency had retained £12.1 million due to be paid to EDS, because of performance problems between 3 March 2003 and 19 September 2004.

The CSA's Doug Smith admitted to MPs later that he had not attempted to make a specific calculation of the amount of CSA staff time which had been lost as a result of IT problems, at which MPs were aghast. But Mr Smith also had some news. During a question and answer session on 17 November 2004, he told the Commons work and pensions select committee that he was quitting. DWP Secretary Alan Johnson, who was sitting alongside Mr Smith, said: 'Doug has decided that now is the time to stand aside and allow a new chief executive to tackle the challenges ahead.' Mr Smith had overseen a truly dreadful performance. Since March 2003, only 61,000 absent parents had made payments out of 478,000 applications for support. The CSA had reached a 'natural break-point', Mr Johnson explained, and it was a good time for him to go, having exceeded the four-year time limit for civil servants in the same senior position. Mr Johnson was playing his own game of hard ball – he was even said to be considering the 'nuclear option' of scrapping the system.

By the end of 2004, there was a backlog building up in the system. Some applications were disappearing altogether. Michelle Counley, of the National Association for Child Support Action, said: 'There are many cases where we have complaints from parents with care, where applications are simply lost. They go months and months before the parent with care is told "Actually we don't have your application here" and she has to start the whole process again.' EDS blamed the IT problems on management, staff culture and a lack of training. Government consultants found that officials in charge had simply not acted on warnings and were acting at the edge of what was achievable. The CSA had the opportunity at this point to terminate the contract and start all over again. It chose, however, to stick with EDS and try to learn from its mistakes.

In April 2005, the CSA's new chief executive, Stephen Geraghty, commissioned a major review of the agency's problems, leading to a new 'operational improvement plan' which started in February 2006. Costing another £120 million, it was targeted at the huge tail of legacy cases. An estimated 500 defects in the computer system would be fixed. Yet by October of that year, one in four applications received by the agency since 2003 was still waiting to be cleared and the backlog was an eye-watering 250,000 cases – 36,000 of which were simply classed as being 'stuck in the system'.

The agency was now described in newspapers as 'broken-backed', after it emerged that the amount of uncollected maintenance had crossed the £1 billion mark. The backlog of parents waiting for a maintenance assessment increased by a fifth in just six months. Four in ten of all applications for child support on the new computer system were waiting for an assessment. That is not to say that the CSA had been a complete failure. The agency was in some cases securing regular payments from absentee parents. An estimated 100,000 children had been lifted out of poverty by receiving the correct amount of mainte-nance. Yet that modest success had to be set against the cost of what was going wrong. The NAO estimated in 2006 that one third of 'non-resident' parents were not paying maintenance. Some £3.5 billion of maintenance had not been collected by the agency, 60 per cent of which was now considered to be 'uncollectible'. Of the £3.5 billion figure, £2 billion was owed to parents who were looking after children, and £1.5 billion was owed to the government. The CSA had by now worked out how to prioritise absentee parents who owed the most, and was targeting them with enforcement action. Half of the debtors owed less than £1,000. One parent owed £50,000.

The agency's record at collecting money was woeful. In 2004/05 the agency's enforcement teams recovered £8 million in direct payments. But getting back this money cost the agency far more – £12 million. Private debt collectors were hired to collect more of the outstanding cash which was owed. This also cost money, of course – the debt collectors were allowed to keep 20p of every pound they collected, although the very fact of using debt collectors prompted 10 per cent of absen-tee parents to pay up straightaway. But there were still too few parents paying their fair share, with a virulent non-compliance culture among absentee parents and a caseload that swamped the agency. By 2007, 19,000 cases were being dealt with by the agency's enforcement teams – a fraction of the 127,000 completely 'non-compliant' cases.

The vultures were circling over the body of the CSA. In September 2005, veteran Labour MP Frank Field said the agency was now 'in meltdown'. Mr Field, a former welfare reform minister, told Prime Minister Tony Blair in a September 2005 letter that EDS's new IT system, introduced in 2003, had merely added to the CSA's 'general level of chaos we inherited. Indeed in practically all respects the CSA now performs worse than it did a year after the 1997 election.' He suggested that the CSA should be scrapped and its work carried out by the Inland Revenue. Mr Field's intervention prompted a debate about the CSA's future. The PAC's chairman, Edward Leigh MP, said: 'I don't think it [the CSA] can be salvaged. I think we're going to have to go back to the drawing board, although it is difficult to think of an alternative system.' Hannah Lownsbrough, a researcher at centre-left think tank Demos, added: 'It's no longer looking like an agency which absent parents take seriously. I've dealt with parents waiting months for payments who are in real despair.' Kate Green, the chief executive of the Child Poverty Action Group, accused the government of failing to overhaul the agency and instead merely tinkering with it. She said: 'The CSA is a total shambles and the system is failing the very people who are in most need.' Mr Blair's response came two months later in November 2005, when he conceded that the CSA was 'not properly suited' to its job. The following February, Work and Pensions Secretary John Hutton performed the last rites for the CSA, saying that it was 'not fit for purpose'.

In June 2006, the NAO pronounced on the CSA's IT systems. The EDS contract had been signed in 2000 and then amended in 2002 following a series of disputes about technical delays and faults, increasing the overall value of the contract to £456 million. The cost had now risen to £539 million and was expected to rise to £800 million by 2010. It said the agency was 'continuing to fail many parents and children in a big way'. It was costing 70p to collect every £1 in maintenance. An astonishing £3.5 billion of maintenance had not been collected and this would 'continue to rise'. The DWP had 'ignored ample warnings'. A further 300,000 cases were waiting to be cleared, while 36,000 cases were still 'stuck' in the system. Applications were taking nine months to clear. Paul Cannon, the director who wrote the NAO's report, said: 'The government has already stated that it is not fit for purpose. It is a pretty stark fact that that judgement is correct.' An editorial in the *Birmingham Post* the next day described the shambolic CSA as 'one of the most loathed institutions in Britain'.

Another PAC report, in July 2007, set out the CSA's failure in clear terms: 'Since it was established in 1993, the Child Support Agency has consistently underperformed.' The MPs concluded gloomily: 'A significant consequence is that anyone considering not paying maintenance knows that they have a good chance of avoiding detection or serious penalty.' The CSA was working in possibly the most contested and difficult areas of public policy. Yet by virtually any measure it had been a failure. Edward Leigh was withering in his condemnation. 'The reform of the Child Support Agency has been one of the greatest public administration disasters of recent times,' he said. 'The agency threw huge sums of money at a new IT system which was intended to underpin the reforms.' The problem, he said, was that 'the Department for Work and Pensions never really knew what it was doing in dealing with the contractors EDS and the system was a turkey from day one'.

In all, £91 million had been spent on external consultants – but records existed to explain where only a third of that sum went. Edward Leigh added: 'It is hard to think of a body in which the public has less confidence.' In 2005/06, he said, 55,000 complaints were lodged about the CSA. In that same year, 423,000 phone calls to the CSA – 9 per cent of the total – were abandoned while a parent waited to speak to an operator. Leigh concluded: 'It took thirteen years of failure for the department to reach the conclusion that the agency was not fit for purpose. During this time, thousands of children suffered, as thousands of absent parents have neglected their duties.'

In July 2007, MPs on the PAC claimed that the failure to reform the CSA properly had cost nearly £1 billion; their report was described in one newspaper as 'one of the most damning Commons reports ever written'. The report set out a legacy of failure, overseen by seven different ministers since 1997. The bill for outstanding maintenance was £3.5 billion – 60 per cent of which was deemed to be 'uncollectible' – and parents faced a long wait for any money. Overall the cost of trying to reform the CSA had been £850 million. Around 2,500 parents owed more than £50,000 to the agency. Edward Leigh sounded a warning note about the plans to replace the CSA, suggesting that merely swapping brass plates on buildings might not be enough. He said: 'It is by no means clear how this will benefit citizens or regain the confidence of those the agency was intended to help. The government must keep an iron grip on this organisation to ensure that the lessons have been learned from the CSA debacle.'

By now the CSA had already been junked. A year earlier, in July 2006, Sir David Henshaw, a former chief executive of Liverpool City Council, was asked to carry out a thorough-going review. He concluded there had to be a fundamental change in the way that child support was administered and recommended a clean break. At the same time, John Hutton, the Work and Pensions Secretary, said the CSA would be replaced with a smaller, more focused organisation. This 'son of CSA' – the Child Maintenance and Enforcement Commission – would be much tougher with fathers who were failing to pay their fair share. 'I will come down like a ton of bricks on dads who think they can use the changes as an excuse not to pay up,' he said. Debt collectors and bailiffs would be allowed to track down absent fathers using credit checks, while fathers who were dodging their responsibilities were liable for community sentences and curfews imposed by civil courts.

The old CSA had been doomed from the start. In a foreword to the White Paper preparing the way for the commission, Hutton wrote:

Despite the best efforts of its staff, the performance of the Child Support Agency has been and remains unacceptable. However, the problems go much wider and deeper than the Child Support Agency itself. The history of child maintenance in the UK is a case study of well-intentioned policy designs that were incapable of being administered on the ground. The current system often works against parents – obstructing them from carrying out their parental responsibilities instead of supporting them to achieve the best outcomes for their children. And not enough children get the maintenance they need. The system needs root and branch reform.

The new commission would allow parents to come to their own private arrangements about looking after their children – and would not overturn them, as the CSA had done. This was vital. In the comparable system in Australia – which had formed the basis for the CSA when Mrs Thatcher helped to devise it – more than half of the cases were settled privately. By allowing parents to settle their own terms, agency staff would have more time to deal with non-compliant parents. The new commission would also allow the latest tax year information to be used as the basis for calculating child maintenance, as was happening in other countries.

Peter Hain, now the Work and Pensions Secretary, promised MPs in July 2007 that the commission would 'mark a clean break with the past', adding: 'Never again will the system be frustrated by relying on non-resident parents to provide information on their earnings.' It was intended to be a 'tough and effective maintenance regime', provide a 'cost-effective and professional service that gets money flowing between parents in the most efficient way for the taxpayer' and be 'simple and transparent'. The commission came into existence on 24 July 2008, as a result of the Child Maintenance and Other Payments Act 2008. Its objective was to 'maximise the number of effective child maintenance arrangements in place for children who live apart from one or both of their parents'. Yet it inherited many of the old problems of the CSA. An assessment by the NAO of the agency's 'operational improvement plan', published in 2009, found that 350 of 500 defects on the new IT system had been remedied. Yet the remaining 150 defects had generated over 1,000 other problems, 400 of which had no apparent solution. An MPs' report in February 2010 found that the commission was experiencing around 3,000 IT incidents a week, 70 per cent of which were caused by about sixty of the problems.

The computer problems led to tens of thousands of cases being 'managed clerically, outside the IT system'. There were 19,000 of these cases in March 2006. Three years later in March 2009 the figure had more than trebled to 60,000. By September 2010 the figure was forecast to be 108,000. The MPs reported that they were concerned about this 'exponential rise'. The cost of managing each clerical case was £967 – more than three times that of a computer case. Still, finally complaints were falling, from 61,000 in 2005/06 to 27,800 in 2008/09, and the number of children receiving maintenance payments was rising, from 623,000 in March 2006 to 797,000 by September 2009.

The commission's head, Stephen Geraghty, had spent some time mulling over what was going wrong. He decided that two computer systems from 1993 and 2003 were the wrong sort, because of a misunderstanding about the nature of the CSA. 'We are effectively ... a bank – we take money in, we give money out – so a banking system [is needed],' he told MPs. One system – an off the shelf one used by the National Bank of China – was on order, he said. This of course meant more change. From 2011, the commission was suggesting, there would be a further period of transition, as the clients on the old and current schemes were moved onto the new one. Most of the clerical cases – which sat outside the IT – were due to have been moved across by the end of 2012. The MPs called for six-monthly progress reports, concerned at the prospect of the CSA being able to manage three systems at once, given its track record. 'The transitional period will post a formidable administrative headache,' they warned.

The collection of owed money remained problematic. The

commission hired more debt collection agencies to collect
£357 million in 63,500 cases. Yet by September 2009, a paltry
£26 million had been collected, out of a hoped-for £113
million. The agencies were paid £3.5 million for their work.
Mr Geraghty described this as 'disappointing', and said that
the process was being taken back in-house. There were other
powers that the commission were yet to try out. The Child
Maintenance and Other Payments Act 2008 and the Welfare
Reform Act 2009 included powers to ban parents from
driving, and to seize goods. Some money could even be recover-
able from the 3,000 'non-resident' parents who die each year
owing around £14 million. Yet MPs on the work and pensions
committee detected a whiff of history repeating itself. 'We are
concerned that the new statutory scheme, and its reliance on
private arrangements, will see a return to the pre-1993 situation
regarding child maintenance,' they said. The MPs feared that a
reliance on more parents making their own arrangements 'may
recreate the problems associated with the child maintenance
system before the Child Support Act 1991 came into force'.

And still there was more upheaval to come. The new coalition government came to the conclusion – at least, initially
– that the Child Maintenance and Enforcement Commission
should be turned into an executive agency with closer ministerial oversight. The change – which was part of the coalition's
'bonfire of the quangos' – was to increase accountability. The
government said:

> For too long unelected officials have been taking decisions
> which affect the public and spending billions of public money.
> We believe there should be a clear presumption that functions
> carried out by the state should be accountable through demo-
> cratically elected structures, unless there is a compelling reason
> for them being carried out by an independent body.

Ministers were to have more direct control and responsibility
for child support policy and delivery, as well as for ongoing and

future reform. Eventually, it was decided that instead of trying to turn the Child Maintenance and Enforcement Commission into an executive agency it would simply be abolished entirely. Staff would be integrated with the Department for Work and Pensions. The commission's statutory powers would transfer directly to the Secretary of State. Rather than leaving the issue of child maintenance at arm's length, accountability and decision-making responsibility for holding errant parents to account was being taken back into direct ministerial control. It was as though the previous seventeen years' experience – which had cost billions of pounds while causing misery to thousands of taxpayers – had never happened.

2

PASSPORT AGENCY

This is a disgraceful failure by a government agency.
Alan Beith, Liberal Democrat home affairs spokesman

Until quite recently it was common for Britons to go through their lives without ever needing to get a passport. Only a few needed to venture abroad for work purposes, while for most people overseas holidays were prohibitively expensive. But the arrival of cheap air travel in the late 1970s and early 1980s changed all this. An inevitable consequence was a dramatic increase in the need for passports. The government was unprepared. Long delays were common as the passport office, which was part of the Home Office, struggled to process large volumes of applications on time. As a result, holidays were ruined and business trips cancelled. Ministers tried to up their game. In 1985 a feasibility study by the government set the passport office the target of processing applications for passports within five working days.

Yet the processing of travel documents in a timely manner continued to be a hit and miss affair, and in 1989 the passport office decided to computerise some of its clerical systems. But as an unpublished review commissioned from accountancy firm Coopers & Lybrand later that year concluded, the passport office 'had been optimistic to press ahead with the implementation before problems had been resolved'. The review noted that there were 'inadequate contingency arrangements to deal with a surge in applications', while emphasising that 'computer-based systems must not impede their users' and that 'more might have been done to manage risks better within resource constraints'. The study offered a template for what would go woefully wrong ten years later.

The backlogs continued. Finally, in April 1991, the government announced plans for a new United Kingdom Passport

Agency to solve the problem once and for all. Peter Lloyd, a Home Office immigration minister, promised that taxpayers – or 'customers' as they were being called – would see rapid improvements, such as a better telephone enquiry service and easier application forms. The agency was established under the government's 'Next Steps' initiative, which tried to improve delivery by setting up agencies to deliver public services.

John Hayzelden, the agency's new chief executive, said he wanted to vary passport charges between peak and off-peak months to smooth the flow of applications and cut waiting times. It started well. In 1992 the agency even won a Charter Mark from Prime Minister John Major for the 'excellence' of its service. Yet a year later a report from the National Audit Office – entitled *Manpower Planning in the Home Office: The Passport Agency and the Nationality Division* – found that the creation of the new agency had made little impact on the problems faced by holidaymakers and business travellers. Applications were taking up to four times as long as they were meant to.

The agency was failing on all counts. Attempts to 'smooth' applications through the year had failed. Instead of offering incentives, such as reducing the fees during quiet periods, the agency had only paid for expensive adverts to encourage people to apply for their passports in the off-peak months from August to December. The charges remained the same. Officials were reluctant to introduce cheaper off-peak charges because of a fear that all applications would migrate to the cheaper months. The NAO found that between 1988 and 1992 the number of people employed at the agency rose by nearly a third to 1,316, with salaries accounting for £17 million of the agency's £48 million budget during 1991 and 1992. Despite this wealth of job creation, the agency's management had failed to carry the staff with them. Absenteeism was running at 7 per cent – more than twice the rate in the private sector – and walk-outs were common.

John Hayzelden left in 1994 and was succeeded as chief executive by David Gatenby, who wanted to turn the passport agency into something akin to British retail institution Marks &

Spencer. One of his first actions was to seek changes to opening hours to let more applicants in earlier, after seeing his 'customers' waiting in the rain for the local passport office to open. He said:

> For a service supposedly dedicated to the customer this didn't seem right. So I called for opening the office at 8.15 a.m. instead of 9 a.m. Immediately there was a strike ballot and when that failed there was a walkout. We have to become more like Marks & Spencer, a business that reacts efficiently and cost-effectively to public demand. I realise that many of the staff are hostile, but we are doing everything to win them over.

In 1995 alone, there were four strike ballots and one walk-out. This was clearly not good enough. So in May 1996 – more than five years after it was first established – the agency published a new framework document setting out its aims and objectives, together with specific targets, and a new mission statement: 'to provide services for British nationals in the United Kingdom promptly and economically'. There were new targets including one to process applications within ten days for 'straightforward, properly completed applications'. Another key objective was 'to meet customers' declared travel dates for at least 99.99 per cent of passports issued' and to bring in private expertise. The search for the private firms started in 1996. Officials wanted two private firms to work with them: one to process passport applications, and another to print and despatch them. The prize would be two ten-year contracts, worth £120 million.

Four private companies bid for the processing contract – Donnelly Pindar, IBM, Siemens Business Services and EDS. It was finally awarded to Germany's Siemens after Donnelly Pindar and IBM were knocked out in earlier stages and EDS's final bid was ruled to be non-compliant. Under the deal Siemens would be paid £2.39 for every passport it processed for the agency. Three firms bid for the printing and despatching contract – Security Printing & Systems, International Data and De La Rue. SPS were awarded the contract after De La

Rue's bid was ruled to be non-compliant and International Data was knocked out. Like Siemens, SPS was to be paid per passport, based on annual volume and on whether the agency was using a 24-hour or 48-hour turnaround service. For the 48-hour service, the fee charged by the company to the government was £3.21 per passport. Overseeing both companies' contracts, the agency retained its duty to examine and authorise the issue of passports. The hope was that applicants would see a much-improved service. The other major change was that photographs and signatures of applicants would be printed digitally onto the passport documents themselves.

The responsibility of the contractors was to check and correct all key information within fifteen hours of receiving a completed application before giving it to examiners at the agency. The new system would also provide more checks to improve security and better facilities for tracking the progress of applications, as well as an electronic archive to retrieve applications if necessary.

The government established a project steering committee to oversee the setting up of the computer system, which included representatives from the contractors. The intention was to roll out the new service between October 1998 and February 1999, starting with the largest passport offices at Liverpool, Newport and Peterborough. The government ditched a less ambitious plan to start at a smaller and quieter passport office, because it would have led to the roll-out in larger offices starting just as the 'peak' season for applications was getting underway. However – just as the steering committee started its work – the government decided to axe the twelve-month British Visitor Passports. These short-term passports had been available for decades from the local post office. They had been used by millions of people for short trips to the Continent, as a quick and cheap alternative to the rigmarole of applying for a full passport. More than two million British Visitor Passports were issued annually at a cost of £12, compared to the £18 fee for a ten-year passport. But Spain announced that from 1 October 1995 onwards it would no longer accept British Visitor Passports. Other countries followed suit, though confusingly the ban only took effect in France, Belgium, Portugal and Turkey from 1 January 1996. Chaos ensued, with reports of hundreds of British tourists being turned back on their way to Spain because their passports were invalid.

There followed a near-doubling in applications for full passports from 3.2 million per year in 1991/92 to some 5.1 million in 1996/97. The growth continued the following year, when 27 per cent more passports were issued than expected. On the surface the agency appeared to be coping, despite trying to modernise at the same time. In a review of the performance of government agencies, the agency met 80 per cent of its targets.

Yet behind the scenes, the timetable had been slipping since the beginning. The agency had originally hoped to award the contracts in April 1997, but talks with the bidders were still going on through the summer until July 1997. This should still have left an ample fifteen months for the new computer system to be tested adequately before the go-live date in October 1998. Plans for the secure printing contract with SPS were proceeding on time. But the Siemens processing contract, which would provide the 'content' for the passport, was a completely different story. While it was clear how to print the passports, what was still not clear was how to process the information that would go in them. This was because the design of the new IT programme took four months longer than expected and was only completed in April 1998, just six months before the October 1998 deadline. The NAO subsequently found that too much time was wasted in negotiations over what the computer system was for. It said: 'Discussions between the agency and Siemens took longer than expected as each party sought to clarify the other's intentions and to reach agreement on the systems' specifications.'

Factory-testing the new software started at Siemens's own offices in July 1998, and carried on at the passport office in Liverpool during August and September. The NAO later found that by the time the system went live in October 'most of the system's core functions had been delivered on schedule', although it found that some – such as management reports – were 'not fully developed'. One key area was the examination stage of passport processing. During tests at Siemens over the summer, officials noted that this stage was taking much longer than expected. The agency had planned to carry out more tests on productivity at the Liverpool office before giving the green light on 5 October to start the pilot tests. However, the NAO noted sorrowfully that 'although terminals had been set aside for this to happen, the tests did not take place due to shortage of time'. Despite this, the Home Office's internal audit team gave the delivery of the new computer system a qualified endorsement in a report in early October: 'Given the tight timescales under which the project has been developed it has been well managed with sound controls in place to ensure the quality of the end products.' However, the need to hit the start date of 5 October meant that not enough testing had been carried out. The Home Office said:

> There has been a compression of testing timescales. We understand the compelling reasons for wanting to meet the 5 October 1998 pilot start date and acknowledge that the functionality of the system was largely proven. However, the risk is that the pilot may need to have its timescales extended to ensure that robust operational and user procedures and controls are in place.

There had also been problems with training staff to process the passports. While Siemens had successfully coached them to use the new software, not enough time had been given to instructing staff on the 'clerical procedures' necessary to support the new passport-issuing system. The agency's plan to roll out the new software was ambitious. At each passport office, computer systems were stripped out, building works carried out and office lay-outs reconfigured, allowing for space for staff from Siemens. On 5 October, as planned, the agency's

office in Liverpool started to issue new passports using the new
IT system. The tight timetable meant that there was just five
weeks to reflect on the experience at Liverpool and see if it was
working properly, before work started on stripping out the old
computers in Newport as the new IT system was rolled out
across the agency's other offices.

However, two main bottlenecks emerged. Siemens's way of
scanning application forms, which were then corrected manually, had delayed the issuing of passports. A consultant had
warned the agency that this might happen when the bids were
originally assessed. The consultant wrote that there would
be a 'high error rate in reading hand-written letters [and]
numbers [which] would lead to a high correction level and all
the resulting problems'. Trials during the summer had picked
up this problem, although Siemens and agency staff dismissed
it, believing wrongly that 'this was because the forms had not
been completed with the same care as real applications'. There
were also problems affecting a small percentage of applications
because of the quality of ink used by applicants.

The roll-out was also criticised because of a delay in installing
a counter service at the passport office in Liverpool for personal
callers trying frantically to chase a passport application on
site before hoping to go on holiday. The agency had wanted
Liverpool to hit a target of 30,000 passports a week within
six weeks of its launch. Yet on 14 October, nine days after the
launch, officials realised this would not be possible. There was
a risk that the roll-outs at the two offices in Peterborough and
Newport would be delayed, pushing the introduction of the
system at Peterborough until the New Year.

Rather than try to hit the stretching target, managers moved
the goalposts. The target for issuing passports at Liverpool –
which would trigger the roll-out of the system to Newport
– was cut by two thirds, from 30,000 per week after six weeks
to just 10,000 per week at the four week point, while still only
rising to 20,000 per week after six weeks. Yet on 9 November,
five weeks after the start of the service at Liverpool, the

agency's management board approved plans to start the service at Newport, which appeared reckless. Output at Liverpool was running at just 6,200 passports per week, yet by expanding the system to Newport before ironing out problems on Merseyside, the agency turned a local problem into a national one.

The agency's board felt this risk was worth taking. On-site testing at Newport had gone well, and the board felt that the Liverpool office might not have been fully prepared for the scale of the change. Testing the service on more than one site had its advantages, and – as the NAO noted – 'delay at this stage, only five weeks into the roll-out programme, would almost certainly have meant delaying the remainder of the roll-out programme until the following autumn'. But the gamble failed. The Newport office saw similar delays to those that had plagued Liverpool, and David Gatenby and his team had little room for manoeuvre. Timescales were so tight that they had only a small window of opportunity in which to act. The board decided to postpone the roll-out to Peterborough on 7 December 'until revised performance criteria for the two pilot sites had been met'. It would be a long wait. Newport and Liverpool did not achieve the chief criterion – to issue 30,000 passports per week – until the following June, six months later. This failure was central to the oncoming crisis. The NAO later concluded: 'If the planned output at these offices [Liverpool and Newport] had been achieved according to the original timetable, the agency would have issued around 400,000 additional passports, enough to avoid the serious backlogs that occurred.' The clock was ticking, with the agency heading inexorably towards its peak time in January, like the *Titanic* towards the iceberg.

And things were about to get even worse. The government had announced in April 1998 that separate passports would be required for children under sixteen, who would no longer be able to travel on a parent's passport after October 1998. This was to prevent child abductions. Only the previous year, in 1997, some 285 children had been kidnapped and taken over-seas. But the requirement for separate child passports would kick in at precisely the same time as the new computer system went live. The Home Office was already aware that this would cause a huge surge in applications. In September 1997, the department's own research and planning unit had forecast that 800,000 child passports would have to be issued in 1999/2000 – compared with 400,000 in the previous year. This turned out to be a significant underestimate – the forecast annual total was achieved in just the first six months of 1999, greatly aggravating the problems at the agency.

It was not a happy Christmas for David Gatenby. His officials were faced with two of their six regional offices – Liverpool and Newport – running at well below capacity going into the busiest time of the passport-issuing year. To make matters worse, the Peterborough office – which had already shut down processing to prepare for the introduction of the new system – suddenly had to fire up its old computers. Applications were being transferred between offices to try to smooth the workflow. But the offices in Glasgow and Belfast were also struggling with their normal intake of applications, along with extra work transferred from other offices. Siemens hired extra staff and brought in 'specialist work planners' to help out at Newport and Liverpool. By February 1999, as applications increased, waiting times deteriorated markedly. By the end of that month, the agency had 'serious concerns about its ability to cope', the NAO said later. Managers tried to flex the system. The agency focused on trying to process passports in time to meet customers' travel dates, while more staff were paid overtime to cope with the increased workload. Yet the combination of increasing numbers of applications and longer processing times became insurmountable. Between March and July, members of staff on average worked overtime totalling an extra four days per month, or nearly an additional day per week each. And the cost of all this activity was starting to hit the agency's bottom line. At the end of February its managers authorised a £5 per hour bonus in addition to normal overtime rates. This was bumped up to £10 per hour in March, and then £20 per hour in July and August. It was no good. The NAO noted bleakly: 'Despite the transfer of applications between offices and extensive use of overtime, the agency was not able to generate the sufficient extra output to deal with the volume of incoming applications, leading to a growing backlog.'

The agency's public relations strategy was to say nothing. Press releases had been issued in October 1998 to publicise the changes to the child passports, but not one press notice was promoted by the agency between January and July 1999. Even when problems emerged, the supposedly arm's-length executive agency did not have a press office to deal with journalists' enquiries, which were referred to the Home Office throughout the crisis.

The agency had contemplated reassuring the public that everything was fine, but feared this would only stimulate demand and panic holidaymakers. Unions later said that by February 1999 they were advising the agency to place adverts in the press telling people about the problems. It was obvious that the situation could not stay hidden from public view for long and by March 1999, MPs and the press started to pay attention to the unfolding drama. The sudden spotlight on delays prompted even more people to apply for a new passport, to be sure of getting one before they went on holiday.

The agency's call centre, which had just seventy lines, went into meltdown. By the end of March more than half of all calls were not being answered. The NAO's 1999 report into the sorry affair was unpitying:

> As the backlog of applications built up, telephone queries took longer to resolve as more applications became urgent. In March the agency decided to withdraw some staff from telephone duties in order to devote more resources to processing applications. At peak periods in Liverpool, the telephone enquiry service was virtually shut down.

Telephone callers were told to send a fax instead, on a new recorded answer phone message. Not surprisingly, a survey by the agency during 1999 found this telephone service was 'one of the biggest sources of frustration and complaints'.

Having given up waiting at the end of a telephone line for an answer, thousands of people voted with their feet and turned up at their local passport offices demanding answers and their passports. Soon long queues were building up, providing excellent television pictures for the gawping media and only fuelling the sense of panic. In May 1999, for example, the number of personal visitors to the office in Liverpool alone increased by 50 per cent to 15,000 – or 500 per day. The average waiting time was two and a half hours. The agency spent £5,000 on free luncheon vouchers and splashed out £16,000 on 1,200 umbrellas for queuing customers (the Home Office later said that 'regrettably one or two' of the brollies were not returned).

The fun for the watching media was only just beginning. Mohammed Al Fayed, the owner of Harrods, who had famously been denied a British passport, soon appeared with green and gold-liveried delivery vans packed full of refreshments from the famous Harrods food hall for people queuing outside the agency's Petty France headquarters office in central London. Then the formidable Ann Widdecombe MP, shadow Home Secretary and a former Conservative Home Office minister, arrived to lend support to the queuing customers before heading back to the House of Commons, where she laid into Jack Straw, the Home Secretary, for 'changing the rules' so that families had to get passports for their children if they wanted to go on holiday. A furious Widdecombe, rippling with anger, told him: 'Queuing in the rain, in many cases since dawn, were mothers with very tiny babies, some as young as six weeks. They were there because the government have changed the rules. All those mothers said to me, in different ways, that they thought that the government must be barmy!'

In a leading article, *The Times* newspaper was withering in its condemnation:

Ministers and civil servants have cobbled together poor excuses

for the fiasco. Like bad workmen they are blaming their tools ...
The agency has belatedly admitted that it was caught unawares
by the new regulation which requires children under the age of
sixteen who are not listed on one of their parents' passports
to get a passport of their own. But such a confession reveals
managerial incompetence of the highest order.

By June 1999, the backlog had reached 565,000 passport applications – nearly double the 300,000 backlog of the previous
year. The slowest regional office was Liverpool – the first to be
modernised – which was taking a glacial forty-one days to issue
a passport. Jack Straw decided special measures were called
for and authorised 300 extra staff to help clear the backlog.
However, this was to little effect. On a visit to the office in
Liverpool some time later, Straw asked officials where the 300
extra staff he had ordered to be hired were. One newspaper
reported: 'The silence lasted a minute and a half; the official
started making excuses about procedure and promotion and
security vetting.' It seemed the 300 extra staff who had been
drafted into the agency were making no appreciable difference,
largely because the agency typically needed at least ten weeks
to recruit, train and obtain security clearance for new staff.
Passport clerks were told to overlook errors in applications
to keep them moving through the system. Staff were to 'give
the benefit of the doubt' to applicants, and the 'widest possible
interpretation' to some rules to ensure passports were being
issued quickly. Kevin Sheehan, the agency's operations director,
wrote to staff to ask them to ignore the normal requirement
that a person witnessing the signature of a passport applicant
should be a professional, such as a doctor, lawyer or accountant.

Gatenby and Straw were by now said not to be on speaking terms. And the agency chief executive's public comments
did not inspire confidence after he told his 'customers' to stop
trying to make contact with his agency. Using the formula
which would be heard some years later by farmers trying to
contact the ill-fated Rural Payments Agency, Gatenby said: 'The

delays have understandably led to increased customer enquiries, particularly by telephone and fax, which is itself adding to the problem. I would urge people not to contact us unless it is really necessary.'

The Home Office admitted to some responsibility for the agency's very public problems. Mike O'Brien, the immigration minister, conceded that the agency's situation was 'extremely serious', blaming 'the new high technology-driven passport-issuing arrangements'.

In July 1999 the Home Office took direct control of the crisis from the agency, ordering emergency measures to alleviate the problems, including a new call centre to deal with telephone enquiries and an extra 100 staff in passport offices. The Home Office also brought in new powers for staff at post offices manually to extend the expiry dates on passports for up to two years, free of charge. Broadly, the plans to deal with the emergency worked. By the end of August 1999, the backlog had been reduced to 82,500 and the maximum processing time was cut to within the ten-day period. In September this was cut to five days and by October the Post Office's powers to extend the expiry dates of passports had been removed altogether.

The final bill for the summer of misery at the Passport Agency was eventually estimated by the NAO to be £12.6 million. From this, £6 million had been spent on hiring additional staff and paying staff overtime to process the backlog. There were also compensation payments to the 500 people who had missed travel dates. Between October 1998 and August 1999, the agency paid out £161,000 in compensation – more than three times the £52,000 in the previous year, but hardly a significant figure. Indeed Gatenby admitted in August that these payments were so low that they had not materially dented the agency's budget.

Siemens escaped relatively lightly. The agency decided to cut fees paid to Siemens from £14 million to just £5.4 million in the year from October 1998 because of the failed rollout of the IT system to all of its offices. The agency could have fined Siemens at least £402,000 for the problems with the computer system, yet it waived fines worth £275,000. Perversely it had even agreed to pay Siemens 14 per cent more (£2.72 instead of £2.39) for every passport processed. The NAO report concluded that problems with Siemens's computers were the 'initial' cause of the fiasco. It strongly criticised the agency for 'insufficient contingency planning in the event that implementation of the new system might not go according to plan'. The report also criticised the agency's disastrous PR strategy and its inability to communicate effectively with the public.

MPs on the Public Accounts Committee were appalled by what had happened. In a report published in June 2000, they condemned the agency's flawed system for the drastic reductions in productivity, with delays to the production of 400,000 passports, stating:

> We consider that the Passport Agency's inability to provide an adequate service during the summer of 1999 represented a deplorable departure from the high standards of service the public has a right to expect. We believe this case offers salutary lessons for all organisations providing services direct to the public.

Between March and the end of June, at the height of the crisis, they found there were around 3.5 million 'unsuccessful attempts to get through to the agency by telephone. The public should be able to obtain prompt and accurate information about public services quickly from a variety of sources, including the internet.' At fault, the MPs said, lay unfocused cost cutting at the Home Office, which had slashed costs by 17 per cent in the two years before the new system was implemented. 'As a result the agency had few or no resources to cope when implementation of their new system started to go so badly wrong in late 1998. The Home Office should have exercised better oversight of the agency, and should have been more alive to the risks and the agency's capacity to deal with them, before the agency embarked on this ambitious project.'

3

TAX CREDITS

If you cannot follow the legislation, why should the ordinary punter do so?
Edward Leigh MP to Dave Hartnett of HM Revenue and Customs

My first report ... raised some more fundamental issues for government and Parliament to address, not least whether a financial support system which included a degree of inbuilt financial insecurity could properly meet the needs of very low income families and earners.
Ann Abraham, Parliamentary and Health Service Ombudsman

There used to be just two certainties in life: death and taxes. In the past decade, the British government has added a third – tax credits. From a plain English point of view, tax credits are a hard sell. Their name sounds like an oxymoron. If a tax is a debit of funds from an individual, then how can it also be a credit? Yet for some, their prospect was a panacea, a way of allowing the government to integrate fully the tax and benefits system.

The idea was not new. Indeed a 'negative income tax' was first proposed in the 1960s by a future Conservative Chancellor of the Exchequer, Geoffrey Howe, based on an original idea from the Nobel prize-winning economist Milton Friedman. The Tories then suggested the idea on two occasions in government, first in 1972 and then in 1985, when a Green Paper called 'Reform of Social Security' described it as a long-term aim. The new Labour government picked up the idea in May 1997, when its Chancellor, Gordon Brown, set his sights on a complete overhaul of the tax and benefits system, which it was hoped would save billions of pounds in administration costs. The new tax credits were billed by overexcited newspapers as Brown's 'big project'.

Martin Taylor, chief executive of Barclays Bank, was

appointed to see how it could be done. His terms of reference were 'to examine the interaction of the tax and benefits system so that they can be streamlined and modernised, so as to fulfil our objectives of promoting work incentives, reducing poverty and welfare dependency and strengthening community and family life'. Taylor concluded that Britain could look to America and consider adopting its 'earned income tax credit' as a model for a British tax credit. He said: 'Although the differences between the UK and US tax and benefit systems need to be recognised, there is no over-riding reason why the UK should not have a tax credit payable through the pay packet to families in work.' The government hoped, too, that the tax credits would reduce the dependency and 'stigma' among those claiming in-work support and be more acceptable to claimants and taxpayers as a whole, as well as helping to lower the very high effective marginal tax rates affecting those who faced the withdrawal of benefits. So it was that the Working Families Tax Credit and the Disabled Person's Tax Credit replaced two existing benefits – the Family Credit and the Disability Working Allowance – in October 1999, with the main difference that they were paid through wages by an employer or directly from the Inland Revenue into a bank account or a Post Office Card Account. Within four years, some £6.46 billion was being paid out every year through these two benefits.

This was just the start. In the 2000 Budget, the government set out plans for a new 'integrated child credit' called the Child Tax Credit, to replace the still new Children's Tax Credit, and an 'employment tax credit' called the Working Tax Credit, which from 2003 would replace the newly minted Working Families Tax Credit, Disabled Person's Tax Credit and the New Deal 50+ Employment Credit. There was no time to lose. In July 2001 the government issued a consultation paper and a partial regulatory impact assessment to examine the plans in more detail. The consultation closed in October 2001. The government's statutory response to its own consultation was published after MPs had considered the Tax Credits Bill on

28 November 2001. The legislation became law on 8 July 2002 and people could claim the new credits from April 2003. This was a near record from consultation paper to the statute book in Whitehall terms, where the progress of legislation can often appear glacially slow.

There was a rush, too, to get the information technology ready in time. This was no easy task, not least because the Inland Revenue – a department traditionally known for collecting taxes – was being asked to start doling out benefits as well. The government only confused matters by trying to claim that tax credits were not public spending, a ruse which was soon dismissed both by the courts and by auditors. Judge Michael Harris, the Chief Social Security and Child Support Commissioner, said: 'Whatever their title, Tax Credits are benefits not tax.' Sir John Bourn, head of the National Audit Office, stated that a tax credit 'is a form of social security'.

The Inland Revenue called on favoured IT provider EDS, a company with which it had worked closely for nine years, to set up an entire system to process the new tax credits. The new computer system needed to have links with other Inland Revenue databases and also with computers at the Department for Work and Pensions to check new tax credit claim forms. All seemed to be going well, with the Office of Government Commerce, which vets large projects, describing the scheme in December 2002 as 'an exemplar of good programme management', while noting there was much to be done in a short timetable. This was not the whole story, though. It later emerged during an MPs' inquiry that the committee in charge of the scheme at the Inland Revenue had rated the programme at 'red status' since May the previous year, meaning that it faced significant risks which were supposed to be clarified and addressed before considering further progress.

System testing had been due to start on 25 November 2002 but this was then delayed, cutting nineteen weeks of testing to just thirteen weeks. The time allowed for volume testing was also slashed, from twelve weeks to four, because of a problem matching National Insurance numbers with claimants. And in the end, just seven weeks was set aside to test 'end-to-end functionality'. Bill Thomas, EDS's president for Europe, Middle East and Asia, said that it was 'a massively challenging programme', later telling MPs: 'We knew we were dealing with one of the hardest business and IT programmes the British government had ever introduced.'

The problems with the computers came amid growing warnings of how the existing system for the still relatively new Working Families Tax Credit and Disabled Person's Tax Credit were working. Bourn sounded his concerns on 8 November about

> the problem the department experienced in reconciling the amount of tax credit paid via employers with that actually authorised by the department ... It is important that the department are learning the lessons from their experiences of current tax credits so as to minimise similar problems in the new tax credit schemes that are to operate from April 2003.

MPs on the Public Accounts Committee reinforced this point in the following month, highlighting that there were only limited checks on whether the right Working Families Tax Credits were being paid by employers, and then recouped out of tax and National Insurance payments to the Inland Revenue.

In February – two months before the new tax credits were introduced – David Willetts, the opposition Work and Pensions spokesman, gave a speech in which he complained that the excessive complexity of the tax credits system was encouraging fraud. He estimated that 'of the £6 billion a year spent on the Working Families Tax Credit, £1.5 billion is wasted on fraudulent claims'. Willetts warned that the new credits were also overly complicated. The new Child Tax Credit had five different parts: a family element, a baby addition, a child element, a disabled child element and an enhanced disabled child element. Families applying for tax credits had to fill in a twelve-page form, after reading forty-seven pages of instructions. The Working Tax Credit was even more complex. It had seven parts, including a basic part, an element for couples and lone parents, a thirty-hour element, a disabled worker element, an enhanced disabled worker element and an over-fifties worker element. There was also a childcare element, depending on numbers of children. Claimants were 'baffled by something which really ought to be pretty straightforward', Willetts complained. 'It has been like watching a professional footballer with an open goal who darts round the ball, dribbles it up and down but refuses to do the obvious thing of kicking it at the goal.'

Willetts pointed to a further weakness – that the credits were being administered by the Inland Revenue, traditionally a department more used to collecting taxes, and not by the 'poor old Department for Work and Pensions', whose traditional job was to run the benefits system. 'There is a real danger that this will distract the Inland Revenue from its core task of collecting revenues efficiently and running the tax system smoothly,' he said. 'One place where the pressures from the new tax credits might show up is in further administrative failures at the Inland Revenue.'

The Child Tax Credit and the Working Tax Credit were introduced in April 2003. Some 4.5 million applications had been received by June. Almost immediately problems began to emerge as the computer systems started to fail. Hundreds of thousands of people had not received the payments to which they were entitled. Staff were inundated and a special helpline set up by the Revenue had to change its number because it was swamped with calls. The Revenue had hoped that the relaunched tax credit scheme would be 'wholly IT-based'; however, in practice, a great deal of significant human intervention was required. The unexpected problems caused the department to issue 500,000 cheques 'manually', worth £170 million, despite only having inadequate supporting documentation in some cases.

Accuracy was initially poor. A little over three quarters of claims were processed accurately in that first year, the NAO found, compared with nearly 97 per cent in the following year. Some 1,600 people 'who could demonstrate that they incurred expenses as a result of delays and to recognise worry and distress' were further compensated. The NAO later discovered that software errors resulted in overpayments worth £184 million in 2003/04 and 2004/05. In the first year of the new credits, £37 million worth of payments, each totalling less than £300, were written off. In the following year, 2004/05, the Revenue wrote off £33 million 'because the records were not good enough to cost-effectively match them to claimants'.

The civil servants in charge were called to account publicly in December 2003. Sounding like a driver who had just bought an old banger that he thought was a Rolls-Royce, Sir Nick Montagu, the Inland Revenue's chairman, told MPs: 'I can honestly say that it came as an equal shock to EDS and ourselves that a system which we had every reason to believe would perform to standard turned out, when it came to live running, to be unstable and not fit for purpose.' By the end of the first year of the scheme, the Revenue had fielded 32,000 complaints. The reputation of the entire department was severely damaged.

There were also the first stirrings of a wider problem of over-payments. In the first year some people who realised they had been paid too much in tax credits because they had received a pay rise tried to send back a cheque to the Inland Revenue. The department declined the offer and told them to repay the following year. The MPs on the Public Accounts Committee warned that this could be just the start: 'From April 2004, the department will adjust tax credit awards for the past year and make new awards for the next year which will take into account changes in claimants' circumstances. The process will probably bring to light further overpayments which the depart-ment will seek to recover.' The MPs were not mistaken. It was inherent in the tax credits system that every year hundreds of thousands of people would be overpaid and a similar proportion would be underpaid, because claimants were paid a provisional 'tax credit award' based on a family's income during the previous year. The award was finalised after the end of the tax year when the actual income and circumstances of the recipient of the credits were known. The figure was then adjusted for the following year, with any overpaid money being clawed back. Overpayments were part of the landscape *by design* for any claimant whose income turned out to have risen during the year, although the first £2,500 of an income increase was disregarded.

MPs found in a later inquiry that overpayments were 'significantly higher than that predicted' in the first twelve months of the new scheme. One third of the awards paid out – nearly one million in total – overpaid claimants by nearly £2 billion. Of the 1,879,000 claimants who were overpaid, 41,000 received more than £5,000 in overpayments. Half of the total overpayments related to 283,000 families who had been overpaid at least £2,000 each. Full recovery of overpayments from the first year of operation was expected to take at least five years. The figure for this year was always going to be higher than expected, because the awards for that year were based on income for 2001/02, not 2002/03, yet they still came as a shock. Ministers had been budgeting for a degree of overpayment every year – but not this much. A government policy paper published alongside the 2002 Budget entitled 'The Child and Working Tax Credits: The Modernisation of Britain's Tax and Benefit System' had forecast that 'in a steady state' one million people would receive more tax credits each year because of a fall in their income, while 750,000 people a year would receive less because of a rise in their income. It said that people who did receive a pay rise 'would be advised to ask for an adjusted award during the year to reduce the risk of overpayments'.

The chaos from the complexity forecast by David Willetts before the scheme launched was becoming reality. Many of the recipients of the new tax credits were bewildered by how the system was working. One woman explained how she had been awarded tax credits worth £3,251, based on eight months' work in the 2001/02 tax year. When her part-time salary rose to £10,300 in the following year, her award was cut to £2,554. Yet the payments continued until she was sent a notice informing her she had been overpaid £1,911. 'It is craziness, a complete farce,' she said.

In truth, the difficulty of trying to recoup wrongly paid tax credits from people on low incomes, many of whom were unlikely still to have the money, had been known in Whitehall for some time, following a sampling exercise on mistakes under the old tax credits scheme carried out in 2001 – yet the government sat on the data for two years before finally passing the results to the NAO in August 2003. Sir John Bourn published the results in his review of the annual accounts of the Inland Revenue in November 2003. The incendiary findings were delivered in the dusty tones of an experienced auditor:

> The Working Families and Disabled Person's Tax Credit schemes began in 1999, ended on 6 April 2003 and spent some £17.8 billion. The department were able only in August 2003 to provide me with the results of their examination of samples of tax credit applications made during part of 2000/01. Error rates for a full year were 10–14 per cent by value, and the estimated level of overpayment for a full year was between £510 million and £710 million.

This meant that over the four years of the two credit schemes, nearly £3 billion could have been paid out in error. Bourn was so alarmed by the findings that he refused to give the accounts a clean bill of health – a major embarrassment for a government department that was in charge of collecting taxes. He wrote:

> [T]he department have not undertaken similar exercises for 2000/01 or 2002/03. The department emphasise that they had incorporated the lessons learned into their design of the new tax credits. For these tax credits the department must consider undertaking an exercise each year to determine the effectiveness of their

controls in detecting error and ensuring that payments are properly
calculated to reflect claimants' circumstances. The level of overpayment identified by the department is cause for serious concern
and as a result I have qualified my opinion on the Trust statement
for 2002/03. The improved controls in the new tax credit system
should help to reduce overpayments. But the department are not
yet able to assess the likely extent of that reduction.

Bourn's concern about the degree of overpayments of tax
credits was horribly prescient. Over the following years, many
billions of pounds more in public money were overpaid to
claimants. The annual reminder through the publication of
successive reports by committees of MPs of the scale of public
money wrongly paid out through tax credits was set to become
part of the Westminster calendar, along with the Budget and
State Opening of Parliament. In 2004/05, two million out of
the five million families receiving tax credits were overpaid by
£2.1 billion. A further 900,000 were underpaid by £556 million.
So it continued in 2005/06 and 2006/07. In the first four years
of the scheme, £85 billion was paid out to claimants. Of that,
£7.3 billion was overpaid and £2 billion was underpaid. By
the end of March 2008, HM Revenue and Customs – the new
name for the Inland Revenue – had collected 37 per cent of this
debt (£2.7 billion) and written off 14 per cent of it (£1 billion).
A further £3.6 billion was outstanding, of which officials had
decided they were unlikely to recover £1.8 billion. This was
becoming a national scandal.

Yet officials seemed to be scratching their heads when asked
to explain what was going on. HMRC confessed in April 2005
that it could not 'easily identify the reasons why an overpayment
arose', and warned that it would be 'prohibitively expensive' to
try to find out why. Mike Brewer, a tax expert at the Institute of
Fiscal Studies, blamed a deficit of reliable information when the
policy was being devised in 2001: 'There was not a good source of
data for them to design the initial policy, when they were thinking
about this in 2001/02. Basically that remains the case even now.'

What evidence there was suggested that tax credits awards were likely to vary wildly from year to year among recipients on very low incomes who were not used to receiving a regular monthly salary and who in many cases were not in regular employment. One study in 2004 found that nearly half of lone parents experienced changes in their financial circumstances between two and seven times in the first year of the new tax credits schemes. Dawn Primarolo, the Paymaster General and minister in charge of the schemes, attempted to shed some light on the problem in December 2005, more than two years after the schemes launched, when she gave the government's first official view on why so much money was being wrongly paid out:

> Analysis of overpayments suggests that they result from a number of factors: income rises from one year to the next; families overestimating the extent to which their income has fallen when they seek extra support during the year; provisional payments made at the start of the tax year, which are based on out-of-date information that is subsequently updated when the award is renewed; and delays in reporting changes in families' personal circumstances.

MPs who visited a tax credits office in Preston, Lancashire, as part of an investigation were told that the minister's first three factors accounted for 70 per cent of overpayments. The Revenue's Tax Credit Office received 51,000 complaints in 2004/05, and 'has had difficulties managing this workload', the MPs found. Staff numbers were doubled from 200 in April 2004 to around 400 in April 2005, to ease the pressure. In March 2006, the government finally commissioned a study to see how the pay of 'low and middle-income working families with children' fluctuates throughout the year. It would be hard to think of a bigger case of slamming the barn door after the horse has bolted. The report noted that this information 'has not been collected before'. It concluded that 'patterns of income mobility ... involve considerably greater volatility of income within the year (for this particular kind of working family) than many might have expected'. The groups hit hardest were those earning less than £15,000 a year, as well as lone parents and tenants – exactly the groups the tax credits were meant to help. Many of the poorest families were found only to be able to plan ahead financially for a month or less, rather than over a whole tax year. MPs on the Treasury committee welcomed the report, saying, perhaps tongue in cheek, that 'it offers valuable data to those designing tax credits policy'. They concluded that 30 per cent of overpayments were due to delays in reporting changes in families' personal circumstances, such as family breakdown, a new relationship or a child going to school or leaving home, to the tax credits office.

The computer problems that had beset tax credits from the very beginning had not gone away. EDS, which had set up the system, lost its contract on 30 June 2004 and agreed to pay £71.25 million to the government in compensation, of which £47 million was paid in cash. The remainder was in staged payments set against any future work EDS was likely to win from the government, although there was of course no guarantee that this would happen. MPs on the Treasury committee were appalled. The deal had 'the appearance of impropriety, if not the fact' because it appeared to place an onus on government departments to give work to EDS just to claw it back in compensation payments owed to taxpayers because of earlier failure. Later other MPs would describe the arrangement as 'invidious'. Indeed, there was no guarantee that EDS would win enough work to pay back its 'fine'. The company finally paid its fine in full in January 2009, shortly after it was taken over by Hewlett-Packard. EDS's replacement Capgemini was swiftly locked into a contract with a series of tougher penalty clauses, should they be required.

Yet the departure of EDS did not solve the IT problems at the heart of the tax credits system. In June 2004, an IT mistake, known as a 'Red A' computer error, caused the miscalculation of hundreds of thousands of awards in Northern Ireland. Sir David Varney, the chairman of HMRC, told MPs in October 2005 that his department had 'been trying to stabilise – and I think have been successful – the IT system. It is still potentially fragile and therefore every time we have had to do something, I approach it in the spirit that we do not want to lose any progress we have made in stability.' Three hundred improvements were made between April and October 2003, but there were still another 199 known software errors in the tax credit computer system. Most of these were resolved by April 2007.

The Revenue appeared to have been caught out by the temptation – ever present in Whitehall – to rely on computers too much. The tax credits office in Preston which had been visited by MPs, for example, found that staff had to intervene manually in three out of every four new applications. Judging by the evidence from both the Inland Revenue and the staff, it is hard to conceive of a more ill-suited system to so complex a task. The Public and Commercial Services Union, which represents civil servants, was furious: 'The computer system is not user friendly and continues to be unavailable at key times' (although this was denied by the government). One of the key problem areas was the 'interface' between the tax credits computer system and information provided to HMRC staff about a claimant's change of circumstances. Volunteer groups reported that applications were being lost by the computer system at the Revenue. A representative from the Citizens Advice Bureau said: 'I used to think [the problem] was a lot of administration, a little bit computer, but I personally now believe it is a lot computer and a little bit administration, particularly with this issue of losing clients.' When claimants phoned the hotline, they were told there was a software error. MPs on the Treasury committee noted: 'From the perspective of helpline users, it is often difficult to tell whether it is official error or software error which is the problem.' An IT system that lacked flexibility was a recurring theme – 'staff may accept that information is wrong, but still be unable to correct the information'. In some instances, the computer system had produced tax credit award notices in which the number of children was not the same in different parts of the notice. In another, a constituent had complained to an MP that she had put a line through a section which asked if she had a disabled child to indicate it was not relevant to her. The computer, needless to say, interpreted this as confirmation that she did have a disabled child. Three quarters of the claims had to be handled manually. One solution offered at a meeting was drastic: 'To change people's national insurance numbers because that way you could put them back on the system with a new national insurance number.'

Staff at HMRC, who were used to applying pressure to ensure taxes were paid in full, sought to balance the books. But they were soon accused of excessive zeal in clawing back the overpaid benefits. MPs on the Treasury committee recommended in a report in June 2006 that there was a 'pause before recovery of an overpayment ... in the interests of natural justice'. Ann Abraham, the Parliamentary Ombudsman, who deals with complaints about government departments and agencies in England, called for a 'reasonableness test' which would be 'consistent with the test that is currently applied to social security benefits ... in general an overpayment of a social security benefit must be repaid [only] if the claimant had misrepresented or failed to disclose a material fact'. She found that HMRC's 'internal system for determining whether sums should be repaid' did not operate 'in a fair and transparent manner'.

Other groups warned that HMRC was assuming too great a level of knowledge among claimants. The Low Income Tax Reform Group drew attention to the fact that many claimants had a reading age of just eleven years old, arguing: 'It is simply not reasonable for them to be able to understand a lot of this stuff.'

To make matters worse, evidence soon emerged of high levels of fraud among people claiming the credits. From the first year, in 2003/04, the fraud rate was running at 'significantly more' than 3.4 per cent, officials admitted. The temptation was clearly there, say, to invent a fictitious child or an imaginary single parent, to bump up a claimant's entitlement. The Institute for Fiscal Studies estimated tax credits or out-of-work benefits were being paid to 200,000 lone parents who did not exist. The IFS said that a proportion of the credits were probably being paid to co-habiting couples. It said: 'If one disregards the threats of fines or penalties, it is often financially worthwhile to pretend to be a lone parent, rather than a couple, when claiming tax credits or out-of-work benefits.' MPs on the Treasury committee were outraged that more than two years after the end of the 2003/04 tax year, HMRC still had no final figures for error and fraud among tax credit claimants.

The internet was one particular way to defraud the system. The NAO's Sir John Bourn, by now an irritating thorn in the side of the government for the way he relentlessly examined and published reports about weaknesses of the system, disclosed on 7 October 2005 that serious fraudsters were using the internet to submit fake claims for tax credits. HMRC had evidence, he said, that it was being targeted by organised criminals, particularly when they were able to submit claims over the internet without having to prove who they were. The Revenue's own internal audit team had concluded worryingly that 'there was a lack of comprehensive information to allow a robust analysis of the problem'.

Soon after, on 2 December, HMRC's tax credits e-portal was suddenly closed and it emerged that a criminal investigation was underway. The following month Dawn Primarolo revealed that 8,800 DWP staff identities 'may have been stolen' in the first year of the new tax credits' operation, and 6,800 of them had been used to try to defraud the system. Around 4,100 stolen identities were 'fully intercepted' before any payment was made and, of the remaining 2,700 stolen identities, payments were suspended as soon as the fraud was discovered. Primarolo estimated that £2.7 million had gone missing as a result of fraud. Yet this could have been avoided. In September 2002 measures had been introduced requiring new controls on government services that were provided electronically in order to prevent fraud. MPs noted: 'Central government departments and agencies were required to comply with these requirements. But the department did not apply these to the tax credit system, despite the fact that they were mandatory.'

More evidence of criminality emerged. Identities stolen from rail operator Network Rail resulted in 16,000 claims being stopped. HMRC staff intervened in 17,164 incorrect cases where fraud was suspected before payments, in 2004/05. More than twice that figure – 38,924 – were stopped between April and November 2005. Half of these were from 'organised attacks'. In all the NAO estimated in December 2005 that £15 million was lost to organised fraud, of which twenty-five cases involved sums of more than £25,000 each. The NAO added grimly: 'The department believes that the £15 million figure will increase but it is too early to give a firm estimate at the moment.' Sir David Varney said the scale was 'pretty unprecedented'. Part of the problem was that fraudsters were able to open thousands of bank accounts using stolen identities. In one instance 2,200 bank accounts at nineteen banks and building societies were used by the fraudsters to spawn a further 6,000 sub-accounts. Two arrests were later made, and the individuals charged with money laundering offences.

That same month the government stepped in with what it hoped would be major changes to the way tax credits were administered, by announcing that the 'disregard for increases in income' from one year to the next was increasing ten-fold from £2,500 to £25,000 from April 2006 – thereby cutting the numbers of those who might have needed to have their awards reassessed. The government hoped that this would cut overpayments by a third. This clearly added an extra cost to taxpayers because ministers were effectively writing off hundreds of millions of pounds in overpayments, but the government declined to put a figure on it. Indeed, payments described as 'overpayments' did fall from £1.9 billion to

£1 billion in the year after the changes, although they were still higher than planned when the scheme was introduced. MPs on the all-party Treasury committee were less convinced, saying that the ten-fold increase in the disregard level would be 'costly'. The NAO justified their concern by estimating the cost of the disregard at between £400 million and £600 million a year.

If that was the carrot, the stick was in the form of fines of up to £300 for claimants who did not tell HMRC about a change in their circumstances that resulted in an overpayment or who supplied incorrect information on their claim forms. There was a further possible charge of £3,000 if a claimant had negligently not taken enough care to ensure that information sent to the Revenue was correct. HMRC was back to doing what it did best – chasing money owed. And here was the reason why the government thought that increasing the disregard level would be 'revenue neutral'. Charities were somewhat concerned about the prospect of a tougher enforcement regime. The Child Poverty Action Group warned that the changes could foster 'a climate of punitiveness as opposed to encouraging people to report appropriately', adding that it was 'not credible to start by talking forcefully about fining people who are already in difficult financial circumstances'.

Yet in the year following the changes, 2006/07, tax credits continued to be hit by high levels of error and fraud, with between 7.2 per cent and 8.4 per cent of awards (£1.31 billion and £1.54 billion) paid incorrectly. Some 1.3 million families were affected by overpayments and were being asked to repay hundreds of pounds each. The NAO's fearless Sir John Bourn was forced to question the accounts for HMRC for the sixth year running. By March 2008, the Revenue was chasing £4.3 billion in overpayments, £1.8 billion of which was unlikely to be recovered. In 2007/08, £337 million of incorrect payments on 157,000 'highest risk' claims were stopped.

HMRC tried to improve its game. More staff were hired, with numbers swelling from 7,300 in 2003/04 to 10,120 in 2006/07, and helping to push up the administrative cost from

£406 million to £587 million. In January 2008 the department published a new code of practice for recovering overpayments involving official error. Principally this meant that the 'department no longer considers whether it was reasonable for the claimant to have believed the award was correct. Instead claimants must check information that the department is working with, based on what it has been told.' Yet MPs on the Public Accounts Committee found in March 2009 that 'in too many cases the department had not taken account of individual circumstances and has blamed claimants for not noticing something which they were unlikely to be able to do. There have been too many cases where the department continued to recover overpayments where it could not support its case.'

Worse still, it emerged that in its desperation to recoup some of the lost billions HMRC had acted unlawfully, overreaching its powers under the 2002 Tax Credits Act 'by adjusting some final awards when it is not entitled to do so'. In some cases Revenue officials had looked into awards without asking the claimant first, as they had to do by law. In others they recovered overpayments that were the Revenue's fault, when in law they could not do this unless any adjustments were in the claimants' favour. The result was that the department owed 20,000 people between £800 and £1,000 each. Again, the computer system was blamed for this because there was not an inbuilt warning system 'to prevent staff taking such actions'. MPs were aghast when they learned that Revenue staff had effectively broken the law to claw back credit payments. An incredulous Edward Leigh, the committee's chairman, asked Dave Hartnett, acting chief executive of HMRC on 8 October 2008: 'If you cannot follow the legislation, why should the ordinary punter do so?' Hartnett said it was 'a matter of enormous regret' and blamed officials for using guidance from the 'design of the system rather than the legislation'.

The basic problem remained that tax credits relied to a large extent on claimants ensuring for themselves that they were receiving the correct payments. The MPs on Leigh's committee observed with understatement:

> Claimants faced with household breakdown are unlikely to give their highest priority to contacting the department about tax credits. At the time it was developing the tax credits system, the department failed to appreciate the variety and frequency of changes in claimants' circumstances that would occur in practice.

The system was simply not working for the people it was meant to help.

> Too many claimants have had to cope with the anguish and irritation of trying to get reliable information out of the system. For example, claimants have had to cope with contradictory letters from the department, and find that staff providing the phone service do not have the necessary information to deal with their enquiry.

Figures appeared to show that the sheer hassle of claiming the complex benefits was putting people off. In 2006/07 only eight out of ten families who were entitled to Child Tax Credit actually claimed them. For the Working Tax Credit, the proportion was six out of ten. PAC member Don Touhig told Dave Hartnett about one of his constituents: 'Mrs T' had received an overpayment because the tax credits' computer could not read four words written on her application form – 'Finished 19 January 2003' – to describe the ending of her income support on that date. Parliamentary Ombudsman Ann Abraham investigated and blamed the Revenue's computer system. Despite this, Mrs T was pursued for payment. Mrs T, whom Touhig described as 'not a lady to be bullied, she was a lady in command of all the detail', met with HMRC staff at Touhig's office and left 'in tears'. A chastened Hartnett apologised. Between 2004/05 and 2007/08 the Revenue dealt with 1.19 million disputes involving overpayments, of which 187,700 were written off. Three quarters of complaints dealt with by the Parliamentary Ombudsman in 2005/06 were upheld. MPs on the PAC reported in February 2008 how 'claimants may not understand why they have to make repayments, especially where they find themselves owing money to the department when they were not previously in debt'. The scheme was described as 'unduly harsh'.

HMRC proposed tailoring support more closely to people's needs and making it easier for them to claim, receive and renew their tax credits. The plans, introduced from April 2009, were intended to give claimants greater certainty and more control over how they managed their tax credits and support those whose income fell or whose circumstances changed. Officials were even told to contact people who they had not heard from for a while to ask if there were any changes that the department needed to know about. In addition, call centre operators were trained in how to deal with claimants.

Billions are still being paid out every year in tax credits. In 2008/09 more than six million families in the UK were paid £24.1 billion in the Child Tax Credit and Working Tax Credit. Part of the problem, as Jesse Norman observed in a recent book, is that the government had wrongly assumed that 'ordinary people would actually understand and be able to react rationally to massive complexities of the new system – in other words, they assumed people were far more economically rational than they actually were'. In fact the system was too complex even for experts to explain. Then, when it went wrong, tax collectors chased after the recipients of the benefits, people on low incomes who might have already spent the money, and asked for some of it back.

According to Sir John Bourn, who had consistently warned publicly about the schemes, the government simply failed to understand the lives of the people it was trying to help. As he told MPs: 'How crazy to set up a system where you're going to pay people more money than they really deserve and you're going to get it back from them!' Bourn blamed a disconnection between the comfortably well-off officials who devised the scheme, and the people they were trying to help.

Now we might say that most middle-class people that you find in the Civil Service would be prepared to pay it back and able to pay it back, but when you think of who gets the tax credits, they are often very poor people without very much experience in handling money and budgets. So they get tax credits over the odds, and they spend it and then the money is not there to pay it back. Therefore, of course, you do not get the money back. But you leave the evidence of a failed project and disappointment all round.

PAC chairman Edward Leigh had pinpointed the heart of the problem in January 2005 in a rhetorical question to David Varney, HMRC's boss: 'I just wondered whether MPs, when they voted for this to go through the House, would have done so if they had realised that the people in difficulties were, as a matter of course, being required to pay back money to the Inland Revenue?'

4

INDIVIDUAL LEARNING ACCOUNTS

It should have been possible to design a scheme to encourage new providers that was not wide open to fraud or abuse by unscrupulous people posing as learning providers, but the lack of quality assurance made it almost inevitable that it would be abused.
House of Commons Education and Skills Committee report

Many governments face a basic problem: how to get millions of people without the most rudimentary qualifications into the labour force. Improving Britain's productivity per head has been an intractable issue confronting successive governments. For the new Labour government that took office in May 1997, part of the answer was 'Individual Learning Accounts', an idea which seemed to dovetail perfectly with the new consumer-empowering mantra of the late 1990s. The party's general election manifesto was brimming with ambitious, horizon-scanning brio: 'We will invest public money for training in individual learning accounts which individuals – for example women returning to the labour force – can then use to gain the skills they want.' There was even a ready pot of cash to pay for these new accounts, initially from reserves held by the Training and Enterprise Councils (TECs). The manifesto stated:

> We will kick-start the programme for up to a million people, using the £150 million of TEC money which could be better used and which could provide a contribution of £150, alongside individuals making small investments of their own. Employers will be encouraged to make voluntary contributions to these funds.

The idea was straightforward enough. For those wanting to be trained, hundreds of pounds were to be made available through new virtual accounts modelled on the sort of product you could open at a high street bank. People would apply for an account and would then be sent a card through the post, containing a unique account number. This card, and its number, would act as a key to allow the customer to access thousands of different training schemes, although many were aimed at helping the computer illiterate to hitch a ride on the new and exciting information super-highway. The way into this magical world of knowledge would be controlled by firms known as registered training providers, whose job was to match customers to the different training courses. Customers would go along to training providers and hand in their account number, which the providers would then use to log onto the Individual Learning Account website and transfer the payment for the course they were about to provide. Yet there were prophetic warnings that it might not all go to plan. Similar plans had been proposed by the Conservative government in May 1994 and rejected two years later as unworkable. The government's 1996 competitiveness White Paper said: 'The government is not convinced that individual learning accounts, linked to employer tax relief or incentives, are likely to broaden participation. In practice they would be over-complex and more likely to subsidise existing activity.' Yet a confident new government believed it could do better. Plans for the new accounts were given prominence in the first 100 days after Labour's election victory with the publication in July 1997 of a consultative document, optimistically titled 'ILAs: Making Them Succeed'. The plans were then fleshed out in a Learning Age Green Paper, published in February 1998, which declared: 'We propose to support up to one million learning accounts, funded by £150 million from the TECs' resources.' The paper explained that the accounts would be both universal and targeted. The new accounts were to be offered to all who wanted to have one, as long as they invested a minimum amount of their own cash which was topped up by £150 of public money. A proportion of the accounts would also be offered to 'people without qualifications and in low-skill jobs, areas of skills shortage, employees in small firms and those seeking to return to work'.

In June 1998, the government announced twelve pilot schemes to run over the next two years at a cost to taxpayers of £2 million. In April 1999, TECs started to offer a limited number of accounts to particular groups, such as those trying to re-enter the labour market and those people with few or no qualifications. By the following August the system was working quite well – it was proving possible to attract unskilled people to sign up to the new accounts. One month later, by the end of September 1999, 56,917 new accounts had been opened, costing the TECs £2.9 million. The trials were judged to be a success. This was partly because the TECs were able to handle the new money for the training through their own network of established training providers. Private firms well versed in training people were full of praise. They succeeded 'because they understood who they were dealing with', one of the providers from Pitman Training Group later told MPs on the Commons education committee.

The government had originally supposed there would be a 'real' account where people could bank and save their own money, in addition to other cash contributions from government, employers and trade unions. Officials had therefore hoped to persuade banks and building societies to become partners in the project, running the new accounts and allowing people to bank and save their own money in addition to the other help on offer. Yet this key part of the plan soon foundered. Market research showed that customers were not particularly interested in saving for learning, while financial institutions were not especially interested in developing such a product. Derek Grover, director of adult learning at the Department for Education and Skills, later admitted that despite 'really very extensive discussions' with the banks and building societies 'we were not able to develop a business proposition' with which these financial institutions felt comfortable and secure.

It was time for a change of plan. Officials decided to scrap the savings element from the plans and, instead, base the accounts on offering discounts for training schemes. The theory was that in order to attract the one million customers the government was aiming for, the new scheme would need to give people the maximum amount of control and freedom of choice. The new idea was that people would sign up to a new Individual Learning Account to manage their training for life. Yet the absence of the banks created a glaring problem. How could they be called learning 'accounts' when no one could do any saving? They were nothing to do with savings. They were hardly 'accounts' at all. In reality, the so-called Individual Learning Accounts were actually more like training vouchers. As MPs on the Commons education committee later noted: 'This was the point where there should have been a fundamental rethink about the whole ILA project.' Instead, the adapted plans proceeded briskly. Throughout 2000, several seminars were held with learning providers and other partners, with advice from auditors and consultants KPMG. In June 2000, the department awarded a five-year contract worth £55 million to a private firm, Capita, to run a new Individual Learning Accounts Centre, after a full tendering process under European Union rules.

Yet, as the department was later to admit, there were no discussions about the vulnerability of the new accounts to systematic fraud. There had been warnings here, too. Two years earlier, in its 1998 report *Ghost in the Machine*, the Audit Commission had advised that 'computer crime is on the increase and while key risks remain, new dangers are emerging'. Tony Blair, the Prime Minister, had himself acknowledged these risks. In a foreword to a Green Paper called 'Beating Fraud', Blair had observed that 'all kinds of fraud, from petty "fiddles" through to criminal gangs setting out to defraud the system of hundreds of thousands of pounds, take money away from where it is needed most'. What was more, the government would work across all departments and councils to try to share expertise on tackling fraud.

All these worries were ignored. Sections 104 to 109 of the Learning and Skills Act 2000 gave new powers to the Education Secretary to set up a framework for the new accounts. On

1 September 2000, the first Individual Learning Accounts were opened. The accounts were available to anyone resident in Britain, aged nineteen years or over. To open an account, the customer had to register with a training provider and then make a modest deposit of £25. Individuals could choose how to 'spend' their ILA on training (subject to some exceptions) which could amount to a government subsidy of £200 for certain courses priced at £250. From the individual learner's point of view, it was a fairly simple proposition: if you signed up for an ILA, you could get up to £250 worth of computer training, for example, for only £50.

The first one million accounts would receive a grant of £150 each. After that, account holders would be able to claim discounts which would vary depending on the course chosen. Some courses attracted an 80 per cent discount worth up to £200 in any single year. The Commons education committee later identified that the 'introduction of the 80 per cent discount was a crucial step in widening the attractiveness of the ILA to unscrupulous operators'. Or in other words, there were holes in the system big enough for conmen to drive an articulated lorry through, fill it with cash and then drive away, with lights on and horn sounding.

The government wanted to use the new accounts to create a market for hundreds of new training providers, a market it was trying to manipulate. This was a marked departure from the pilots in which the TECs had employed reputable and well-established training providers. The department's Derek Grover later told the education committee: 'There's an old saying – "if you do what you always did, you get what you always got" – and we really wanted to get some different learners involved and some different providers.' The company enlisted to help to deliver the new model was Capita, which was hired to implement 'a policy design and delivery model drawn up by the Department for Education'. In effect, as the education committee found, this meant the risks were not shared with a private sector company, as might have happened in a conventional

Private Finance Initiative project; rather, the risks 'always remained with the department'. The MPs said: 'Surprisingly the potential expertise of Capita in designing systems to be fraud-resistant was neither called upon, nor offered. The opportunity to use private sector expertise in policy design fell between the two stools of policy [retained in-house by civil servants] and delivery [narrowly defined by the contract as performing operations to a required standard].' Indeed there was little evidence that the various policy, finance and procurement teams at the department, as well as external consultants and commercial lawyers, discussed the vulnerability of the scheme to fraudsters. Ministers were kept informed throughout the tendering process.

Capita's job was simply to match the applicant's account number with his or her entitlement. The brief was explicitly not to be an expert in training. Officials later claimed that IT security was discussed with Capita yet other training providers saw little evidence of it. The education committee found that Capita 'gave any provider who joined the system unlimited access to individuals' accounts'. Roger Tuckett, from private training company Henley Online, described the level of security as 'pitifully low'. The fact that a provider 'could enter a single number and not even have to cross-relate it to the surname, for example, was crazy'. The implication of this was clear. As the MPs found, a training provider could simply log on and then 'trawl the database and submit claims for having trained an individual on the system whose account had not already been spent'. This is exactly what happened.

At the heart of the impending chaos lay a confusion about who was vetting training firms that signed up to administer the accounts. The government had muddied the waters by offering a fig leaf of respectability for anyone who fancied themselves as a bit of a trainer through a new database run under the brand name 'Learndirect', containing details of 500,000 courses. Any learning provider was able to have its courses included on the database free of charge by applying via the website. Capita, for its part, understood that as part of the deal to administer the scheme it would be 'hooking up to a database which was accredited'. Yet by the time it was clear that there would be no accreditation of quality, the system was built.

Without a quality threshold, the government was in effect telling customers, clutching their training money, to decide for themselves which courses were most appropriate and offered the best value for money. In effect, they were put straight into the arms of the fraudsters. Yet customers had assumed – quite reasonably – that a government scheme would only use accredited, honest training providers. Reputable training providers, for their part, were flabbergasted at the lack of checks and balances. Caroline Lambie, of Hairnet, said the lack of vetting of providers was 'shocking'. James O'Brien, from Pitman Training Group and the Association of Computer Trainers, said he was 'astounded' at the lack of quality accreditation. The first official warning was sounded on 20 September 2000, when O'Brien wrote to ministers at the Department for Education to protest that the programme was open to abuse. Indeed, it later emerged that there had been private concerns two months earlier, in July 2000, that the accounts might not be subject to the usual rigorous quality arrangements.

To make matters worse, there was no cap on the eligible course costs that could be claimed. The department later lamented: 'Regrettably, some unscrupulous providers exploited this to charge inflated prices.' O'Brien later said that 'the scheme was abused from day one'. On 20 October 2000, officials decided to cap the cost of one training 'episode' at £200. Yet the fraudsters were one step ahead: they would make multiple false claims.

With a very rapid increase in the number of Individual Learning Accounts being opened, the scheme was soon spiralling out of control. Some of the new training providers were themselves vague about how the new accounts worked, asking customers to fill in the account application forms and then send them off and 'wait to see what happened'. By 2 May 2001, the commitment to reach one million Individual Learning Accounts had been reached, one year early. An average 3,000 accounts were being opened every day. At least on paper, the accounts seemed to be targeted at the right people – more than half a million of the people who had opened an account since January 2001 appeared not to have received training of any kind in the previous three years.

However, the bulk of applications were from so-called 'non-personalised forms' which indicated that they were most probably completed *en masse* by a training provider. Alarm bells were raised by the sheer volume of these forms being sent in, and in September 2001 they were banned. The fear was that many of the names on the forms were simply made up. MPs on the education committee found: 'One of the reasons for withdrawing the use of non-personalised application forms was doubt about whether the individuals in whose names the applications were being submitted really existed.' This was the fault of the officials who drew up the plans. As Denyse Metcalf of Capita explained, this form of 'self-certification' (without a requirement of proof of an individual's existence) was an amendment introduced in May 2000 'so that it was not deemed necessary for people to provide additional documentation to prove they existed'.

By September 2001, some 2.6 million accounts had been opened – compared with just over 109,000 in the same month the year before. The cost of the scheme soared. Expenditure had now reached £180 million, doubling since May 2001 and exceeding all expectations. Excited officials at the Department for Education had commissioned research from a private firm, York Consulting, to compare and contrast results from people who were early adopters of the programme and those who opened accounts after May 2001. The research, which was due to be published in October 2001 but which was only made public in January 2002, threw up some curious results. The group's researchers were puzzled to find that more than a quarter of those contacted about their account said they had not opened it. The researchers initially blamed a 'data issue'.

The questions over the 'ghost' account holders dovetailed with increasing complaints. Paddy Doyle, also from Capita, put

it succinctly when he described the growing concern as something 'that crept up on us over a number of months. In the first
nine months [September 2000 to June 2001] we were getting no
evidence of learning providers misbehaving or not getting the
right calibre of learning providers through, volumes were right,
the level of complaint was low.' Yet by the end of July 2001,
some 3,000 complaints had been received, increasing to 6,053
by September and 8,500 by October. Some of the complaints
were about money being taken from people's accounts without
their knowledge. There were even allegations of potential fraud.
By now trading standards officers were fielding complaints
about 'mis-selling, aggressive marketing, poor learning, poor
value for money and alleged fraud', MPs later found. Ministers
were shocked that the system was being exploited by unscrupulous people. John Healey, the minister in charge, said that
some learning providers were breaking the rules of the scheme
and 'very much after a quick buck'. Healey admitted that 'they
were the problem for us'. It subsequently emerged that the
rules were so loosely drawn up that there was actually no need
to break them in order to subvert the intentions of the scheme.
A 'training provider' could send nothing more than a £5.99
introductory computing booklet to an applicant who signed up
for 'training' costing £200, and yet not break any rules.

It was Capita's job, as part of the company's original service
provider agreement, to provide a system 'that can receive,
monitor, report on and resolve complaints'. Yet the Association
of Computer Trainers described the performance of Capita in
operating the learning accounts as 'woeful'. MPs found there
were problems even in counting the number of complaints.
Caroline Lambie of Hairnet said: 'If you phoned Capita you
got people in the call centres who were just there to put information into the system, they were not there to deal with any
complaints. There was no complaints mechanism at all.'

Legitimate training companies hated phoning the call centre.
Keith Humphries of Dataplus Computer Services found the
staff 'young, impersonal although not impolite', but he added

tellingly: 'It just seemed that they did not have a complete grasp of the job they were doing.' To make matters worse, the software used by Capita to scan the applications meant they were often misread by the firm's computers. Capita's Paddy Doyle admitted that take-up had been so successful that 'some early indications of fraud were too readily dismissed as "computer error"'.

While the numbers of complaints were rising, they still only represented a fraction of the account holders – 5,732 complaints out of more than 2.6 million account holders. Yet examples of frauds were emerging. A Sunday newspaper disclosed tales of bogus promises of City & Guilds diplomas, the unlicensed use of Microsoft software and unqualified tutors. MPs reported a 'massive fraud' involving up to 80,000 accounts in a single case. There was anecdotal evidence of 'door-to-door selling of [accounts] to sign up applicants in return for a worthless CD'. One rumour suggested that at least one training provider was doing business of more than £1 million a week. Under the rules to cap funds at £200, a provider would have to find 5,000 students each week – the equivalent of a small university – to generate such business. In another case a bank reported that a customer had opened an account in July 2001, into which poured £2 million, solely from ILA payments, which the account holder then asked to be transferred to an offshore tax haven. Legitimate training companies had to try to win business competing against fraudsters. One provider told MPs that '*bona fide* trainers had to fight arrivistes whose only interest in training was its ability to earn them quick money for no effort'. Such was the scale of the distortion in the industry caused by Individual Learning Accounts that legitimate training companies either had to get involved with the accounts or simply go out of business. At one stage, there were claims that fraudsters threw caution to the wind and asked training providers straight out if they could buy large numbers of completed application forms.

Whitehall moved with all the speed of a startled turtle. A compliance steering group was established which asked all training providers involved in the scheme to sign a new Learning Provider Agreement by the end of June. A leaflet was issued. Blank application forms were no longer sent to third parties. And from 28 September, no more new providers were allowed to register. Yet the attempt to close the stable door failed. The department had to admit defeat in the face of the systematic and sustained fraud. Its officials told MPs that 'the rules and robustness of the scheme were simply not sufficiently strong to allow us to prevent the misuse, at the margins, outright abuse and some fraud that clearly was creeping into the system'. Throughout October officials wondered if they could call a temporary halt and relaunch the scheme. One said: 'The judgement that we took was that it was too risky an option to stop and patch and re-launch as soon as possible. We had to get to the bottom of all the problems.' It turned out that the entire design of the accounts meant that it was impossible to eradicate fraud.

On 24 October 2001, the government formally announced that Individual Learning Accounts were to be withdrawn by 7 December. More than 8,500 providers and 2.6 million holders of the accounts were informed individually in writing. In public at least the government was still painting the accounts as a triumph. Estelle Morris, the Education and Skills Secretary, trumpeted that the scheme had been 'a great success in bringing down the financial barriers to learning. ILAs have opened up access for a great many people to a wide range of learning opportunities.' The scheme was being withdrawn because it was simply too successful for its own good, she said. 'The rapid growth of the scheme has exceeded all expectations, causing us to think again about how to best target public funds in this area and secure value for money.' The abuse of the scheme was given second billing in the press release. Morris continued: 'I also have concerns about the way some ILAs have been promoted and sold. There is growing evidence that some companies are abusing the scheme by offering low value, poor quality learning. We are keen that this does not undermine what has been a very successful programme and we are acting quickly to protect the interests of individual learners.' Therefore, she said, the scheme would be shut down on 7 December. This would not have been an easy decision to make. At around the same time, officials at the department were putting the finishing touches to a new strategy paper. One of only two milestones for the following year, 2002, was to 'expand individual learning accounts'.

Yet this planned withdrawal soon came unstuck. A few days earlier, on 21 November, a provider had told officials at the department that a third party had tried to sell them a large quantity of ILA numbers. Inspectors looked into the matter the next day. They found a computer disc containing nearly 1,000 names, addresses and contact details, as well as ILA numbers. The accounts were live, and some of them had not been used – meaning that whoever had control of them would have been able to draw down public money supposedly to pay for training. Two days after learning of the apparent fraud, on 23 November, the department officials presented the findings to ministers. Proof that people's details from the central ILA computer were being hawked around to the highest bidder, in large volumes, prompted ministers to call in the police. Their advice was straightforward: shut the accounts down now, to protect public funds. The closure of the scheme, two weeks early, was announced later that day. This time there was no varnishing of what was going on. 'The Department for Education and Skills today called in the police to investigate alleged fraud and theft involving Individual Learning Accounts. Officers from the Department's special investigations unit had discovered irregularities on Thursday after being contacted by an ILA provider. This afternoon the ILA programme was shut down, two weeks earlier than planned. The ILA programme was to have been suspended from 7 December.'

What soon became clear was the fraud had been able to take place, not by the traditional methods of hacking into a computer, but simply walking through the system's virtual front door. Capita later confirmed that there had been 'no evidence of a breach of security nor hacking of the system' as well as 'no evidence' that any employee from Capita had been up to no good. Respectable providers, which had been using the system in good faith, were left high and dry by the sudden shutdown. Some reported that the website just suddenly crashed, while others said the site was taken down at 5 p.m. 'for essential maintenance'. A promise to reinstate the site at 6.30 p.m. was never delivered. One provider estimated that he lost £10,000 simply by being unable to post his claims on that day.

The Association of Computer Trainers accused the department of reneging on its promise to accept legitimate training in the days up to 7 December. Three quarters of its 250 training centres, which had expanded their business to meet the government's requirements for the ILAs, were forced to lay staff off over the following six months. The National Extension College, which specialises in home learning, said that it was 'dismayed' by the decision. Many trainers attempted to honour training commitments despite the certainty that they would lose tens of thousands of pounds. One provider estimated that the sudden closure would lead to up to 5,000 job losses. Total losses to respectable colleges were later estimated at £1.2 million, with one college in Preston losing £260,000.

The government refused to compensate any of the training companies for the early closure because there was not a formal contract between the government and the training providers (although validated, eligible bookings up until 23 November, were honoured until the following May). John Healey told MPs on the education committee: 'If I have been tough about that it is because I do not want anyone to mistake what I have said or to be misled that somehow it can be a lifeboat of public money which will continue to support their operations.' The MPs were not impressed, concluding: 'It is difficult not to see this "agreement" as introducing reciprocal obligations between its signatories.' By the end of January 2002, total complaints received had reached nearly 18,300 (0.7 per cent of account holders). Of that figure, 5,800 of the complaints related to people having cash taken from their accounts without their knowledge. The complaints related to 670 out of 8,910 providers. By March, 117 registered providers were being investigated by the department. Eighty of them were being probed by police officers in nine force areas.

A project's success depends on one's standpoint. In just over fourteen months, more than two million people had signed up to the new Individual Learning Accounts; many of them were genuine; and many received some useful training. However, this was at a very high price. In the West Midlands, a gang was ordered to repay £500,000 after using the names of members of the England football team and the cast of *EastEnders* as well as 'Bill Clinton' and 'Harry Potter' in order to defraud the ILA scheme. In just one case on Teesside in 2008 following a six-year police investigation and a 4½-month trial, a director of the 'National Distance Learning College', Michael Smallman, was convicted on three counts of fraudulent trading and one of money laundering after cheating the government out of £6 million by claiming Individual Learning Account grants. This was only one part of wider fraud in which he tempted 80,000 students to sign up for home study courses, though only eighteen students ended up with genuine qualifications. This netted him a further £10 million. He used the money to finance a lavish lifestyle including the purchase of forty racehorses. Smallman was sentenced at Teesside Crown Court to seven years in prison. The judge said: 'Unlike Robin Hood, who robbed the rich to give to the poor, you robbed from the poor to make yourself rich.' Two other directors of the company were cleared of fraudulent trading charges. In another Teesside case, in July 2011, after what a police inspector described as 'one of the longest running criminal investigations in Cleveland Police's history', five ringleaders behind another ILA fraud were convicted on charges ranging from fraudulent trading and money laundering to conspiracy to defraud. The fraudsters had obtained amounts varying from £126,000 to £266,000.

But the scale of criminal prosecutions does not reflect the

scale of the losses, nor does it account for the colossal cost in police time and manpower to investigate crimes that could easily have been prevented. The exact size of the losses through fraud against the Individual Learning Account scheme will probably never be known, but estimates have been put as high as £90 million. Scandalously, as John Healey, the minister in charge at the time admitted, 'the design of the scheme did not allow us to stamp out abuse'. It is likely that many fraudsters simply got away with it.

5

CRIMINAL RECORDS BUREAU

The consequences of the Bureau's problems were far-reaching.
Employers could not recruit, voluntary organisations lost poten-
tial volunteers and delays occurred for those applying to foster
or adopt...
House of Commons Public Accounts Committee report

O ne of the most important responsibilities for any government is to ensure the education of children in a safe
environment. The Criminal Records Bureau (CRB) was
established in 2002 to protect children from predatory adults
who might exploit their innocence and vulnerability. Schools,
companies, charities and voluntary groups all needed a quick,
easy and cheap way to check whether adults whom they wished
to employ had criminal records. The CRB appeared to be the
answer, a new government agency to vet the backgrounds of
anyone wanting to work with children, or vulnerable adults.
Its intention was surely not to close schools because of the
panicked early mandatory introduction of these checks but that
is exactly what happened in September 2002.

Obtaining reliable background checks on an adult's criminality or otherwise should theoretically be easy. Police have kept
records going back decades. Yet until very recently, retrieving
this was no easy task, largely because local intelligence was
held by forty-three police forces. Prior to the existence of the
CRB, such checks were patchy and local with no central unify-
ing body to bring them all together. It could take months for
enquiries to be completed because an employer had to gain
access to many different sources of information, and such
checks were only carried out on those who wanted to work
with children, not those people wanting to work with vulnerable adults. In the pre-internet era one had to ask the local
policeman whether an adult who wanted to work with children

had a questionable past. Forces were happy to oblige but they were hardly geared up for it, and often vitally important checks were subordinated to more pressing police work. Nevertheless, despite these difficulties, by 2001 up to a million checks were being carried out in this way every year.

Officers verified conviction details against information held on the Police National Computer – although alarmingly this was not reliable. An internal audit by the Metropolitan Police in 1999 found that 80 per cent of its records on the computer contained errors. Her Majesty's Inspectorate of Constabulary found that the problems extended across the UK, with the error rate running at between 16 per cent and 65 per cent in other forces in England and Wales. There were other ways to vet adults' pasts. Local authorities could cross-reference prospective teachers against the so-called 'List 99', a database of abusers and suspected abusers held by the Department for Education. Across Whitehall, the Department of Health also held a list of people deemed to be unsuitable for working with children. Not surprisingly, some organisations were less than happy with these haphazard arrangements and decided to set up their own vetting procedures. For example, the Scout Association developed a database of unsuitable people based on press cuttings. If ever there were a need for a joined-up, centralised government agency to pull this spaghetti-like morass of half-baked vetting procedures together, this was it. And so the CRB was conceived in the 1997 Police Act, which placed the Home Secretary under an obligation to disclose criminal records to anyone who made a request using a specified form and paid a set fee. A new agency would be set up with the main objective to strengthen the safeguards for protecting children and – later – vulnerable adults.

The Home Secretary, Jack Straw, set the bar very high from the outset. He told MPs that millions of job applicants would have to provide proof that they had no criminal record when they applied for sensitive jobs. If they had a criminal background, it would be disclosed. As many as a third of the workforce would be vetted. The Home Office was expecting to process ten million certificates each year, costing between £5 and £10 each. It was not the first time a politician had exaggerated the capability and underestimated the cost to the taxpayer of a new government agency.

A team from the Passport and Records Agency – itself going through its own crisis that year – was given the job of setting up the new Criminal Records Bureau for the Home Office. During the summer of 1999, this team drew up what in Whitehall-speak was called the 'User Requirement of the Bureau'. By October 1999 the team had issued a business prospectus that laid the foundation stones of the new CRB. First, it would be based in Liverpool, creating 1,200 new jobs, which would lessen the impact of other Home Office job losses feared on Merseyside at the time. Second, the new agency would be self-financing and based on a public–private partnership. Third, the bureau would be 'e-enabled', focusing on government targets to drive more people to use the internet. Fourth, the number of applications would mean that the CRB would have to be computerised. Lastly, and crucially, a call centre would be needed to handle applications, 85 per cent of which were expected to be by telephone.

In order to establish the working methods for the new body, the team ran a listening exercise in a 'customer forum', in which trade associations and other bodies took part. These bodies were vital because to run the service each one would have to register with the CRB. In May 2000, more focus groups were organised. Some of the private companies which hoped to be involved in setting up the new body were invited to attend. Soon, an agreed way of working for the new CRB was hammered out.

The idea behind the CRB was simple. People wanting to work with children or vulnerable adults would apply for one of two types of criminal check: a standard disclosure or an enhanced disclosure. A standard check was for anyone in regular contact with children or vulnerable adults and would look for convictions, cautions, reprimands or warnings on the Police National Computer, regardless of length of time since the incidents. Checks could also be made against names on List 99, held by the Department for Education. An enhanced disclosure would be similar to a standard check, but was for anyone who had greater contact with children or vulnerable adults (such as doctors, social workers and nursing home staff). These types of disclosure included any relevant intelligence on a 'no smoke without fire' basis. Typically, they would involve details held by police forces of investigations in an area where the applicant had lived for the previous five years, which might not have led to a criminal record.

For a standard disclosure, the process would go something like this: Bloggs Academy, a sixth-form college, decides to hire Joe Smith to work as a teaching assistant. Smith has never worked with children before and so must apply to be checked by the CRB. Bloggs Academy gives Smith an application form. Smith fills it in, signs it and gives it back to Bloggs Academy, which is registered with the CRB. The headmaster of Bloggs Academy counter-signs the form, and sends it to the CRB to be checked. The form is processed. Disclosure forms are sent to both the headmaster of Bloggs Academy and to Smith himself. Then, if cleared, Smith starts work.

The plan was for the Passport and Records Agency to run the CRB as a new joint venture with a private company, chosen in a competitive bidding process. By June, the bids were in. The main contenders were PricewaterhouseCoopers and Capita, which each bid for the ten-year contract. In most procurement processes, bidders have a reasonable idea of each other's costs and margins, both because staff move around within the industry and also because the parameters for any given project are set by the government. As a result, private firms generally bid roughly within the same range, depending on how badly they want the business. So there was some surprise that while PricewaterhouseCoopers were asking for £380 million to run the project, Capita said it could do the job for £250 million. Capita's super-low offer, £130 million cheaper than the next bidder, sounded clanging warning bells at the agency. How could the firm bid so little? Capita was Britain's biggest 'outsourcing' company, running services contracts in business and central and local government including management software for 23,000 UK schools and 158 education authorities and collecting the council tax for local authorities. Concerned that the process must have gone wrong in some way, the agency hired consultancy firm PA Consulting to check whether all of the bids were compliant with the terms of reference in the original tender documents. Pocketing a £300,000 fee for its trouble, the firm assured the government that all the bids were compliant. But PA had been set the wrong question: the agency failed to ask whether the tender process itself was fit for purpose. It wasn't – as would become abundantly clear within a matter of months.

Much later the National Audit Office revealed what had happened. The two firms had apparently 'made different assumptions about the application channel customers would prefer'. Put simply, PwC had assumed that 40 per cent of applicants would want to send in applications by post. Capita thought that the figure would be just 15 per cent. Capita priced accordingly and was confirmed as winner of the contract at the end of 2000. Capita had merely sought to convert into reality the CRB's original pre-determined assumption that four out of five people would apply by phone or over the internet. With hindsight it now appears that government officials' heads were turned by what was going on in the world of business and on the stock market. Away from Whitehall, a revolution was underway. The first internet boom had well and truly arrived. Companies were being set up by youths in polo shirts and then sold within months for millions of pounds. Values of dot-com firms were soaring based on hopelessly optimistic financial forecasts. Insurance and banking companies were embracing the new internet age with gusto; why couldn't central government?

In January 2001, the team at the passport agency ran the first of twenty-three roadshows to explain the purpose of the new body to 5,000 of its likely users. However, the feedback was negative. A wide range of organisations told officials again and again that their volunteers and members would want to apply for their checks in writing. In the era before super-fast broadband, when the internet was accessed over a dial-up connection, posting documents was still by far the preferred option. Organisations complained 'they felt they were ignored', particularly 'over the bureau's proposed use of call centres when customers' preferences were for paper and online routes'. Their concerns were hardly surprising. Given that the ID checks required original birth certificates, passports and other original documents, it was inherent in the design of the scheme that a phone-based call centre would not be adequate and that applicants would need to send supporting documents by post. There were also questions over whether the CRB could cope with seasonal peaks and troughs, such as the start of the school year when new staff were being vetted for new jobs, and the 'likely high level of inaccuracies on paper forms'. In May 2001, the team setting up the CRB finally woke up to the inevitable: plans to allow more people to apply using paper applications were introduced, just weeks before the CRB was due to start operations in August 2001.

The launch was marred by a series of delays, officially due to problems with the computer systems and other technical issues. One of these was the need to find a way to process paper application forms quickly, even though the agency had formally agreed in July to introduce such forms. A new contract was agreed with Capita in September – with extra payments that were not disclosed for reasons of 'commercial confidentiality', though believed to be in the region of £50 million to £100 million – and the start date was pushed back until November. Soon there were more hold-ups. By the autumn, the November start date was pushed back again, this time to March 2002. By now it was panic stations at the CRB. Tests were being run and they were not going well. With characteristic understatement, the NAO observed: 'System tests took place in November/December 2001 but were not fully successful.'

The Office of Government Commerce stepped in. An

independent government body (now merged into the Cabinet Office), the OGC monitors how contracts are awarded and run by Whitehall departments. It carried out an audit of the CRB's readiness to start work in February 2002 and examined the robustness of the CRB's computer system, the business case and the readiness to go live. The news was not good. According to the NAO report, the OGC found that the 'full end to end assembly of the Information Technology production environment would be put in place for the first time just days before 1 March 2002'. There was, quite simply, no time left. Yet calling the whole thing off was not an option. As the NAO noted later, the CRB would have to start work come what may, 'given the confusion and bad publicity that would result from delay'. And so it was that the first applications to the CRB started to be processed on 1 March 2002.

There were immediate problems. Within two weeks, it emerged that half of the applications sent in by organisations and companies had mistakes on them. Just as officials had been warned eighteen months earlier at the roadshows, the predicted large surge in paper applications had overloaded the system. The assumptions of Capita and of the CRB could not have been more wrong. Far from 80 per cent of people applying for CRB checks by telephone, in fact more than 80 per cent were applying by post. To make matters worse, the call centre was not working properly and the 'online authentication process' was failing because it relied on customers filling in a long list of questions. Real-time access to other databases was required by people who were using desperately slow dial-up internet connections. The system, quite simply, could not cope.

By May 2002 voluntary sector bodies were boycotting the CRB, accusing it of reneging on a deal not to charge volunteers a fee for being vetted. Home Secretary David Blunkett had said that charges would not apply to voluntary groups but volunteers were being billed £23 plus VAT. Susanne Rauprich, chief executive of the National Council for Voluntary Youth Services, told him in a letter: 'We are deeply concerned that the CRB will

be unable to function effectively. The consequences of this failure could be extremely serious, both in relation to ensuring the
safety of children and vulnerable adults and also to the avail-
ability of volunteering opportunities in England and Wales.'

Things kept going wrong. The CRB was forced to publish an
apology on its website for losing 100 forms that had been filled
in as part of a consultation exercise. By August 2002, only 50 per
cent of standard disclosures were being issued within the two-
week target. New problems were springing up by the month.
Checking information against the Police National Computer
was not going smoothly. The Metropolitan Police complained
that its computer was not communicating properly with the
CRB's technology. The problems soon impacted upon an
ambitious timetable to widen the scope of the CRB to vet those
working with vulnerable adults. Ministers had wanted to put in
place checks for all health and social workers by 31 March 2003,
by issuing a Protection of Vulnerable Adults list. Yet in November
2002 the necessary legislation – which had been due to be introduced in early 2003 – was postponed due to the problems at the
CRB, and the checks did not finally start until late 2003.

Organisations and voluntary groups were now reporting soaring administrative costs incurred by chasing delayed
or lost application forms. Recruitment agencies supplying
schools, colleges and other bodies were losing income because
they could not supply unchecked staff and in some cases care
workers were taken on without any checks. A children's nursery in Brighton waited three months before checks began to be
performed on its new staff. By June 2002 the nursery was still
waiting for the results on two forms which had been submitted
in April. One of its trustees complained: 'We had no choice but
to give employment to unchecked staff, because of the shortage
of people with clearance certificates.'

But there was far worse to come. In August 2002, the country
was shocked by the horrific killings of ten-year-olds Holly Wells
and Jessica Chapman in Soham, Cambridgeshire. Ministers'
response to the arrest over the killings by school caretaker Ian

Huntley, who had been able to take up his job despite a string of undetected rape and underage sex allegations, was far from sure footed. Neither Education Secretary Estelle Morris nor the department's Permanent Secretary, Sir David Normington, were available for comment. Margaret Hodge, the department's on-duty minister, was working from home. Yet on 21 August – less than a fortnight before the start of the new school year – the Department for Education suddenly ordered that all teachers had to have been vetted by the CRB. Head teachers swiftly had to get hold of all their colleagues, deep in the school summer holiday, and ensure that they had filled in their forms, sent them to the CRB and got them back in time for the start of term. Large numbers of staff from the passport agency were drafted in to help the embattled CRB deal with thousands of extra new applications. Capita decided to send tens of thousands of applications for processing in India, where they could be stored on computers before being checked. The turnaround time for this was six weeks.

The result was inevitable. When the new school year started in early September 2002, schools across the country stayed shut because they did not have enough employees with CRB clearance. One head teacher in Leeds was outraged. 'It's an extraordinary idea that we should even think of sending 1,100 children home because of this,' he said. 'It's treating schools as if they are breeding grounds for paedophiles. Pupils would be at far greater risk if I shut the door on them because we're waiting for vetting confirmation on some of our fifteen new teachers. I can tell you from past experience, we may still be waiting by the time we get to half term.' Fearful of the consequences if they failed to obey ministers on such a crucial child safety issue, many schools complied with the government's instruction.

No official figures are available for the total impact of such measures. However, based on a close analysis of local press coverage across the country, we estimate that at least 14,000 pupils missed school because of closures. To take a few examples: more than 1,500 pupils at schools in the Stockport area missed classes for several days at the start of term as well as 1,000 students at a college in Leicester. Nearly 600 pupils in Derby and 400 in Morecambe were unable to return for the first day of term, while 400 students in Coventry were told to stay at home when classes were cancelled for pupils in years eight, nine, eleven and twelve. In Cheshire 250 pupils could no longer get the school bus because ten bus drivers were still awaiting CRB clearance and the county council asked parents to take their children to school instead. In Hillingdon, west London, 1,200 children were told to stay away from school; up to 3,400 students had to stay away because of closures in West Bromwich, Oldbury, Smethwick, Great Barr and Tipton; and 2,300 stayed at home in Wolverhampton and Solihull. Staff at the CRB were said to be working through the night to process a backlog of 6,000 applications for vetting. Eventually, Morris stepped in and said that teachers could work in schools so long as they were checked against the List 99 database of potential or convicted child abusers held by her department.

There was another fall-out from the Department for Education's hasty decision. Thousands of parents who helped out at their local schools were told to stay at home unless they had been vetted and cleared by the CRB. The need for vetting depended on the 'regularity and type of contact', officials said. Parents were furious. One said: 'It's madness. Parents are allowed to look after their own children at home but are not to be trusted in a classroom of thirty children with a qualified, vetted teacher.' There was further dismay when it emerged that taxpayers would be paying extra to clear the backlog.

By the end of September, after weeks of uncertainty, the worst of the chaos was over, despite a backlog of 198,000 unprocessed checks, of which half were more than three weeks old. But there were still long delays. By the end of the following month, the number of checks was running at 40,000 a week – nearly twice the figure at the beginning of August. The problems were still having an impact many months later. Ministers soon announced that plans to check 300,000 people in care homes and nurses' agencies were to be suspended. By the following February, Home Office ministers were insisting that the situation at the CRB had now stabilised and was under control. Yet the backlog still stood at 51,000.

Heads had started to roll at the CRB. Keith Broadbent, the agency's director of operations, left the CRB once the scale of the crisis had become clear, moving to the Home Office's Immigration and Nationality Directorate, which was having its own problems. Bernard Herdan, the CRB's chief executive, who had been in charge of setting up the agency, stayed on for a year to sort out the mess until he went back to the passport service in September 2003. The government, for its part, commissioned a report into the crisis at the CRB by businessman and trouble-shooter Patrick Carter, now Lord Carter of Coles (nicknamed 'Get Carter' in Whitehall for the frequency with which he was commissioned to help ministers out of a fix). Extraordinarily, Carter decided to lay some of the blame at the door of the taxpayers. His report, published in February 2003, stated that 'unreasonably high public expectations' had contributed to the bureau's eventual problems. Yet these very same expectations had been originally set in 1999 by Jack Straw when he launched the new agency.

There was more trouble for the battered CRB in October 2004 when it emerged that its contract with Capita would now cost taxpayers £400 million in its first ten years. The revised estimate was £150 million more than Capita had originally bid, and even more expensive than the price offered by Capita's second-placed rivals, PricewaterhouseCoopers. MPs on the Public Accounts Committee concluded that the Home Office and Capita had found no effective way of tackling problems until they reached 'crisis point'. Even in October 2004, some two and a half years after the CRB's launch, they concluded that the bureau 'is not yet providing the standard or range of service originally envisaged'. Officials at the CRB were casti-gated for failing to listen to the warnings from the firm's rival bidders that most people were likely to want to apply for their

CRB disclosures in writing. For Capita, the price paid for the scandal – which involved thousands of children missing out on education because of school closures – was little more than a rounding error. The firm was fined £3.8 million for failing to meet its targets, loose change for a business that in 2004 made pre-tax profits of £143 million on a turnover of £1.28 billion, especially when the government ended up paying £3.6 million extra to Capita for the unexpected overload of paper applications, albeit the contract was later renegotiated to give the company a lower price per application.

The new reliance on computerised criminal records threw up another problem, which emerged just a year after the establishment of the CRB. In its first year, the Home Office admitted that 400 people had been 'mistakenly matched' with criminal convictions. The cases included those of a supply teacher whose work had dried up after the CRB wrongly described him as a career burglar with convictions for grievous bodily harm. There was also a case of a retired RAF pilot, who was vetted when applying for a voluntary job driving for the disabled and who had been wrongly accused of using an alias and having been jailed for theft. These problems have not gone away. In July 2008, the CRB revealed that it had wrongly branded 680 people as criminals in just one year. The CRB maintains that it clears up errors as soon as possible (normally within three weeks) and points out that the figure is a fraction of the total number of CRB disclosures issued annually by the agency. But none of this does justice to the embarrassment and difficulty for people who apply for a CRB check and then are wrongly told that they are criminals. Once the word gets around that someone has been given a criminal record by the CRB, the taint is hard to shake off. The Home Office said this was 'regrettable'.

Little wonder, then, that Professor Frank Furedi, a respected sociologist from Kent University, warned that adults were increasingly being seen as 'potential child abusers' by the system. His report, 'Licence to Hug', published in 2008 by the think tank Civitas, detailed how adult–child relationships were being distorted by the need for CRB checks. In one case, he revealed how a mother was banned from a school disco because she had not been vetted. Such checks, he said, did not 'provide anything like a cast-iron guarantee that children will be safe with a particular adult. All it tells us is that the person has not been convicted of an offence in the past.' The result has been a decline in people's willingness to volunteer. The Children's Commissioner, Sir Al Aynsley Green, revealed a 50,000-strong waiting list of teenage girls who cannot become Girl Guides because of a shortage of volunteers. No wonder ministers called for charities not to carry out CRB checks 'unnecessarily'. Phil Hope, a Cabinet Office minister, tried to calm the situation in late 2008: 'Risk has to be managed properly and proportionately,' he intoned.

The CRB's annual 2008/09 business plan boasted of how it had increased the number of checks per year from 1.5 million in 2002 to nearly three million by 2007, even though this was still well behind the ambitious target set by Jack Straw of 10 million per year. The bureau claims that CRB checks have 'directly prevented over 80,000 job offers being made and acted as a deterrent to many more unsuitable people working with children or the vulnerable'. The report stated that 93.6 per cent of enhanced disclosures were issued within four weeks. Yet this masked the fact that more than 50,000 people waited for more than two months for the same checks. An astonishing 240,000 people also filled in vetting application forms incorrectly. And there were hints of morale problems at the CRB, with 450 people taking 5,000 sick days in 2007 – more than two working weeks each. The CRB had been delivered £150 million over budget, eight months late and clearly not fit for purpose, failing tens of thousands of the people it was meant to protect. There were other loopholes, too. The CRB was not able to check for crimes committed by foreigners overseas who had since moved to Britain to work. There were reports that thousands of foreigners were being allowed to work 'airside' in Britain's airports without being vetted properly. Relatives of vulnerable adults might also be alarmed, given that many of the nurses and care workers in the UK are from overseas.

The CRB had shown that it couldn't cope properly and had failed to deliver on its original promise, yet at the start of 2010 it was preparing to get even busier. There were signs that the government wanted to go even further and was determined to push forward with plans for a new vetting and barring scheme run by the newly established Independent Safeguarding Authority. This would result in millions of people in England being vetted for any criminal record and registering with the new Independent Safeguarding Authority before being given approval to come into contact with children under sixteen. Nine million people who wanted to work with children or vulnerable adults would have to register on the database, or face a £5,000 fine. The plan was heavily criticised by nurses, teachers and actors such as Sir Ian McKellen, who said the measures were excessive. It would even affect parents taking part in school driving rotas for weekly sports events or clubs.

In June 2010 the new coalition government halted the plans, a month before they were due to be implemented, and said that they would be scaled back, saving £100 million a year. Theresa May, the new Home Secretary, said that in future the protection of children and vulnerable adults would focus on 'common sense' rather than form filling. Ministers feared that the previous government's vetting and barring scheme would drive a 'wedge between children and well-meaning adults'. Tens of thousands of employers, charities and voluntary groups were informed of the sudden change of plan. Eight months later, in February 2011, a Home Office review recommended the merger of the CRB with the Independent Safeguarding Authority, into a single 'stream-lined new body providing a proportionate barring and criminal records checking service'. This more 'proportionate' approach would affect 4.5 million people who work closely and regularly with children or vulnerable adults. Teachers would continue to be vetted but those doing occasional, supervised volunteer work would not. Unveiling the plans, Deputy Prime Minister

Nick Clegg said: 'Most people accept we were treated with too much distrust and suspicion ... It's still going to be a scheme of some considerable size but one which does not cast that atmosphere of distrust over adults who are simply trying to do their best by their own children, by children in their own community.' Barnardo's, the children's charity, said the change of heart was 'a victory for common sense'. Chief executive Anne Marie Carrie said: 'There is already enough safeguarding in place for people who have unsupervised, substantial access to children.' In 2013 the Court of Appeal ruled that trivial crimes committed by people when they were young should not be allowed to stay on their criminal record years later and frustrate people's attempts to get work if they were not relevant. Gradually, the scope of the CRB was being reined in. Time would tell if the new approach would work.

6

RURAL PAYMENTS AGENCY

Ministers were being told it was possible when it was not in fact possible.
Dame Helen Ghosh, Permanent Under-Secretary, Department of the Environment, Food and Rural Affairs

The problem was summed up by Bill Duncan of the Rural Payments Agency: 'If we choose anything other than the simple historic or simple regional average payment we will have a nightmare on our hands.' The senior agency official who was responsible for overhauling the system of EU farm payments had issued a very clear warning. Guess which option ministers chose to take?

Working out how to distribute billions of pounds of subsidies to farmers under the European Union's Common Agricultural Policy has never been easy. Until mid-2003, EU officials had grimly weathered the controversy that was never far from the CAP, by running a myriad of subsidies linked to production, such as the beef special premium, the suckler cow premium and the sheep annual payment. The more meat and crops farmers produced, the more cash they received in subsidies – with the resulting creations of infamous mountains of butter and lakes of wine.

Then in June 2003, after six months of talks, European Union farm ministers voted to change the system, reforming the CAP by scrapping nearly a dozen subsidies for livestock and crops, and simplifying them into a single payment scheme administered across the EU. The breakthrough was agreed, after years of haggling and delay, at a marathon all-night meeting of EU agriculture ministers. Within hours a jubilant Margaret Beckett, the Secretary of State for the Environment, Food and Rural Affairs, was telling MPs: 'It is hard to overstate the importance of this morning's agreement in transforming the core elements of the Common Agricultural Policy and laying down a new direction for its future evolution.'

Beckett outlined significant changes, in particular the breaking of the link between farm subsidies and production. Farmers would still receive payments but these would now be for stewardship of the land. Subsidies would also be dependent upon meeting standards in key areas such as the environment and animal welfare. The most radical and important element in the package was the new 'Single Farm Payment', which would facilitate the 'decoupling' of subsidy payments from production of food. Beckett told MPs that this would 'greatly simplify' the bureaucracy. Crucially, there would be no more incentives to produce particular types of food; farmers would now have to grow crops and raise livestock that they could actually sell, rather than just to rack up subsidies. A revolution was underway. The new scheme replaced nearly a dozen production-linked subsidies with one new single payment based on land area. Landowners and farmers in England who kept their land in good agricultural and environmental condition would be eligible (there were different schemes for Scotland, Wales and Northern Ireland). The United Kingdom was one of the prime movers of change within the EU – and thus it wanted to be seen as one of the first EU member states to implement the new scheme.

But how would this happen? It was not to be straightforward. There would be a choice of two 'simple' methods for replacing the old production subsidies: the first was 'historic payments', based on the sums that individual farmers had received in the past under the old CAP schemes; the second was 'regionalised average area payments', based on a new flat-rate subsidy per hectare of land. But it did not end there. Member states were allowed to apply a 'mixed model' under which they could use different calculation systems within different geographical areas; it was this that enabled Scotland, Wales and Northern Ireland to use a different system from England. Furthermore, member states could also use more than one payment method within the same geographical area – under what was known as a 'hybrid' system – so that payments would be calculated both by splitting the new flat-rate subsidy among farmers and also by taking account of the historic payment which they would have received under the old CAP schemes. This was called the 'static hybrid'. And that was not all. The scheme could be varied even further, so that over the years the proportion of the new single payment based on the historic subsidy payment declined while the proportion based on the flat-rate payment increased; this was known as the 'dynamic hybrid'. The dynamic element of the hybrid meant that the exact sums would vary from year to year, as the flat-rate portion took an increasing share every year of the total subsidy paid. Payments would initially be mostly historic, based on what farmers had received in the past, with only a small fraction based on the new flat rate for a specified amount of land. This flat-rate payment would then take a greater proportion of the total subsidy, from 10 per cent of the total in the first year, increasing in increments each year until it finally eliminated the historic element. Readers who have now reached for a glass of whisky would not be alone.

The hybrid options were a laughing stock in Whitehall, a way of overcomplicating something which was already complex enough. In meetings between farmers and officials following Beckett's announcement, it was described as 'an object of some entertainment'. Civil servants in Beckett's own department were dismissive. When David Hunter, a senior Defra official, chaired a private meeting on 17 October 2003 at which options were discussed, he said that the hybrid options were the 'most complicated', that dynamic hybrid options would present the 'most difficulty' and that it would be 'madness' to go down a hybrid route. Meanwhile Bill Duncan from the Rural Payments Agency was no less emphatic, and his approach won admirers, including George Dunn of the Tenant Farmers Association, who later told MPs: 'I have to say that Bill was excellent in terms of the advice he was giving to us and to Defra. Bill Duncan's view was stark: "If we choose something other than a simple historic or a simple regional average system it would be a nightmare to administer."' Duncan also made it clear that the 'worst of all worlds' would be a dynamic hybrid.

Yet almost unbelievably, support for the dynamic option hardened among ministers. Why was this? As Jeremy Moody, secretary of the Central Association of Agricultural Valuers, told MPs: 'You could see a world in which obviously entitlements were going to move between farmers.' This meant that using historical data to set future subsidies would soon look outdated, and the farming minister Lord Whitty was deeply concerned about the long-term consequences if the government opted for the straightforward historic approach. The Tenant Farmers Association suggested that Whitty veered away from a purely historical approach 'for a fear as to how it might look in years to come'. At the Oxford Farming Conference, Whitty quoted the Hungarian farming minister as saying 'I can see why I might have so many entitlements because I had twenty cows, but why after a period of transfers should I have an entitlement based on the fact that you had twenty cows?' Moody described Whitty's position: 'He was almost quixotically anxious about what would be the right decision for five years' time. Clearly, he went through a process of agonising, one of the reasons why I think the decision took so long to arrive at, and ultimately he chose perhaps the purity of theory over the practicality of delivery'.

So it was that a few months later, on 12 February 2004 – a date described by George Dunn as 'a dark day' – Margaret Beckett announced formally that the government had chosen the 'dynamic hybrid' method to pay the subsidies. Dunn had been present when David Hunter had referred to the hybrid route as 'madness'; Dunn had also heard the 'excellent' Bill Duncan say that it would be a 'nightmare'. At a subsequent meeting when Dunn asked why the RPA's advice had not been taken on board he was told by David Hunter: 'The RPA will do what the RPA is told to do.' So was David Hunter to blame? Actually, he was just doing what civil servants are supposed to do, which is to implement the wishes of their ministers. And no matter how 'mad' or 'nightmarish' the experts knew the hybrid route to be, this was what ministers wanted. The National Farmers Union believed the final decision was 'very ministerially-driven'.

Farmers were left scratching their heads at the sheer complexity of such an approach. James Jones of the Royal Agricultural College said that using the 'dynamic hybrid' method made establishing the appropriate levels of payment 'about as complex as it could conceivably have been'. Jeremy Moody added that 'arguing over the hybrid system was rather like wrestling with a bar of soap; it started in one place and by the time you got an answer on that it was somewhere else in the bath'. The Rural Payments Agency, chosen to imple-ment this complex new system, was a novice executive agency which had only taken over implementing farm subsidies from the old Ministry of Agriculture, Fisheries and Food in 2000, and was itself only half-way through a complicated 'change' programme. The government had high hopes for this new agency. Agriculture minister Nick Brown had told MPs in July 2000 that it would take 'full advantage of the benefits of electronic services delivery'. Farmers would benefit from 'a reduction in red tape and more efficient and rapid processing of payments', he said. Brown pledged that there would also be 'significant benefits' for taxpayers, with 'a 10 per cent cut by March 2004 in unit costs of administering payments and further savings in subsequent years'. He wanted farmers' views on the best ways of ensuring a smooth transition to the new arrangements, assuring them: 'We will work very closely with our customers to help them reap the benefits which electronic service delivery offers.'

Subsidy payments would be handled under one roof in order 'to provide top quality customer service using electronic systems'. Some £130 million was set aside for a 'change' programme. Yet even then it was not to be until 2005 that 'all the new structures and systems are in place and the benefits the new agency can bring ... will be fully realised'. Much of this work was to be done by computers. A committee of MPs did no more than state the truth when it observed: 'The importance of the new IT system cannot be exaggerated. It will facilitate all the activities of the agency.'

The new man in charge of the RPA was Johnston McNeill, a tough Ulsterman who then ran the government's Meat and Hygiene Service. McNeill arrived after an open competition and then interviews in which initially he had been reluctant to participate. He was persuaded to take part after being repeatedly urged to do so by the government's recruitment consultants. Strangely, given that familiarity with information technology was a pre-requisite in the job specification, McNeill had no specialist knowledge of IT systems at all. This might have ruled him out for the new job, but the selection panel was undeterred. Sir Brian Bender, Defra's Permanent Secretary and a member of the panel which had appointed the new chief executive, later told MPs that McNeill had been selected on the basis of his track record in creating new organisations and 'complex mergers in different cultures'. He explained that McNeill had a reputation as a 'robust' manager and that given the culture change that would be needed in creating the new organisation 'it might well be necessary to break some eggs'. The failure to appoint someone with the necessary IT skills for the job was later brushed aside as Bender told MPs: 'I am not trying to mince words, but I simply do not recall the extent to which when the panel had a discussion about whether that was crucial [sic].'

The new Rural Payments Agency emerged, blinking, into existence on 16 October 2001 with McNeill at the helm, becoming the single accredited paying agency for all CAP schemes in England and some schemes throughout the rest of the UK, with responsibility for spending over £2 billion in total each year. Its mission statement was 'to be a customer focused organisation that pays valid Common Agricultural Policy claims accurately and on time'. One of McNeill's first moves was to address a deficiency in his own knowledge about computers. He set in process a scheme to look for an IT director for the RPA to provide the new organisation with the skills that he lacked. Having exhaustively considered some thirty CVs, a selection panel including McNeill and Bender offered the job to an ex-consultant called Alan McDermott, on a salary of £225,000, twice McNeill's own salary.

Just over a year later on 31 January 2003, the RPA agreed a new contract with a large IT consulting and services firm, Accenture, to provide a new computer system, the RPA IT Application, known as 'RITA'. The contract would include a land register, a customer register, a 'claim processing engine', a customer service centre, a document management unit and a 'customer on-line capability'. The new computer would supposedly increase efficiency and make payments under the existing CAP. Crucially, adapting to any changes to the CAP was excluded from the contract. Yet only ten days earlier, on 21 January 2003, the European Commission had published its plans to reform the CAP under the heading 'A Long-Term Policy Perspective for Sustainable Agriculture'. The new contract for RITA was already looking out of date.

At the top of Defra, Margaret Beckett was sailing full steam ahead towards a dynamic hybrid system. Britain had a choice of when to introduce it – 2005, 2006 or 2007. Beckett chose the earliest possible date – 2005, despite other member states choosing to go live with their systems in the following year. It meant that 96.14 per cent of the £1.54 billion to farmers in England had to be paid by June 2006 to avoid late payment penalties. Beckett and her officials had picked the most compli-cated system of all and then chosen to implement it in the shortest possible timetable. And within two months, the hybrid was being varied further. On 22 April 2004, a third region – 'moor land' – was added, to try to channel more subsidies into poorer parts of England. RITA was forced to adapt – after all a computer system designed for CAP subsidy schemes based on food production was no longer much use – and a new contract worth £20 million more was agreed, to include the new Single Payment Scheme.

In public, all was calm. On 17 June 2004 Andy Lebrecht, Defra's director general for sustainable farming, food and fisheries, told his department's management board that the RPA would be able to make payments under the payment scheme from 1 December 2005 – at the very beginning of the possible payment window stipulated by the European Union. The following month Defra published a regulatory impact assessment of the implementation of the dynamic hybrid model. This concluded that starting to make payments from 2005 'was a demanding timetable taking into account the work that has to be done in redesigning computer delivery systems'. It added that 'if Defra fails to deliver or delivers a poor service, there will be a considerable risk to the ongoing reputation of the department'. Then in August, the department bravely gave the European Commission 'formal notification that England would implement' the scheme in 2005. As MPs reviewing the saga later noted sombrely: 'The department was thereby locked into its policy choice.'

Within a few months, Defra narrowed its options further by mothballing a contingency scheme which would have allowed it to start to make payments based on the old way of calculating them in case of a major IT failure. Despite costing £8.4 million, this 'Plan B' was seen as a stop-gap measure that distracted from the main work of developing the Single Payment Scheme. In the early part of 2005, Beckett and her team were given the option of developing another system to make advance payments to farmers in the case of delays, but the EU insisted that Defra obtain a bank guarantee from each farmer. This was deemed out of the question.

There were further problems. The new IT contract had been agreed before Brussels had hammered out the detail of the payment scheme (there was some dispute among the Eurocrats about the definition of a 'farmer'). By December 2004, the RPA had managed to distil sixty possible changes to the specification of the RITA computer system into twenty-three critical IT changes. Software deadlines were extended, sometimes by months. IT capability was being developed before the policy had been fixed.

The computer programs were eventually delivered in 'bite-sized chunks'. The rural land register arrived in September 2004 and the customer register in February 2005. The manual system went live in May 2005 and the rest of the software was up and running in October 2005. The RPA later complained that the rural land register 'was not able to perform as intended', while the IT system was not 'as user-friendly'. However, there was no time to make changes, so the programs were never tested 'end-to-end'. Accenture was later largely cleared of any blame by MPs on the Defra committee, although it was criticised for 'not venturing comment on matters which they deemed beyond their contractual observations', during their later inquiry.

The pressure was now on – but who was in charge? As so often in Whitehall, this was not a straightforward question. Two committees oversaw the new scheme: the CAP Reform Implementation (CAPRI) board and the Executive Review Group (ERG). The CAPRI board was alternately chaired by Johnston McNeill and Andy Lebrecht to ensure the leadership was 'joined at the hip'. The ERG was chaired by Sir Brian Bender and was intended to provide a 'critical challenge function' of the work of the CAPRI board. This was far from ideal. The National Audit Office subsequently reported that the ERG took over too much of the decision making from the CAPRI board, confusing officials who were desperate to know where responsibility lay. The same decisions were put to the CAPRI board, then the ERG, then to ministers for approval. Sometimes these important papers were long and complex and only circulated just before meetings.

The Single Payment Scheme 'year' started on 1 January 2005, with applications due in by mid-May. Yet already, in late 2004 and the early part of 2005, Johnston McNeill and Bender were holding a number of informal meetings to discuss the risk that the project might not be delivered on time. Then came a public hint that all was not well. The RPA announced that the first payments under the CAP scheme would not be made until February 2006, not in 2005 as had been planned. Margaret Beckett was furious, reportedly telling the National Farmers Union's conference in the following month that she was 'bloody livid' about the delay. The Secretary of State's intemperate language had repercussions at the RPA. McNeill complained that it caused 'confusion' among staff, 'given that she should have been aware of the background to the decision and that the delay was a consequence of SPS [Single Payment Scheme] policy decisions being finalised later and adding to the scheme's complexity'. He also told MPs that the comments were 'not very helpful in terms of staff morale'. Beckett herself tried to explain her remarks in an interview three months later, when she said she had not been 'livid' with the RPA's work, but the fact that payments would be later than planned. She had been aware of the pressure on staff with this 'absolutely massive change'. MPs on the Defra committee were still not impressed. 'The committee very much regrets the former Secretary of State's attempts verbally to distance herself from the consequences of policies which she herself must have approved. Expressing annoyance or dismay was no substitute for her need at the time fully to engage in her department's efforts to deliver the SPS on time,' they concluded.

Bender believed that even committing to a February 2006 start date was a mistake. Bender later said he privately warned colleagues:

> While we said 'as early as possible in the payment window' there was vagueness, but once we went to February 2006 we had to be confident. Once ministers made that decision not only would they be disappointed that it was not December, which became clear, but we risked being hoisted on a petard.

Indeed there were suggestions that the RPA itself had asked to make all the payments by the end of the payment window in June but were told by Defra that this was 'totally unacceptable politically' because farmers were traditionally paid in December. Despite the concerns, in May 2005 the February start date became a formal performance target for the RPA in that financial year.

The RPA's new 100-strong customer service call centre was opened on 14 February 2005, and almost immediately went into meltdown. At its peak the call centre was receiving 12,000 calls a day from worried farmers. More staff were needed, yet the agency had committed to a job reduction programme, with 1,800 posts set to go – including 1,000 permanent jobs – from the 3,950-strong workforce. Experienced staff, with years of dealing with the complex subsidy system, were being allowed to leave when the agency needed them most. The RPA tried to fill the gap with temporary staff. But unions complained that they were brought in and paid the minimum wage to work unsocial hours. MPs later lambasted the RPA because it had 'failed to reduce its overall staffing levels as intended, while losing a large number of experienced people who would have been particularly valuable to the agency and its customers in this time of major change'. The Public and Commercial Services Union complained that 900 staff had been 'temporarily promoted into higher grades including entire management chains'. As the trade union explained, the consequence was that 'during times of crisis inexperienced managers found themselves in authority'. The call centre was 'staffed by untrained managers and staff brought in off the streets'. At the other end of the scale, it was not unusual for a contractor or consultant 'on £2,000 a day' to occupy a civil service post.

The scale of the staffing crisis was not at all clear to the RPA's top officials, though, because of inadequate management information about the rate of progress in dealing with claims. This information vacuum meant that they underestimated the work involved in processing each claim and therefore underestimated the number of staff required. It was the worst of both worlds. McNeill confessed that he had 'wondered why it did not cross his mind that there would be a problem if the RPA lost staff

with experience in dealing with farmers when customer relations were going to be so important'. To stem the flow, a second
wave of voluntary redundancies was cancelled. But the damage
had been done. Farming minister Lord Whitty later conceded:
'In retrospect I think it is probably true that it was not sensible
to have reduced staff by that much.'

The way staff were being asked to work had changed for
the worse too. In the past, a single official would have been
appointed to handle an entire claim. However, under the
scheme, staff were given 'tasks' – parts of a claim – to handle.
This meant that farmers and landowners could deal with a
number of officials on a single claim, further slowing down the
process and introducing the opportunity for more mistakes.
The new payments system came as a shock for farmers who had
been used to the previously excellent service of a one-to-one
relationship with officials in regional offices. Even the basics
were not right. There were not enough blank continuation
forms available, which meant that farmers did not provide all
of the information requested in some cases, while in others the
quality of form completion was poor. Some of the information
given by call centre workers was just wrong. Jeremy Moody
reported at the time:

> I was rung by a member two months ago now, who said 'What
> do the letters OE stand for?' Apart from the obvious and flip-
> pant answer, I did not know. I went to the RPA and they said 'It
> means "out of England"', which might be understandable for a
> farmer down on the Welsh border, somewhere on the Shropshire
> boundary; this field was in Lincolnshire.

The dynamic hybrid had enfranchised tens of thousands more
claimants. Anyone who kept land in good environmental and
agricultural condition – such as those rearing pigs on open
land, keeping a horse on a paddock and even growing fruit
and vegetables – found they could now make more significant claims, or apply for the first time. Numbers of subsidy

claimants jumped from 70,000 in 2004 under the old system to 116,000 under the new one in 2005. For example, there were 6,000 specialist dairy farmers who had not otherwise made area-based applications because in the past their claims had related to milk quotas, and not to cows or land. Jeremy Moody added: 'This was the first time that we had undertaken a reform that affected everybody, every acre of land, potentially, within the United Kingdom.'

The new rural land register, which formed the basis of their area-based claims under the Single Payment Scheme, presented its own problems. Many of the maps sent to farmers proved to be hopelessly inaccurate. This was because previously some farmers and landowners had only estimated the size of their holdings, and left out other parts that were not relevant to their subsidies. McNeill conceded that these figures were 'a major shock to us, to be perfectly frank'. The RPA had been advised that it should send a copy of the maps to every claimant for approval, creating further cost and delay. The NFU believed that the software underlying the digital maps 'was profoundly unstable'. Farmers tried sometimes in vain to get mistakes rectified. The RPA made matters worse when it tried to blame the quality of information sent in by landowners and farmers. This led to a big jump in changes to land registrations from claimants worried that even small inaccuracies could affect their subsidies. Around 100,000 amendments were submitted, compared to 9,000 changes in a typical year.

Another reason for the surge in claims was that the government had agreed not to set a minimum figure for claims – even though other countries did. A typical 'de minimis' level was €100, then around £68, which seemed reasonable given that each claim cost more than £500 to process. Setting a €100 minimum claim would have allowed the RPA to disregard 14,000 of the eventual 116,500 claims. The fact that the RPA had not done this caused consternation when it was uncovered by MPs in an investigation of what went wrong. Ian Davidson, the Labour MP for Glasgow South West, asked:

We gave 14,000 farmers – 12 per cent of total claimants – money that we were not legally obliged to give them, but chose to do so in circumstances where it cost us more to pay them the money than they were receiving, and at a time when we were sacking staff yet having to recruit temporary staff? I do not see the logic of that position.

With looming chaos all around, the financial year 2004/05 ended on a positive note for McNeill when he received his maximum performance bonus for his work at the RPA, amounting to £21,062 or 18.5 per cent of his salary.

By June 2005, the likelihood of the RPA hitting its start date had slumped to a lowly 40 per cent. Sir Brian Bender managed expectations when he said the department was intent on keeping the likelihood of success at over 50 per cent. A major red flag was waved by the Office of Government Commerce that same month when it warned that the RPA would require a 'very fair wind to succeed, and recent experience suggests that there will be much bad weather to cope with'. The OGC suggested finding a fallback position if it all went wrong, but Defra did not do this for fear of delaying the payments timetable.

Yet just when leadership was required, it was all change at the top of the department overseeing the work of the RPA. On 30 September 2005 Bender moved to become Permanent Secretary at the Department for Trade and Industry. He was replaced at Defra by Mark Addison on a temporary basis, until Helen Ghosh took over in November. Bender warned his successors with some understatement in his final weeks that the Single Payment Scheme deserved 'quite a lot of attention'.

In public at least, over at the RPA there was optimism about the future. On 10 October 2005 Johnston McNeill told the NFU's council that payments were on course to begin in February, and that most would complete three weeks after that. Two days later the EU decided to allow the RPA to make partial payments, but by now the die was cast. In the same month a private firm called Infoterra was brought in to help with the digitisation of the maps – now badly behind schedule – and help with the workload. There was no evidence that this contract was even put out to public tender, suggesting it might have been a 'hurried decision', according to MPs who reviewed the saga later.

By now Lord Bach had replaced Lord Whitty as farming minister. In early January 2006 Bach told MPs on the Commons Defra committee that he could not give a definitive statement about whether full payments under the scheme would be made on time in the following month, as had been promised. The MPs said they were 'staggered'. Two weeks later on 24 January, the MPs published a report in which they said they were 'dismayed by the "complacency" of Lord Bach in refusing to admit that anything could have been done differently to avoid the problems'. Three days later, the ERG internally decided not to recommend making partial payments – a 'Plan B' if it all went wrong – for fear that this would hold up progress towards making full payments. And in public Lord Bach was still sticking to his guns, insisting on 31 January that full payments would begin in February, with 'the bulk' completed by March.

The process of definitively establishing claims started on 14 February, with the first letters going out to farmers and landowners on 20 February. In Whitehall, the OGC had convinced itself that all was going well. A 'readiness for service' gateway review in February congratulated the RPA on its 'great achievement' of starting the payments in that month, adding that it expected all payments to be made by the end of March. The RPA was congratulated for its 'sterling efforts' towards this 'momentous achievement'. The OGC changed its tune in a review after the chaos had emerged. Its 'programme review case study report' concluded, inter alia:

> From late 2003 through to late 2004 a series of decisions were taken which, in aggregate, invalidated most of the assumptions on which the programme's scope, deliverability and benefits had been predicated. By the end of this period, most if not all

of the original objectives – being customer focussed; having a flexible generic system; data being captured primarily through electronic channels et cetera – were so compromised that the emerging picture was almost diametrically opposed to the vision and indeed to some of the precepts on which elements of the system design had been based.

But on 28 February shocked management at the RPA found that payments were only trickling out to farmers, with a measly 2,400 payments made in the first fortnight. Two weeks later, on 10 March, only 4,484 claims – fewer than 4 per cent of the total – had been paid, with another 39,000 out of 120,000 awaiting authorisation. McNeill wrote to Lord Bach, saying he had expected the figure to be much higher. It soon became clear that Bach's commitment that 'the bulk' of the payments would be processed actually meant only 'more than 50 per cent of the total value of claims'. Payments were sent to the wrong people, others were not 'validated' and those which were 'fully validated' were found to be inaccurate.

Alarmingly, McNeill reported that a 'substantial proportion' of the 39,000 fully validated claims were failing to be authorised. This previously undiagnosed problem stemmed from the fact that even with validated claims there were a further six 'authorisation checks' which had to be carried out before payments could be made. Typically a sample of four in every 100 claims was being vetted. However, this meant that a few claims could hold up the payment of all 100, and they would then all need to be checked individually. 'Extraordinarily', as MPs would later remark, 'this blockage took the RPA and Defra by surprise'. Helen Ghosh said the RPA had been basing its predictions on 'over-optimistic interpretations of perhaps inadequate management information'. It later transpired that five of the six checks were unnecessary and could be abandoned to speed up claims processing. The only retained check – the obvious one – was that the payments went to the right person.

Part of the problem was that no single official was dealing

with an entire claim and senior managers had little idea of how quickly staff were working through applications. McNeill reported: 'As we cleared tasks in a number of cases they generated yet more tasks.' Adopting this task-based approach meant that his staff 'could not even prioritise larger value claims'. Senior civil servants suggested that the lack of an end-to-end testing of the IT contributed to this problem. Managers had little idea about what tasks remained outstanding on claims each week and how much time it would take to complete them. One might have thought it was absolutely essential to provide managers with the right information so that they could monitor progress and forecast future work effectively. But it was precisely this that was not done. Splitting up each claim into tasks performed by different people in different parts of the country had made the whole process more problematic. The computer system too had been downgraded to ensure it was ready on time, which made it difficult to tell how quickly an individual payment was being processed. Almost incredibly, the RPA had deprived its managers of the key information they needed to make sensible decisions. There was no management information because they had not developed those parts of the system which would have provided it in order to make the system work at all.

Customers who phoned up to enquire about the progress of their claims were greeted by a recorded message: 'There is nothing that the call centre staff can tell you about your payment.' The truth was that there was nothing anyone could tell them about their claim. Customers were scolded for even seeking to find out what was going on. Another recorded message stated: 'If you contact us this will divert resources away from the urgent tasks of completing validations and making full payments.' The lack of information was a principal cause of frustration for farmers, who complained about the extraordinary secrecy of the RPA. But for managers, secrecy had one key advantage. It helped them to conceal from the outside world how little they actually knew themselves about the progress they were making in processing claims.

Johnston McNeill had only met Margaret Beckett once. His second meeting was on 14 March 2006. At this meeting, which was attended by other Defra officials, he told her 'for the first time' that it would no longer be possible to make all the payments by the end of March as planned. This was 'particularly dispiriting' for ministers, MPs later judged, because Jim Knight, a minister on Beckett's team, was only five days away from announcing that the RPA was delivering on its promise to make the payments in full, with the bulk by the end of March – repeating Lord Bach's assertion from the previous January. The MPs later reported:

> Johnston McNeill told us later that the Secretary of State thanked him for his honesty and he and other RPA officials then left the room. The next day, on 15 March, the Permanent Secretary, Helen Ghosh, told Johnston McNeill that following consultations between her and the Secretary of State, he was being stood down as Chief Executive of the RPA.

In what was described as an 'administrative rather than a disciplinary act' McNeill was told to speak to no one and to take indefinite paid leave. He was dismissed by Defra on 1 December 2006. Ghosh later explained:

> There had been a loss of confidence between ministers and him in terms of delivery of the scheme, and therefore a significant loss of confidence in terms of his relationship with stakeholders, and that, on those grounds, it would be better if he moved aside and a fresh pair of eyes looked at the situation.

Ghosh too said that she had 'lost confidence' in McNeill, although he said Ghosh had told him he had been totally professional and had given '110 per cent'. The department could find no suitable grounds on which to dismiss Johnston McNeill. He had no disciplinary hearing or correspondence explaining exactly what he had done wrong and was given no opportunity to appeal. The Civil Service Appeal Board ruled that he was unfairly dismissed and McNeill received payments of around £250,000 including £60,000 compensation. Lord Bach nonetheless laid the blame at the door of the RPA:

> On Thursday 9 March we were given advice that the bulk of payments would be made by the first few days of April, not the end of March, but the first few days of April. On the 14th, five days later ... we were told that there was no chance at all of such a thing happening, that the bulk of payments would not be made anywhere near by the end of March and of course ... they were not. I frankly have to say that I do not think that that was satisfactory from senior civil servants whose job is to tell ministers the truth.

But he did also say that he felt he did 'not think that Johnston McNeill as a personality is someone who should be crucified ... My view is that the top management of the RPA was not up to the task on this occasion.' For his part, McNeill believed that Lord Bach should not have been surprised by what happened as he was in regular contact with the RPA's director of operations, and that statistics given to him showed the RPA was 'running into trouble'.

The news was broken to MPs in the House of Commons by Beckett on 16 March. English farmers, already bruised by the difficult application process the year before, now would be experiencing delays in receiving money to which they were entitled. The Secretary of State had outlined new measures to speed up payments by the end of the month, including making staff responsible for individual applications rather than tasks. By the middle of April, Beckett was able to announce that 47 per cent of claims had been paid, worth £362 million. However, she advised MPs that Mark Addison, the new acting chief executive at the RPA, had told her that he could not say with complete confidence that all the payments would be made by the EU's June deadline for payments. She therefore authorised work on another system to make substantial payments to remaining claimants as soon as possible.

It was all change at the top again a few weeks later. During a ministerial reshuffle on 5 May, Lord Bach lost his job, in part – he believes – because of the failure at the RPA, and Beckett was promoted to Foreign Secretary. Sir Brian Bender stayed on at the DTI and Andy Lebrecht remained in post. MPs on the Defra committee later noted disparagingly: 'The action taken against Johnston McNeill by the Secretary of State and the Permanent Secretary contrasts strongly with the fortunes of many of the others closely involved.' That month, Tony Cooper was appointed as the new chief executive of the RPA. He immediately warned that its 'deep-rooted' problems meant that the payments system might take another eighteen to twenty-four months to 'stabilise'. Under Cooper, the RPA refocused its efforts on making payments as quickly as possible. The controversial 'task-based' approach to handling claims was abandoned and individual members of staff were assigned to manage entire cases.

It emerged that staff at the RPA's main regional office in Newcastle had been using unorthodox methods to cope with the high levels of stress facing agency employees. A whistleblower alleged that staff had been filmed on closed-circuit television cameras leaping naked from filing cabinets, while others had taken part in a craze of vomiting in cups and leaving them to fester in cupboards until they were discovered through the horrendous smell. Other pranks included people taking drugs, having sex in the toilets and holding breakdancing competitions during working hours. The whistleblower wrote to the *Newcastle Chronicle*: 'I'm appalled at the level of depravity that is being tolerated at my work place.' The agency immediately launched an internal investigation, which eventually resulted in a statement that there was 'no evidence' to support the allegations. This did not stop the story going global. It was ranked number one in a list of 'The Ten Most Unbelievable Workplace Stories of 2006' by the *Colorado Springs Business Journal*, which commented: 'Next time the boss complains about you managing your fantasy football team during office hours, you can point out that at least you are not leaping naked from filing cabinets.'

The RPA narrowly missed the EU requirement to pay 96.14 per cent of its payments by 30 June 2006. In all the RPA paid £1.438 billion, 94.19 per cent of the total claims. By the end of August of that year it had paid 98 per cent of the claims. In later reports, the spending watchdog found that problems experienced for the 2005 scheme were likely to recur in subsequent years and the RPA did not expect to remedy matters fully until April 2008. The problems implementing the Single Payment Scheme eventually cost Britain £132 million in fines, payable to the European Commission. But at what cost to farmers? MPs on the Defra committee reported that 'this sorry saga has cost farmers about £20 million of their own money', while 'Defra is likely to secure only £7.5 million of the expected £164 million savings in the department and the RPA from the SPS and wider change programme'. It had cost £122 million to implement.

Ministers and officials had chosen to operate the most complicated system on offer in the shortest available timetable, in a way which was certain to increase both the total number of claimants and the total land area claimed, while not having first completed the essential digital mapping exercise properly and refusing to recognise that it was flawed. Furthermore, they had adopted a computer system that had not been fully tested and which was not up to the job, using an approach which split up the work on each claim into separate tasks performed in different parts of the country, making it impossible to track the progress of any individual claim, while cancelling those parts of the system which would have provided management with information on what was happening, and also scrapping the contingency plan which would at least have enabled them to make part payments. And in the meantime they had sacked their most experienced staff and replaced them with temporary unskilled staff who were required to work unsocial hours on the minimum wage.

Yet no one, apart from the luckless McNeill and possibly

Lord Bach, carried the can. The MPs on the Defra committee were withering in their criticism. They concluded:

> The Single Payment Scheme was one of Defra's highest priorities, as it underpinned the financial wellbeing of England's rural economy. If a failure to deliver on such a scale had occurred in a major plc, the chairman and the senior operating executives would have faced dismissal from post. With this in mind the Committee continues to be astonished that Sir Brian Bender continues to hold the rank of Permanent Secretary. If he does not tender his resignation, the Head of the Home Civil Service should explain why a failure such as this results in no penalty.

Margaret Beckett and her team also came under fire. MPs said: 'Defra ministers selected the "dynamic hybrid" model in the knowledge that it was inherently more complex and risky' and that 'no proper appraisal' was made of the volume of work which was heading their way, adding:

> It will seem strange to many in the rural economy that right at the top of Defra no price for failure has been paid by the now Foreign Secretary. Leaving others to get on with the day to day delivery of services should not remove the obligation from the holders of high office to do more than just apologise and mouth the words 'I am taking responsibility'. It should be the case that when a Department fails to deliver a key programme right at the heart of its fundamental responsibilities the holder of the office of Secretary of State should not be rewarded with promotion but its reverse.

In short, they argued, it should be made clear to ministers that 'if individuals are prepared to accept the glories that come with high office they also know precisely what to do if fundamental departmental failure occurs'.

7

FOREIGN NATIONAL PRISONERS

If the Home Office were a horse, it would have been shot by now. This shambles is merely the latest symptom that the department is sick and is in need of a drastic cure.
Financial Times

For the number crunchers at the National Audit Office, it was straightforward enough how the government should be dealing with people from outside the European Union who enter the UK illegally and apply for asylum, but fail to win the right to stay in Britain. In a report 'Returning Failed Asylum Applicants', published in July 2005, the NAO said: 'Asylum applicants whose applications have been rejected have no legal right to remain in the United Kingdom. Failed applicants are expected to leave the United Kingdom voluntarily or be subject to removal action.'

Yet it was not working out like this. The problem was simple enough – the number of immigrants who were returned was half as many as the numbers being allowed to remain every month. In just one year, 2003/04, 13,625 failed asylum seekers were deported, yet another 34,735 were not. In the following year, 2004/05, the number sent home (1,000 a month, excluding dependants) was more than outweighed by the number who stayed in the UK (2,150 a month). The backlog had been growing for years and was reaching unmanageable proportions.

The government's system for dealing with illegal immigrants had long since broken down. This was how it was meant to work: responsibility for assessing the merits of an asylum seeker's case lay with a Home Office body called the Immigration and Nationality Directorate (IND). On arrival in the UK, asylum seekers had to demonstrate to officials at the IND that they had a status of 'refugee' as laid down by the 1951 United Nations Convention. If they failed, they could appeal to a tribunal, delaying any attempt by one of the IND's thirty-two enforcement offices around the UK to remove them. This tortuous process created its own problems as overworked staff at the offices tried to manage busy workloads. The length of time it took to deport asylum seekers created 'significant practical challenges for the directorate', the NAO found. 'Those who have been in the country for some time may have settled into their local community and have made a life for themselves and their dependants. Many applicants may not be willing to go.'

No wonder Sir John Gieve, the Home Office's Permanent Secretary, described the system as 'very generous', telling MPs on the Public Accounts Committee a year earlier in July 2004 that people came to the UK for economic reasons and because decision making was slow: 'It's a very generous system and people have used it to stay during the process ... The law is extremely generous in many ways on the rights of people claiming asylum.' According to Stephen Boys Smith, the head of the IND from 1998 to 2002, it had been 'run down' from 1995 onwards, with at one point only 100 to 150 experienced asylum caseworkers dealing with the growing backlog. Gieve blamed a crisis caused by a computer system that had not worked as expected in the late 1990s, a staffing reduction ahead of the introduction of the new IT and a large increase in asylum applications. This crisis 'had taken some years for us to get out of', he said.

Yet despite Gieve's optimism, figures seemed to suggest that the crisis was still unfolding and the situation appeared to be rapidly spinning out of control. The NAO's report estimated that in the ten years to May 2004 'a maximum of 363,000 applications for asylum were unsuccessful'. Over the same period, just 79,500 failed asylum applicants were removed. This suggested that as many as 283,500 were still in the UK when they should have been repatriated. More worrying still, the IND did not know where nearly half of them were. A database held by the IND only contained the details of 155,000 asylum seekers who were due for removal. Of those, 12 per cent were from Iraq, Zimbabwe and Burundi – countries which the UK had agreed at that time not to make forced returns to. What had happened to the other 133,000? They could have simply left the UK. No one knew because the immigration service discontinued the practice of recording people entering and leaving the country at ferry ports, small and medium-sized airports in 1994 and at large airports in 1998. There were random attempts to find out if any asylum seekers were going home of their own volition, but the numbers detected were a tiny proportion of the overall figure. During spot checks at Heathrow airport in the week before Christmas 2002, a week in February 2003, ten days around Easter in April 2003 and ten days in December 2003, a total of 191 'immigration offenders were detected' of whom forty were failed asylum applicants.

The simple truth was that no one knew how many failed asylum seekers were wandering around the UK. The NAO concluded: 'The actual number of failed asylum seekers still in the United Kingdom is not known and therefore the number of people due for removal is not known.' This was hardly optimal for an agency whose main job was to manage immigration into the UK. Edward Leigh MP, the chairman of the Public Accounts Committee, was appalled. Quizzing top officials from the directorate, he exclaimed: 'There is no target for dealing with the backlog of cases! It is shocking that the IND cannot give a solid estimate of how many failed applicants are still in the UK.'

The IND itself appeared dysfunctional. The NAO found that 'the application, support and enforcement processes have operated as largely separate systems, leading to poor communication and co-ordination within the directorate, thereby reducing the prospect of quick removal of newly failed applicants'. There were 'bottlenecks' in the removal process, and a lack of 'adequate management information leading to insufficient control over how resources are deployed against its various objectives' while not enough attempts were made to help failed asylum seekers return home voluntarily. Within the IND there were also separate systems for handling applications and enforcement. Often an applicant's case could be dealt with by a number of different teams, leaving the potential for chaos and for records to be lost. This degree of failure was costing the taxpayer hundreds of millions of pounds every year. A sample carried out by the NAO for its report on 800 'non-detained' applicants who had been required to return after exhausting the appeal process found that just 3 per cent of them had left within twelve weeks. Failed asylum applicants spent an average of 403 days in the country from the point of having their application turned down to being removed.

The length of time it took to deport failed asylum seekers meant that many of them effectively disappeared, leaving no forwarding address and making it extremely difficult for the immigration officers to find them. Only a small proportion was detained while their cases were considered. The rest were left to their own devices in the community. There were other ways to frustrate the removal process, not least from lawyers who were able to find ways of challenging the legal process. Even for those who were told to leave, it was far from easy to send an asylum seeker home. The NAO found that 'difficulties obtaining emergency travel documents [could] thwart removal'. This was no idle concern. Two thirds of recorded failed asylum applicants were from countries that required nationals without a passport to obtain emergency travel documents from their embassies. It was perhaps understandable if officials at embassies might be reluctant to help someone to return home who had been seeking asylum from their government and did not have the right travel documents to travel. Added to that were the practicalities of arranging the removal, co-ordinating more visits from lawyers, buying plane tickets, booking flights, arranging escorts if required. If any of these did not happen, on time, at the right moment, in the right order, the failed asylum seeker could not be sent home. Such delays were fatally undermining the system. The NAO observed coolly:

The prompt departure or removal of applicants refused permission to stay in the United Kingdom plays an important part in maintaining the integrity of the asylum process. Prompt departure reduces the cost of supporting failed asylum applicants and potentially reduces the incentive for those without a valid claim to come to the United Kingdom.

Every year that passed it became harder to remove failed long-term asylum seekers, as they became more embedded in British society. Some started families. The NAO estimated that 50 per cent of the backlog cases in May 2004 were people who had applied for asylum three years before.

The cost to the taxpayer of this failing branch of government was mounting. In 2003/04 the IND spent £1 billion on 'supporting asylum applicants', of which an estimated £308 million 'was attributable to an estimated 18,500 failed asylum applicants with dependent minors under the age of eighteen and no further right to remain in the UK', the NAO found. A further £285 million was spent on supporting voluntary repatriation of some failed asylum seekers or enforcing the deportation of others. These 'voluntary assisted returns' had been introduced in July 2000, in a bid to find a cheaper way to persuade failed asylum seekers to go home. In 2003/04 they were costing around £1,100 per asylum seeker, compared to the average cost of a forced removal of £11,000. One in four failed asylum applicants were paid to go home in this way in 2003/04.

The IND and the Home Office were aware of the problem – and had been throwing money and resources at it. The number of removals and enforcement staff doubled to 3,000 in the two years up to 2003/04. Then in 2004, officials started again to count passengers who were coming to the UK in a bid to give officials at least a chance to identify anyone who might be tempted to become an overstayer (they still did not count people as they left the UK). In February 2005 the Home Office published a new five-year strategy on immigration and asylum which outlined new plans to fast-track decisions and hold more applicants in detention centres while they were being deported. Yet, despite all this activity, the number of actual removals remained stubbornly low. In 2000 the government had set itself the target of removing 30,000 people a year. It was dropped two years later in 2002. The IND never got close. Excluding dependants, there were 13,625 removals in 2003/04, 12,110 in 2004/05 and 3,093 in the first quarter of 2005/06. In September 2004, the government set itself another target, this time for the rate of removal to be the same as the number of newly unsuccessful applications every month by the end of 2005, essentially to get to a position where the system was just treading water. Little wonder that the MPs on the Public Accounts Committee, reviewing the NAO report, would warn in March 2006 that at current rates of removal it would take between ten years and eighteen years for the asylum backlog to be cleared and all failed asylum applicants to be removed from the UK. Edward Leigh MP said: 'Failed asylum seekers are in increasing numbers staying in this country knowing that there is very little likelihood they will be apprehended and removed. The fact is that no one really knows how many of them remain in the UK or where most are living.' Tony McNulty, the immigration minister, insisted that the government had taken 'some very important steps forward in recent weeks, by significantly increasing the number of removals, and now believe we have reached the point where they are exceeding the number of unfounded applications'.

But the truth was that the actual number of failed asylum seekers in the UK was almost certainly higher even than the NAO estimate of between 155,000 and 283,000, and so would take longer to clear. The lower figure was based on a government database that excluded cases from before the database was established in 2000. McNulty defended the government's record, insisting that asylum applications had fallen: 'In 1996 the number of removals was equivalent to only 20 per cent of predicted unfounded claims. Now that proportion is around 50 per cent.'

The clue to the unfolding scandal that would shine a spot-light on the failing policy was in a single sentence, buried at the bottom of page twenty-two of the NAO's July 2005 report. It said: 'The Criminal Casework Team did not have figures available on how many failed applicants had been released from prison because removal could not be arranged.' Under Home Office rules, prisoners from outside the European Economic Area, including those seeking asylum, were supposed to be considered for deportation if they were sentenced to at least one year in a British prison. Yet the IND did not know if this was happening. Supposedly, any foreigner convicted of a serious offence should be considered for deportation on release from prison. The Prison Service had a duty to inform the IND when the offender's release date was approaching. IND staff would then run checks and consider the nature of his offence, as well as previous convictions, before making a decision. If the IND decided to deport him, the prisoner was given ten days to lodge an appeal, a process, which once started, could take several months. If the offender lost the appeal, the IND would get a travel document and take the foreign national prisoner to the airport, or to an immigration centre, to await deportation.

This was not happening as it should. Warnings had been sounded by successive prisons' inspectors including Sir David Ramsbotham, who said as early as 2001 that the government's system for dealing with the growing number of overseas inmates in the country's prisons was not satisfactory. His successor, Anne Owers, took up the theme three years later, warning in her annual report in January 2004 that the Home Office had an 'institutional blind-spot' towards them. Many of the prisons she had inspected had no idea how many foreigners they were holding until the inspectors tried to find out. She complained that immigration officers seemed indifferent to the problem, leaving many offenders stuck in prison, after serving their sentences, with no idea when they might be released and allowed to leave the country. Owers accused immigration staff of a 'dilatory attitude' and criticised the immigration service, which, unless pressed, was not monitoring those liable to deportation. Foreign prisoners were nicknamed the 'forgotten prisoners' and 'second class inmates'. Four months later in May 2004 a report from the campaign group the Prison Reform Trust warned that individual jails did not record on their computer system which prisoners were eligible for deportation. It found that many prisoners were held in a 'bureaucratic limbo' as documents passed between the Home Office and their home countries. Many foreign prisoners had legitimate rights to British residency, if for example they had families in this country or dual nationality.

Ministers had attempted to get a grip on the problem. David Blunkett, as Home Secretary, had made it mandatory under the 2003 Criminal Justice Act for the immigration service to consider deporting any foreign criminals who had served a sentence of more than twelve months. But then a promised detailed audit of the numbers of foreign national prisoners in British jails, which was due to be carried out in 2004, never took place, leaving officials still unsure of how many they were dealing with. Pressed in September 2005 for the figures, Paul Goggins, the prisons minister, told MPs: 'Information on the number of persons held in prison who are the subject of a deportation order is not available except by examination of individual case files, at disproportionate cost.' In November Tory MP Philip Hollobone asked the Home Office what plans it had to deport foreign convicted criminals held in British prisons. Tony McNulty replied: 'The Prison Service notifies the Immigration and Nationality Directorate of all prisoners identified as foreign nationals so as to enable consideration of their liability for deportation in accordance with the immigration rules. We are looking to ensure that foreign national prisoners liable to deportation are removed promptly.' McNulty appeared to contradict his colleague Goggins from just two months earlier. Something was clearly not quite right.

So the uneasy situation might have continued, had MPs on the Public Accounts Committee not intervened in October 2005.

This was how the foreign national prisoners scandal began, eventually resulting in the public flailing and then sacking of a home secretary and contributing to the scrapping of a government agency. Arraigned before the MPs were Sir John Gieve, Brodie Clark, the IND's senior director of operations, and Jeremy Oppenheim, director of the National Asylum Support Service. Richard Bacon, an MP on the committee and co-author of this book, had spotted the paragraph on page twenty-two of the NAO report which mentioned the deportation of failed asylum seekers and wanted to explore its ramifications further:

Richard Bacon: Could I ask you to turn to page twenty-two where it refers to the position of failed applicants who have been released from prison. How many failed applicants have been released from prison because their removal could not be arranged?

Brodie Clark: We would think around 500.

Bacon: So these are people who have no right to be in this country, who have committed a criminal offence, who have served time in prison and who you have now released from prison back into the community because you cannot remove them. Is that right?

Clark: Pending their case being dealt with.

Bacon: Pending their case being dealt with?

Clark: Yes.

Bacon: Do you know where all these 500 people are?

Clark: I am not sure what the answer would be. There will be some who we believe have absconded.

Bacon: What proportion of them has been in prison for failure to comply with the terms of the previous order to leave and what proportion has been committing criminal offences of other kinds?

Clark: I do not know the answer to that question.

Bacon: Quite a lot of them are criminals, they are people who have committed theft or—

Clark: They have committed offences and, as with any other prison sentence, when they come to the end of that sentence they have been released from prison having served that sentence. The case is then considered and the continuation of consideration of that case carries on after they are released from prison.

Bacon: But you have deemed that they have no right to be here. That is correct, is it not?

Clark: In some cases we have deemed they have no right to be here. That is correct.

Bacon: I find it extraordinary that people can commit a criminal offence against citizens of this country, take advantage of the hospitality that is offered them and then we cannot get rid of them. Is the present legislation likely to deal with this area?

Clark: There is a range of reasons why people cannot be removed and quite a lot of this report refers to that. There are some countries to which removal is not possible. The option there is to keep those people in prison for as long as that situation remains or release them into the community with some kind of reporting or other contact arrangements.

Bacon: Are you saying if they are from countries to where they are in principle removable then you cannot keep them in detention once their criminal sentence is up?

Clark: We choose not to keep them in detention.

Bacon: You could do but you choose not to. You have the discretion.

Clark: Not if they are not removable and there is no—

Bacon: No, that is not what I said – 'if they are removable'. You referred to countries to where they are not removable, like Iraq and Somalia, and you said where they are not removable you keep them in prison. Where they are removable in principle, my question was 'do you have no capacity, no power, to keep them in detention', and you said you 'choose not to', so you have the power to keep them in detention but you choose to let them back out into the community after their criminal sentence is finished. Is that right?

Gieve now stepped in, disclosing that there were 3,000 failed asylum seekers in prison 'at the moment'. He said: 'We can

detain people who have no right to be here, including these
people, but we have a limited number of detention spaces so
we have to use them for the people for whom we are most
likely to get a rapid conclusion.' Gieve appeared to be saying
that asylum seekers were being kept in prison not if they were
a danger to the public but if their cases could be dealt with
quickly. Bacon pressed the matter further with Gieve, asking
him if he

> can possibly send a note in, as far as you have information
> on this, about the number of criminals who are failed asylum
> seekers and are then released from prison; how many there are,
> where they are, what type of crime they have committed, what
> sentences they were given and how long they served? Is it possi-
> ble for you to do a note on that?

Gieve had little choice but to agree: 'I can do a note and let you
have the information we have.'

Christmas came and went. In January Gieve left the Home
Office to take up a senior post at the Bank of England. He was
replaced by Sir David Normington. In March the information
Bacon had been pushing for was finally sent to the committee's office, and was made public on 14 March 2006, when
it was published in an appendix to the committee's report on
the NAO study. The Home Office said: 'From 2001 to August
2005, we know of 403 foreign nationals who were released
without deportation proceedings being completed.' Crucially
the letter stated that this was only the figure that officials 'knew
of' – implying that the actual figure might be a lot higher. The
Home Office had also only partially answered Bacon's question
and had left out details of the crimes, whether those released
into the community had committed petty offences or dangerous ones.

Six days later, on 20 March, Bacon wrote to Normington
to ask again for the details of the criminal offences committed
by the 403 foreigners who had been released. A month went

by, with no answer. Then, on 25 April 2006, Charles Clarke, the Home Secretary, stepped in, writing to Leigh and Bacon, stating that the earlier figure of 403 prisoners released into the community was incorrect. In fact, Clarke said, a total of 1,023 foreign national criminals had completed their prison sentences and were released without any consideration of deportation or removal since February 1999. 'I am sorry that the department has previously provided incomplete information,' Clarke told Leigh. A breakdown showed the full list contained a host of serious offenders including three murderers, nine rapists, ninety-three robbers, forty-one burglars, four arsonists, sixty-two drug dealers, thirty-three fraudsters, four kidnappers and twelve sex offenders from more than one hundred countries. The total included 175 prisoners from Jamaica, fifty-nine from Nigeria, fifty-eight from Iraq and fifty from Ireland. Clarke tried to explain the increase: it 'reflects an analysis last month to determine the full extent of the issue. I am reporting this figure, for this longer period, so as to provide the fullest account of the issue.' By way of explanation, Clarke added that the 'absence of deportation consideration before completion of custodial sentences and release reflects the imperfect systems which have existed for dealing with foreign national prisoners'.

The letter was political dynamite. His department had admitted releasing more than 1,000 convicted foreign criminals into communities across the country – and his officials did not know where many of them were. The Home Secretary apologised, claiming the figures were a 'shocking state of affairs'. The system had simply become overwhelmed because the number of foreigners in prison had doubled from 4,000 to 11,000 since 1996, an increase which proportionately was far greater than the rise in the domestic prison population and reflected the big increase in immigration over the period. Of the 1,023 released into the community, only 107 had been traced and found, and considered for deportation. Twenty of those had been deported. The Home Office refused to identify any of them. Clarke said: 'We simply didn't make the proper arrangements for identifying and considering removal in line with the growth of numbers that were there. This is a failure of the Home Office and its agencies for which I take responsibility.' He stopped short of quitting, insisting that it would have been a resigning matter if he were found to have been guilty of 'personal misconduct'. Clarke said he was 'pretty confident' that all of the prisoners would be recaptured and considered for possible deportation. But he told an interviewer: 'A large number of people are involved. I can't say hand on heart that we will identify where each one of those is but we are working on that very energetically.' Clarke was manfully taking responsibility for a festering problem that went back years. Indeed it later emerged that nearly three quarters of the foreign prisoners had actually been released under previous Home Secretaries (twenty-four under Jack Straw, between May 1999 and June 2001, and 711 under David Blunkett, from June 2001 to December 2004).

The stakes were now increasing. Prime Minister Tony Blair described the news as 'deeply regrettable' and was said to be 'privately furious' about the disclosures, although he reportedly accepted that the problems were caused by a 'communications failure' and not a policy decision. One source said helpfully that it would be 'unreasonable to expect ministers to know what is going on in every nook and cranny of their department'. But Clarke's position was not helped when Blunkett called for sackings, although he backed Clarke personally. He said: 'My view is that heads should roll. There are too many people in the system who simply don't care. I fully support Charles Clarke in getting to the bottom of this.' David Davis MP, the Conservative's home affairs spokesman, accused the officials of 'serial incompetence'. Bacon said the news was evidence of 'administrative chaos' at the Home Office, adding that the department had to name the hundreds of former prisoners who were now at large in the community. He added: 'When the Home Office has made such a hideous mistake, you'd have thought they would do everything possible to find them, including enlisting the assistance of the public.' Jan Berry, chairman of the Police Federation of England

and Wales, said: 'This has taken risk management too far. While I recognise these offenders have served their time, they could and should have been deported at the end of it.'

The next morning it became clear why there had been such a long delay before the Home Office had come clean over the problem. Clarke admitted in another radio interview that he had offered to resign over the row before Christmas, once it became clear internally how many foreign prisoners had been released. Coincidentally, shortly after Clarke's *mea culpa*, Sir David Normington and Sir John Gieve were due to be quizzed by the Public Accounts Committee. The session was ostensibly about why the NAO had been unable to give the Home Office's accounts a clean bill of health in 2004/05. But the session was soon overtaken by the escalating row about the release of the foreign national prisoners. Edward Leigh started the attack: 'Can you give us a monthly breakdown of this figure of 1,023 foreign nationals who have failed to be deported month by month?' Normington replied: 'I am afraid I do not know that', promising Leigh that the information would be with the committee by the end of the day. Leigh shot back:

> This hearing might last some time. I understand that you were rung earlier, warning you that this question might be asked. I would have thought in view of what has happened in the last twenty-four hours these figures should be available at the Home Office. The fact that they are not readily available to you, the Permanent Secretary, leads us to question even more whether you are in control of your own department.

Normington disclosed that the rate of release of foreign prisoners was accelerating, with 288 freed in the most recent six-month period to March 2006, compared with 609 in the 4½-year period before that. There was further incredulity when it emerged that officials did not know where the released prisoners were. Leigh said to Normington: 'You cannot say, as Permanent Secretary of the department deputed to protect the public, that you know where those drug traffickers, rapists and murderers are?' Normington replied: 'I can say we are following up those found guilty of the most serious offences and we are going to report back at the end of the week.'

Gieve took the opportunity to apologise to Bacon for not giving him the full picture during the earlier evidence session in October, when his team had suggested that the number was substantially fewer. He said:

> It is only literally in the last day or so that I have become aware that the note that I sent you after that hearing was not correct. I am not in the department any longer so I have not been involved in subsequent discussions. But I do apologise, obviously I apologise. I knew I was not answering the whole question because we only gave some information, but I thought that it was accurate so far as we gave it.

Yet even here it seemed that Gieve was wrong. Bacon had asked during the hearing in October for figures showing how many failed asylum seekers had been released. Yet the Home Office had responded with statistics for all foreign prisoners – not just asylum applicants – who had been wrongly not assessed for deportation at their release. In fact, just 17 per cent of criminals who were deported each year were typically asylum seekers, which would have meant that if Bacon had been answered correctly the figure would have been much smaller.

Nevertheless, the story was rapidly developing its own legs. Gieve then admitted that Clarke had been personally involved in trying to sort out the problem since the publication of the NAO report in the previous July. 'I am pretty sure there were some meetings the Home Secretary had about improving our systems in order to deport foreign prisoners more rapidly,' he said. In that case, asked Edward Leigh, why had more foreign national prisoners continued to be released after August 2005? 'Obviously with the benefit of hindsight it is unacceptable,' Gieve said. This presented more problems for Clarke because it meant that a quarter of the foreign prisoners were released after he knew about the scandal. Clarke then said he had only become 'fully aware' after Bacon started to ask questions at the committee in October 2005, and that he had then set in motion a new set of procedures to change the way the Prison Service worked with the IND, allocating another 100 immigration staff in prisons to do the casework and to identify who should be deported.

Lin Homer, who took over as IND's director general in August 2005, said that in future all foreign prisoners were to be considered for deportation up to twelve months before their release. Hundreds of names from the 916-strong list of unaccounted-for criminals were passed to the Association of Chief Police Officers on the evening of 26 April. Until then, ACPO had only been given the names of eighty criminals – including the most dangerous – to check against data held on the Police National Computer. Yet even this was unlikely to be exhaustive, as the computer only had information on criminals who subsequently reoffended. The risk for Clarke was always that some of the released foreign national prisoners would reoffend.

Days later, on 28 April, Clarke admitted that five of the foreign prisoners mistakenly released had been subsequently convicted of drugs and violence offences. One of these was suspected of rape. Two others were under investigation for sex offences including another rape. In all, at least seventy-nine of the original 1,023 had committed serious offences. Deportation action had started for sixty-three of these. Clarke said: 'The genuine shortcomings which have been revealed in dealing with foreign national prisoners will be repaired and we will learn the lessons to make whatever further changes are needed to improve the quality of what we do across the whole Home Office.' A week later thirty-eight offenders who were convicted of crimes including manslaughter, rape and child abuse had still not been located because they had moved from the addresses they had provided to police.

Tony Blair stepped in to announce plans for the 'automatic deportation' of foreign national prisoners. The only exception would be where deportation could not happen for 'operational reasons' or because someone's life was in genuine danger. Blair also went out of his way to back the beleaguered Home Secretary over what was now billed as the worst blunder concerning the penal system since Labour came to power. Yet the prospect of more revelations about potential crimes committed by those who had been mistakenly released proved too much for Clarke. He quit the government on 5 May, reportedly refusing a move to another Cabinet post.

Within a month, John Reid, his replacement as Home Secretary, in effect turned on his own department, describing it as 'dysfunctional' and in need of a 'full and fundamental overhaul'. Reid declared that the Home Office was simply 'not fit for purpose', adding that it was 'inadequate in terms of its scope, information technology, leadership, management, systems and processes'.

Reid also told MPs that the original estimates of those who had been released had changed. There was more movement in the numbers of prisoners released. The original figure had now fallen by four to 1,019, of whom 186 were serious offenders, itself a rise of seven. Scores more, including sex attackers and violent criminals, were at large.

If anything, the foreign national prisoners scandal helped to signal the beginning of the end of the Home Office's sprawling empire. A commentary in the *Financial Times*, published on 27 April 2006, two days after the scandal broke, presciently recommended separating the department's duties into a 'ministry of justice' and a 'ministry of the interior', adding that 'the Home Office is a Whitehall conglomerate that would do better broken up'.

In April 2006 Brodie Clark was placed on 'gardening leave' and Digby Griffith, a director at the Enforcement and Removals Directorate, had his duties changed. (Extraordinarily, Brodie Clark was suspended again five years later after a dispute about immigration with another Home Secretary, Theresa May. He left the civil service in November 2011).

In June 2006 Sir John Gieve admitted the government had 'lost control' of asylum in the late 1990s: 'I'm sorry I didn't pick up on this earlier and take a personal interest. Obviously we didn't spot this one in time and I regret that very much.'

The following month, John Reid announced a purge of top civil servants at the Home Office, with a quarter of the department's mandarins being removed and a further 250 being retrained and redeployed. The number of civil servants at the London offices would be cut by a third, with 3,300 jobs going by 2010. The resulting savings of £115 million would be redirected into frontline services such as immigration, prisons and probation. But by September campaigners said the problem was getting worse. There were reports of as many as 500 foreign prisoners being held in jail after their release dates because of delays in arranging their deportation.

Just over a year later, in June 2007, an official report into the affair found that only 214 of the 1,013 original foreign national prisoners had been deported or removed. More than 300 had been told they were allowed to stay in the UK. A further 263 were still going through the deportation system, while other criminals were on bail or awaiting decisions. Some 149, including some who had committed serious offences, were still missing. Lin Homer, who moved to be the head of the new Border and Immigration Agency when it replaced the discredited IND on 1 April, told MPs: 'To our knowledge they have not committed further offences.' The review by Stuart Hyde, the assistant chief constable in West Midlands Police, found there were not enough staff to cope properly with the caseload when the numbers of foreign national prisoners was rising so sharply. The Prison Service and immigration officers had failed to co-ordinate their responses when offenders finished their sentences. The team dealing with foreign prisoners was now twenty times bigger than four years ago, with a budget of £10 million – compared with £2 million before the scandal broke. Weeks later, new Prime Minister Gordon Brown decided to remove responsibility for prisons and the courts system from the Home Office and set up a new Ministry of Justice to take on these functions. The evisceration of the Home Office was complete.

The foreign national prisoners scandal had also provided a microscope through which the wider problem of hundreds of thousands of failed asylum seekers wandering around the UK could be viewed. A trawl of cases suggested that between 400,000 and 450,000 failed asylum applicants were still in the UK. MPs on the House of Commons home affairs select committee asked for regular updates about the government's efforts to deal with this backlog, which became known as the Legacy Casework Programme, and Lin Homer committed herself to clearing the backlog by September 2011. Many experts thought that the only way to do this was to declare an amnesty for remaining asylum seekers in this country. This is what happened to 19,000 cases in December 2007.

However, by March 2010 the signs were not good, with suggestions that the agency would have to throw more staff at the problem or change the way in which cases were reviewed and decisions were made. There were claims from a member of one of the agency's asylum teams of racism and inappropriate behaviour at its Cardiff office. Louise Perrett, a former equalities officer, described how she was told by a colleague: 'If it was up to me I would take them all outside and shoot them.' She was then told that 'nobody in the office was very PC, in fact everyone was the exact opposite'. One manager told her that 'when he had young men or children claiming to be former child soldiers from Africa he would make them lie on the floor and demonstrate to him how they would shoot somebody from the bush'. Staff who 'let one through' were given a 'grant monkey' to put on their desk. Perrett later told MPs on the home affairs committee: 'I would raise my concerns with team leaders or my trainer or the other case owners, but I was always dismissed and laughed off.' The UK Border Agency launched an investigation. Asked if her going public had achieved anything, Perrett replied: 'I am aware through contacts that the grant monkey no longer exists in the office ... if that is all I achieve, that is great.'

The MPs also uncovered evidence that 'a new backlog was accruing because UKBA was unable to achieve the targets for resolving new asylum cases within six months'. John Vine, the agency's independent inspector, told the committee that this was at least in part due to the fact that 'unrealistic targets had been set because managers had not adequately consulted the staff processing the applications before setting them'. Lin Homer disputed the use of the description 'backlog' because that meant that cases which were set to one side were not being worked on by officials. MPs disagreed; to them the backlog was caused by cases not being completed as quickly as new cases coming in. It was the same problem as ten years before. It seemed as though nothing had changed.

8

STUDENT LOANS COMPANY

Universities said they were being forced to dig into their reserves to provide loans to students struggling to pay for rent, books and food.
Daily Telegraph

Our students are facing serious problems. Many can't find out the status of their applications. They have bills to pay. Some have families that can help but others do not.
Malcolm McVicar, vice-chancellor of the University of Central Lancashire

The past fifty years have seen a revolution in how we pay for higher education. In 1960 very few eighteen-year-olds went to university – just one in twenty. There followed the great 1960s expansion of higher education, with the creation during this period of new 'plate glass universities' such as the universities of Sussex, Kent, York, East Anglia and Lancaster. By the early 1980s the proportion of school leavers going on to higher education had more than doubled, to 12.5 per cent or one in eight. By 1990 it was one in five, and in 1997 by the time the Conservative government left office, 33 per cent of school leavers went on to higher education. This trend continued under the subsequent Labour governments of Tony Blair and Gordon Brown, reaching the level of 43 per cent by 2010, although this could fall after the coalition government introduced new fees of up to £9,000 a year for students to go to university.

This enormous increase in the proportion of young people going to university cost money – indeed, too much money. While it was possible to finance out of general taxation an 'elite' higher education system from which only a small proportion of the population directly benefited, offering free university places to the students concerned, this was no longer possible when nearly half the population went on to higher education. And in any case, some saw the old system as morally dubious. Why should a taxi driver pay tax for the children of middle-class families to go to university and obtain the education that would land them better, higher-paying jobs – as lawyers, doctors, journalists or engineers – than the taxi driver himself or his children? On this view, it was only right that those who would benefit from a university education should be making a financial contribution along the way. But others were equally worried that a system where applicants were required to pay their own way – in whole or in part – would inevitably deter people from poorer backgrounds and reduce social mobility. Even with student loans to help, some believed that such a system would discriminate against those from poorer backgrounds with an ingrained fear of getting into debt and no experience of taking out loans.

Whatever the rights and wrongs of changing the system of student finance, a political consensus emerged that there would be change. It was financially necessary. As a result, in recent years any aspiring student wanting to go on to higher education has had to rely on a combination of subsidised grants (based on family income) and student loans to fund university education. We are talking big bucks, too. In just one year – 2008/09 – loans and grants advanced to students totalled £5.4 billion, of which £4.2 billion was on new loans and a further £1.2 billion was in grants. No wonder students often leave university saddled with tens of thousands of pounds of debt, which they spend the first years of their working lives trying to repay.

Until 2006, these loans were organised in England by local authorities and administered through a central body called the Student Loans Company, which was then in charge of making payments and collecting loan repayments. The old system had worked patchily and there was a worryingly growing trend of students overpaying for their education, rising from just 600 in 2001/02, the first year in which students could have concluded their repayments, to 20,900 in 2006/07. It was believed that centralising the payments system could help to eradicate these sorts of errors, offer a better service and save money. So in 2006 the government decided to shake up the old system in England and run the whole system through a centralised service, similar to the Student Awards Agency in Scotland. A new centralised system of student finance called Student Finance England would provide information, advice and guidance directly to applicants, as well as assessing their individual applications (previously this had been provided by local authorities).

The changeover was an easy sell to the accountants in Whitehall. Using a central body would achieve faster processing times, provide clearer information for applicants and remove the 'postcode lottery' which saw councils process applications at different rates, giving varying degrees of service to students coming from different parts of the country. Aggregating the processes would cost £41 million in its first year and, the government hoped, save £20 million every year after that. The incumbent Student Loans Company was swiftly appointed by officials to design and operate the new service, leaving the Whitehall department responsible – the Department for Business, Innovation and Skills – in overall charge of how it was to work. The appointment of the company made sense on the face of it. Not surprisingly officials thought it was riskier to give the work to a private contractor, which might be unfamiliar with student finance. Yet there was also a further risk of managing the delivery of an enhanced programme of student finance through an arm's-length public body like the Student Loans Company.

Officials were already well aware of problems at the company. Reviews carried out by the department in early 2006 had uncovered weaknesses in the company's culture and capabilities including – according to a later NAO report – 'its contact centre, stakeholder communications and management capacity'. The company agreed with the department and ran an 'organisational development programme' to improve its ability to deliver, although this programme was not finished by the time the company started to run the system for awarding loans eighteen months later.

Nevertheless, pilots for the new system of administering student loans began in April 2006. The Student Loans Company took control of the centralised administering of student loans for eleven different local authorities. This form of road-testing what would be a major national undertaking was recommended by consultants hired by the department. They had given warning that the proposed plans to centralise the administration of student loans system was 'high risk' and that running a small-scale pilot would be 'extremely useful … in order to avoid surprises when the operational model is scaled to the national level'. Yet this rationale seemed to escape the thinking of the company. In the blame game which started after the process had gone wrong, the company argued that the pilots had been of limited use in part because the amount of work involved in running them was only about a tenth of the full volume.

The pilots continued, by all accounts with little to suggest major problems. Officials did not develop contingency plans if the company should be found not up to scratch. There were no plans either to extend the pilot or to extend the transfer because officials felt 'it would not be possible to obtain the agreement of all local authorities', who had agreed on a three-year transfer period which would see the company start to take over control for running the entire student loans system in England from 2009.

So, the Student Loans Company carried on regardless, leasing and fitting out a new processing and telephone call centre in Darlington in September 2008, at a cost of £8.7 million, and hiring 380 recruits, mainly to staff the new call centre. Although some local supervisors were hired in Darlington, the senior managers in Glasgow – who were familiar with how the student loans systems worked – were not transferred south of the border. This meant that the staff working 173 miles away in Darlington were unable to provide detailed specific answers to queries from students, because they could not easily refer to their superiors. In some cases the Darlington staff offered completely wrong advice. An official review later discovered that after a pilot adviser line was withdrawn 'there was no official direct contact for advisers in student support services at Higher Education institutions'. With managers stuck in Glasgow, there was also a leadership deficit in Darlington which was only rectified later.

But gradually the new system for centrally administering student loans was given the green light in Whitehall. A review in March 2007 by the Office of Government Commerce (OGC) made six recommendations to improve the programme, two of which were described as urgent, resulting in the scheme being given an overall red status, which meant that for the project to succeed 'remedial action' had to be taken immediately. Subsequent reviews were increasingly positive, until by July 2009 the OGC assessed its confidence in the programme being delivered as 'amber/green' – broadly on track to succeed as long as recommendations are implemented.

Yet one glaring problem remained. All applicants for grants or means-tested support had to provide supporting evidence on paper. The process was meant to work like this: applicants submitted a paper or online application form, with evidence of identity and income. The company's staff then checked the details and issued an 'Assessment of Entitlement'. Applicants then had to return a declaration form, accepting the terms and conditions of the loan, and the Student Loans Company returned a payment schedule letter entitling the applicant to funds on enrolment at university.

Bafflingly, the company decided that it should scan all the supporting documents for means-tested applications at its offices in Hillington, Glasgow and then send electronic copies to the processing teams in Darlington. It was not difficult to see how wrong this could go. As the National Audit Office commented dryly in March 2010: 'The risk inherent in implementing a new scanning solution was not recognised by the company and there was insufficient project discipline and executive oversight of the solution.' This was an understatement, given that the executives with any experience of dealing with student loans were marooned in Glasgow, a long way from Darlington.

Time was running out. The system had to go live in 2009 when all new English-domiciled students applying to enter higher education would have their applications assessed and paid by the Student Loans Company for the first time. There had already been a minor hiccup when the new service – which was originally intended to be operational from September 2008 to coincide with the UCAS annual cycle for applications – was delayed because of decisions by the government to alter the regulations for student financial support. This meant that the launch of the new system was postponed until February 2009, further compressing the timetable for processing applications. Sir Deian Hopkin, vice-chancellor of London South Bank University, who independently reviewed the crisis, later accepted that this delayed launch had caused some problems, but he concluded that this was a 'risk that could be managed and that there was sufficient time to process applications before the appropriate deadlines for students to be paid at the start of term'. Hopkin added: 'We believe, moreover, that the risk could have been mitigated through appropriate internal and external communications, and further staff training.'

Undeterred, in April 2009 the Student Loans Company decided to launch the process, including the scanning of documents in Glasgow, before it had been fully tested, in the optimistic hope that any teething problems would be sorted out as they came up. It was soon going wrong. Within weeks there was a huge backlog of unscanned documentary supporting evidence for student loan applications. Hopkin estimated that the problems led to some 100,000 items of evidence being incorrectly indexed, requiring them to be sorted by hand.

On 9 June, after weeks of 'teething problems' the company abandoned the scanning technology and decided to resort to an entirely manual system. Yet the team at the company did not have a Plan B for separating applications and as a result it had to develop these new processes in a 'live' environment. Hopkin found:

> At a critical point the technology failed and the company had to resort to manual processing of documentary evidence, for which it was not fully prepared. The procurement of this technology and the project management of its implementation were, in our view, inadequate. Management indecision and over-optimism in the scanning technology meant that manual processing was not introduced quickly enough, the consequences of which were far-reaching.

There were further internal complications. A restructuring of the management during the summer meant that the centre at Darlington was left 'without a visible and permanent leader on-site holding overarching responsibility for the performance of the whole centre', according to Hopkin's report.

This chaos created intense frustration for students. Documents received by the company were not logged into the system before they were processed, which meant that call centre staff had no idea if supporting evidence from students had been received. This single reason was the cause of 31 per cent of the phone calls to the company in September. To make matters worse, students who had already sent in their evidence were then sent 'reminder notices' asking them to submit their evidence.

Gradually throughout 2009, the pile of unsorted and unscanned applications grew and grew. The Student Loans Company had not helped by failing to manage the flow of applications properly. Deadlines for applications were set – for April and June – but not enough people were told about them. The deadlines were not even advertised on the Student Loans Company's own website where 78 per cent of applicants completed their application forms. 'Consequently,' the NAO found, 'a significant number of students' – estimated to be

60 per cent of new students – applied after the April and June deadlines. And – conversely – 5,600 students who had applied in time for the deadline still had not been paid by 15 November. By this stage it was chaos at the Student Loans Company. Surrounded by piles of application forms, bottlenecks were developing inside the company because staff were too rigidly applied to particular tasks. The consequence was a shambles, a situation made worse because, as Hopkin found, 'arrangements for internal communications regarding application processing were not clear'. Monthly updates on progress were not shared throughout the company, while meetings between processing and contact managers did not take place until late in the cycle. As universities and colleges opened their doors for the start of the 2009/10 academic year, tens of thousands of students were still waiting for their money to pay for rent, books and food. By 6 September, 241,000 forms had been received, but not processed fully. The company decided to make emergency provisional assessments to enable loan payments to be made in time for the start of term. However, these provisional awards were then reassessed over the following months, creating more uncertainty and another mini-mountain of applications to be processed. By the end of January 2010, there were 80,000 provisional assessments still waiting to be completed.

The emerging crisis was fuelled by media coverage, helping to create a sense of panic around the provision of student loans, especially when the company – which had to comply with requests under the Freedom of Information Act – started publishing details of the scale of the backlog. However, Hopkin insisted that while there was widespread media coverage and considerable ministerial correspondence and questions in Parliament, leading to interventions on the floor of both Houses – and that some media coverage may not have always been accurate or helpful – the problems could not simply be attributed to media 'hype' or be explained as a few exceptional cases.

The case for the company was hardly helped by apparently complacent comments from its top managers. In one

interview, Ralph Seymour-Jackson, the company's chief executive, described the problems as a 'telephone issue' and concluded
that while the situation was 'not perfect' it was 'reasonable'.
This 'telephone issue' was the single most public failing of the
Student Loans Company in 2009. Quite simply, if you phoned
the call centre you would probably fail to speak to anyone.
There was some history here. The company's annual report
and accounts for 1999/2000 had recorded that 'the capacity
required to answer all telephone calls at the start of term was
underestimated and unfortunately during this period, call waiting times were longer than our normal service standards. Steps
have now been taken to ensure that this does not recur.' Hopkin
found that similar statements were made in the annual reports
for 2001/02, 2003/04 and 2007/08. He concluded:

> While this may have been acceptable in previous years, the
> nature of the business had substantially changed in 2009 ... The
> company did not change its approach. It continued to resource
> its contact centres well below peak demand, taking a conscious
> decision to provide a service that was, in its view, 'broadly
> acceptable' throughout much of the year and to accept a higher
> number of unanswered calls during peak periods.

The company had set its own bar very low, appearing to think
that a target of picking up the phone to just 55 per cent of calls
within sixty seconds was satisfactory, even though this performance was itself eight percentage points worse than the year
before, with no more than 14 per cent of calls abandoned because
callers hung up while waiting in a queue. Hopkin struggled to
understand why the company had adopted such a ridiculously
low target, observing that this performance measure was 'not
based on any recognised benchmark of customer service used
in other public service delivery organisations'. A more reasonable benchmark used by other bodies was to try to answer
90 per cent of calls at all times. The Student Loans Company
told the NAO that it accepted that its 55 per cent target was far

below industry benchmarks, but 'still considers it to have been challenging given the resources'. But as Hopkin pointed out, 'answering telephone enquiries about the progress of applications forms a key part of the process and customer experience' and that students, their families, schools and colleges had every right to expect better. Furthermore, there was no attempt to identify what Hopkin described as the 'tipping point in terms of manageable call volumes', when the number of telephone calls rose sharply as people unable to get through the first time phoned back again, creating a vicious circle. Eventually when the phones were red hot, the calls disconnected in bulk at a network level.

The answering record was abysmal. Between February 2009 and January 2010, only 21 per cent of calls were answered within sixty seconds, while 56 per cent of calls were not picked up at all. In the peak month of September 2009, the company received more than four million calls from worried students and their parents – of which nearly nine out of ten (89 per cent) went unanswered – including 1.5 million in the first week of September. The NAO said the company's answer rate 'compares unfavourably' with HM Revenue and Customs, where 73 per cent of calls were answered between April and September 2009. Indeed, the report by Hopkin found that 'at its worst the company were answering only 5 per cent of the calls attempted'. The result, he said, was 'undeniable anxiety, frustration and loss of confidence caused by the difficulties encountered by individuals seeking advice, information and answers'.

And even students who did get through were often disappointed with the responses. Hopkin cited 'many examples of customers being asked to submit multiple copies of forms and documentary evidence at their own time and expense, with the company admitting that previously submitted copies had been lost'. In other cases students were 'timed out' from the student loans website, or were unable to progress despite entering the correct information or download a signature form to sign. In a withering verdict, the NAO found that 'the company's actions were responsible for a high volume of unnecessary calls'. Indeed, 52 per cent of those surveyed had placed their call because they had not received a response to their application, while 44 per cent said they had received a confusing message from the company and 42 per cent could not find the appropriate answer on the company's website. The most specific reason for people phoning was to reset a password – because the company had still not developed the necessary IT to allow its customers to reset their own passwords. Overall, as the NAO found, 'communications with stakeholders – schools, universities, local authorities, UCAS etc. – were inadequate in 2009'.

The scale of the problems had only been gradually feeding back to the department in Whitehall during 2009. The NAO established in its later report that although the department was made aware of the scanning problems in May 2009, it was not told of the difficulties processing applications until late August 'by which time it was too late to prevent major problems occurring'. Officials later told Hopkin that 'they often felt risks were not appropriately escalated by the company and that they were not adequately informed of performance issues'. The department was hardly helped by the limp response of the non-executive directors on the board of the Student Loans Company, not one of whom had experience of management in higher education, suggesting that the company's chief executive and chairman of the organisation could have been challenged more robustly. Hopkin also observed that there was also no one on the board 'who would champion the interests of customers' (i.e. the students). The board's response was one of lengthy inaction. It did not meet in August, despite the deteriorating problems, nor were the non-executives informed of the problems by the company's directors. Indeed, the issue of risk to the company was not even addressed by the board, but instead delegated to a subset called the Student Finance Delivery Board. Risk reports were only submitted to the board biannually and to the company's audit committee four times a year. And the problems with the scanning and the growing backlog of applications were not even identified until far too late, when they were finally put in front of the audit committee in September 2009. Written minutes from the various board meetings that took place that year seem to suggest that the company's directors were blissfully unaware of the problems bubbling up around them. The company had introduced what it called a 'balanced scorecard' in 2009/10 to allow the company and directors to judge its performance using a series of internal measures. Yet over the summer of 2009 the scorecard failed to present 'an accurate picture', according to the NAO, to the extent that in July 2009 'the company's board noted that "it was pleasing to see that all the strategic aims were either Green ... or Green/ Amber [satisfactory]"'. The company, simply 'did not create the joined-up reporting needed to run the new service'. What might be considered '*sine qua non*' information from the coal-face at the Student Loans Company – such as processing performance, call centre records and customer satisfaction ratings – was not even part of how the balanced scorecard score was calculated. Indeed, Hopkin observed that for the period from April to September 2009 'a review of the scorecard summary page alone might therefore lead the reader to suppose that all was well'.

The targets by which the Student Loans Company judged itself were found to be hopelessly inadequate. By its own assessment the company had performed well, with the organisation cutting the average time taken for an initial decision on a loan application from seventeen days to eight working days. Yet, as the NAO pointed out, this very target did not tell the whole story and had 'serious weaknesses'. In fact, in 52 per cent of cases in 2009/10 the 'initial decision' was merely a request for additional evidence from an applicant to allow the assessment to be completed.

The inherent weaknesses with the company's targets were not new. A review of student finance in 2006 had drawn attention to it and proposed 'more stretching targets' such as three weeks for online applications and four weeks for paper applications. Independent analysis carried out after the problems emerged painted a much more realistic picture in 2009/10, finding that the new centralised processing system for student loans was actually worse than the previous scheme run by the individual local authorities. The company took 12.4 weeks to process all new applications, compared to 9.3 weeks under the previous system. Online applications took 12.1 weeks, against 10.5 weeks for local councils. Paper-based applications which took town halls just 8.3 weeks took 13.6 weeks under the 'new improved' system. By the start of the 2009/10 academic year, only 46 per cent of applications had been fully processed, compared with 63 per cent under the old system run by the local authorities. This lag behind the previous council-run system continued into January, when only 77 per cent of applications had been fully processed – against 84 per cent under the old system.

By the second week of October 2009, one in six applicants had still not received their payments. The company issued a statement blaming 'a combination of factors, including late applications, of which we are still receiving thousands every day'. Universities themselves decided to step up to the plate. Malcolm McVicar, the vice-chancellor of the University of Central Lancashire, said the institution had been forced to make emergency payments worth £70,000 to 250 students. By November the government had stepped in, writing to vice-chancellors asking them to be 'sympathetic' towards students who arrived at college short of cash. By 17 November, three quarters of universities in England had dug deep and made payments to students. Out of fifty-eight universities surveyed, forty-nine had made hardship payments to help students through the beginning of term. Forty-three of them said the need was because of the loans crisis. John Craven, vice-chancellor of Portsmouth University, which had paid out £80,000 to students waiting for loans and grants, said: 'We are angry on behalf of our students who have been badly hit by this.' One first-year student had applied for his loan in March, but was told he would not get his money till Christmas. And the most disadvantaged of the Student Loans Company's 'customers' – disabled students – received the worst service of all. The NAO found that in this group, which is eligible for additional targeted support (amounting to £91 million in 2009/10), only 5,800 out of 17,000 applications were approved by the end of December 2009. By February 2010, thousands of disabled students still awaited funding to buy basic study aids like Braille paper and computer equipment.

Students were not happy. A survey by the NAO of 1,000 students in December 2009 found 'widespread dissatisfaction' with the service on offer and little more than four in ten students thought that the application and payment process was easy. The survey uncovered a catalogue of incompetence and cock-up. More than half of those surveyed said they had been 'asked to send the same documents more than once', while almost as many had been forced to wait for more than three weeks for a 'substantive reply'. Nearly one fifth of students were told the company had 'lost their documents'. Perhaps unsurprisingly, 11 per cent of those surveyed suggested that as a result of their experiences they were more likely to pack in their studies and drop out of university altogether. The NAO commented, with understatement: 'We cannot say how much more likely these students were to drop out, nor how far the company could be responsible for those who did. The figures are, however, an indication of the potential impact on students who experience difficulties in obtaining their student finance.'

The NAO's study in March 2010 issued a warning: 'The programme continues to be very high risk. Although the company now has the benefit of a year's experience, it expects to process at least twice as many applications in 2010.' This was in part because of an expected rise in the numbers of students, as well as the numbers of returning students it would have to process again from September 2009. The performance of the Student Loans Company was heavily criticised. It seemed to have fallen victim to the old problem which affects many failing businesses: it had completely lost sight of who its customers were supposed to be. The NAO said:

> Crucially, the company did not sufficiently understand its customers, many of whom are inexperienced young people who need guidance. The company's failure to empathise with its customers was particularly apparent in the relative lack of priority given to processing applications for targeted support – i.e. from those most in need.

Overall, despite the government handing an extra £2.8 million to the company to pay for the cost of processing more applications in 2009/10, the company was expected to save money. Having cost £41 million to set up, it was expected to save £20 million a year from March 2011. The company had managed to hit these targets by 'offsetting overspends on implementation, mainly due to higher IT costs, through reduced operating costs (including reduced spend on information, advice and guidance)'. Yet the costs of processing applications remained too high. The NAO said that the Student Loans Company was 'preparing fresh proposals to transform its culture'. Yet it gave warning that 'if these measures do not significantly improve performance in 2010, the department will need to develop the option of contracting part or all of the service to other providers'.

Sir Deian Hopkin found that the company's leadership did not sufficiently appreciate the importance of cultural change, that it underestimated the time, energy and commitment which would be required to transform the company, and that it ultimately failed to deliver the required change. The fact that the company had seen itself primarily as a 'high-volume processing factory' was a clear indication of how it had failed to become the 'customer-focused organisation' it had agreed to become. Hopkin added that the company had 'insufficiently prioritised the customer experience' and that it remained 'inward-looking and process-driven'. Hopkin added that, even in December 2009, the outcome of the next year's student loans round remained 'uncertain'.

A follow-up report by PricewaterhouseCoopers in April 2010 was surprised by the 'lack of focus and urgency' in addressing the concerns raised by Hopkin. A month later, on 25 May, John Goodfellow resigned as chairman and Ralph Seymour-Jackson stood down as chief executive, after it was made clear that their new boss, David Willetts, the universities minister who had watched the saga unfold as a shadow minister in 2009, wanted them to quit. Hopkin became interim chairman of the company with immediate effect.

The PwC report had found there was 'substantial' risk of further delays. It added that the company's executive team was 'under-resourced, stretched and unable to give the breadth of leadership and direction required through the next five months of this year'. By the middle of April 2010, PwC discovered that 264,000 applications had been registered, nearly a third of the expected total, while 114,000 had been processed for payment, 117,000 were pending and 25,000 were being dealt with. In short, it meant that the company had to process an expected 760,000 applications in 100 working days before the start of the new college year. To make matters worse, the company's call centres were 100 people short of those needed to hit the response targets at peak time. For the Student Loans Company, 2010 was shaping up to be another long, hot and difficult summer. In the end, some two thirds of applications from new students were processed on time but for more than a quarter of applicants, the company could not even make an interim payment by the start of the university term. MPs on the Public Accounts Committee were unimpressed. In describing earlier performances as 'completely unacceptable', they recorded a catalogue of failures: the department 'underestimated the risks' and had 'inadequate' monitoring while the programme board 'lacked skills and experience' and there was 'poor communication' between the programme board, the company's board, and the department; furthermore, these failures highlighted 'wider weaknesses in the department's oversight'. 'We expected better,' they concluded bluntly.

9

FE COLLEGES BUILDING PROGRAMME

There was a group of people that we might have expected to know what was going on who did not themselves have a full grasp of it.
John Denham, Secretary of State for Innovation, Universities and Skills

One of the best ways to cement a government's legacy is to invest in education. And for politicians, bricks and mortar offer a good way to ensure that there is something to show for the billions spent. The Building Colleges for the Future programme, launched in 2007, was one such attempt. Its ambition was to provide Britain's children with a college system fit for the twenty-first century. Yet its delivery was an object lesson in how the best-laid intentions can go awry, this time by failing to keep a check on people's enthusiasm for the plans. The programme started out as a flagship project for the Department for Innovation, Universities and Skills (DIUS) and the Learning and Skills Council (LSC). It was essentially an attempt to put right many years of underinvestment in colleges and reform was certainly needed. As far back as 1992 there was a £800 million repair backlog – yet over the following four years, this was barely touched, as millions were poured into dealing with more pressing issues, such as health and safety, in the ageing and deteriorating buildings.

In 2005 a review by Sir Andrew Foster, a former head of the Audit Commission, the councils' spending watchdog, signalled an increase in spending on colleges. His report 'Realising the Potential' called for a 'step change in capital investment in the further education sector'. The effect was to fire a starting gun on an extraordinary and apparently uncontrolled spending programme. It soon went wrong, with the LSC overwhelmed by applications for colleges which were desperate for cash. The end result was enough to make an accountant or a taxpayer weep: a review into the disaster found that seventy-nine building projects had received the first stage of approval in principle, costing £2.7 billion. A further sixty-five colleges were just behind after submitting requests for approval in principle for projects worth £3 billion – six times more than the allowed budget.

MPs who later examined the fiasco described this cavernous funding gap as simply 'remarkable', while Foster – four years after his review had called for more investment – was recommissioned to find out what had gone wrong. He blamed 'a large surge in college proposals [which] opened an untenable gap between the resources identified and the costs of projects underway or in the pipeline'. Foster said the rebuilding plan itself was a victim of its own success: as news of initial successes rippled across the country, more colleges submitted more ambitious plans. This success became self-perpetuating – like an enormous, self-licking lollipop. Yet, while the 'early adopters' were financially robust enough to cope, the colleges which accepted the proposals later 'had relatively less strong balance sheets and narrower financial margins'. New building standards, which came into force in March 2008, and 'inflation in construction industry costs' only made matters worse. Added to that was the inherent Whitehall fear of failing to spend the cash allocated for a particular year, since underspending departments tended to have their budgets cut for the following twelve months to reflect the saving. The result of all this was a 'veritable tsunami' of applications for new building projects – few of which would ever see a building site.

The seeds of one of Whitehall's biggest spending disasters were sown in the LSC's own *Capital Handbook*, published in November 2006, which offered conspicuously little advice to the LSC on how to prioritise spending decisions. If anything, it seemed to suggest that any action would be taken after the event. 'In the event of applications for capital grant exceeding the funds available,' it said, 'the LSC will put in place national

moderation arrangements to determine the relative priority to
be given to competing applications.' There was little evidence
of anyone looking at the national picture either, with projects
assessed individually on merit and financial viability, rather
than on whether they could be afforded and were needed on a
national basis.

Officials entered into the spirit of the spending programme
like Elizabeth Taylor at Asprey's, the Queen's jewellers. Modest
college proposals soon became palace-like structures during
what was clumsily known as the 'bigging up' process. John
Blake, from Sussex Downs College, explained how the process
worked, and how in his case a quite modest £8 million plan
soon ballooned to an eye-watering £175 million scheme. He
said: 'About three and a half years ago we had quite a modest
project of about £8 million to replace one of our sixth form
colleges. At the beginning of the LSC process ... it went up to
£30 million then it went up to £90 million, and at the end it
was £175 million, and in the end most of that was a bigging-up
process, and that happened through the regional Learning and
Skills Council property process.' The problem was that he and
his fellow principals in Sussex were 'too conservative', the LSC
told him. Other principals backed Mr Blake. Graham Moore,
principal of Stoke College, added: 'I knew what my priorities
within the structure were but I was constantly questioned: "You
missed an opportunity. This is a once in a lifetime opportunity
for the sector."' This disastrous grandstanding continued across
many projects until the middle of 2008, when the funding gap
was assuming Grand Canyon-like dimensions. Martin Doel,
chief executive of the Association of Colleges, later said: 'Those
conversations were still going on [in summer 2008] and that
was the National Capital Team coming round to say "No, it
is not sensible for you to leave part of your estate untouched,
you should be coming up with a plan to refurbish the whole
of the estate."' Mr Doel made officials at the LSC sound
like the host of a rather downmarket television gameshow:
'A term which has been bandied around a good deal during

this period – and I understand it and I was there – is that this was a "once-in-a-generation rebuild", a "once-in-a-generation opportunity".'

The 'bigging up' order came from the top. The LSC's chief executive, Mark Haysom, said: 'I was giving very clear messages, as were ministers at the time, that this was a once-in-a-generation opportunity to rebuild the capital estate.' What he did not want to do, he said, was merely to replicate the existing buildings but make them 'just a bit more modern'. In fact the MPs on a Commons committee prised open the lid on

a strange world in which staff at the LSC believed prioritisation would not be needed in the short to medium term because the programme had historically been under-spending. This meant that the programme in the end operated on a first-come, first-served basis, with no consideration given either to need or wider departmental or government policy objectives. Some colleges received funding for iconic buildings when something much cheaper would have served perfectly well. Other worthy projects, perhaps in areas of greater deprivation, will now not be funded at all.

There were warnings of what was going wrong. An internal Capability Affordability Review at the LSC completed in March 2008 foresaw problems between 2010 and 2013, when its capital grant payments programme was set to run £450 million over budget. Yet inexplicably and catastrophically, the report was not seen by either Mark Haysom, the chief executive, or the chairman, Chris Banks, until much later in 2008. This was despite Haysom later insisting he had 'worked very hard in the council to try and create a culture which was really open and where people could actually come direct to me with their concerns'. The MPs who conducted a 'lessons-learned' exercise later said it was 'curious' that there appeared to have been no discussion about looming longer-term problems between Phil Head, the LSC's director of infrastructure, and his boss Haysom, given this 'open door' style of management practised by Haysom, who later admitted that the report 'was never escalated within our organisation to the extent that it reached my desk. So I was never aware of that report and that meant that neither I nor senior DIUS officials nor anyone else was aware that that report existed.' Chris Banks concurred: 'To be very explicit on that, I was unaware of the existence of that report ... No one mentioned it or raised it with me.' Instead the report, a ticking time bomb, was effectively ignored and made its way slowly around the LSC's 'labyrinthine management structure'. The internal communications breakdown was later summed up rather well by John Denham, the secretary of state who had oversight of the work of the LSC: 'I am afraid the problem was there was a group of people that we might have expected to know what was going on who did not themselves have a full grasp of it and therefore could not communicate the problem to us.' The situation was made worse by the narrow belief within the LSC that this was an 'in-year' problem, which could be limited by the end of the financial year. Accordingly £110 million was forward from the budget set for a later financial year – 2010/11 – which just disguised the full extent of the escalating problem.

An added twist to the saga came in March 2008 when the government announced the LSC was to be scrapped by April 2010 and replaced by a new Skills Funding Agency and a Young People's Learning Agency. This hardly helped to focus minds on problems at the LSC. The later review by Foster discovered what he described as 'eye-off-the-ball syndrome associated with organisational change', which meant that at meetings managers were frequently having heated debates about the imminent collapse of their organisation and the possible loss of their jobs, rather than, say, the spiralling colleges programme. Haysom admitted as much:

> The way we were thinking about the future had changed pretty
> dramatically. We were in the business of steering the organisation

towards an end point of April 2010 and that kind of longer-term strategic thinking ... suffered. As a consequence of that the whole organisation becomes focused on that end point rather than managing the way that you would previously.

News of the LSC's abolition also soured relations with the department. Haysom suggested relations became 'more intense' in the wake of the announcement, with officials from the department 'crawling all over' the LSC, ready to take over when the body was wound up, and paralysing its decision making.

The affordability review, which was forecasting such a serious problem, was finally discussed at a meeting of the LSC's Capital Policy Group on 22 April 2008. Then it was passed to the Finance and Resources Board in May – which led to a Prioritisation Working Group being set up. Yet even then dealing with the 'problems' raised by the report was deferred until a meeting of the Capital Committee on 19 September 2008, at which it was agreed that 'further work' was required before any strategies 'could be finalised'. What seems so extraordinary is that the LSC's own risk management systems had failed to pick up the overspend. Running in parallel with the escalating cost overruns was a separate review of – ironically – the quango's own risk management systems, following criticism internally in both 2006/07 and 2007/08. The LSC's management group and the National Audit Office agreed changes in July 2008, which were implemented by the following September. Astonishingly the risk management processes did not include an assessment of the capital building programme. Haysom said there was 'a pretty robust risk management approach' at the LSC, before adding:

Next question: why was the capital programme not on the risk register? I think, well, I know, because it was seen to be a success, that flipping into, in record time, a situation of over-demand was not seen to be an issue on the radar. I am sorry but it was not.

MPs reviewing the affair said this was quite simply 'astounding'.

The National Audit Office published a report titled 'Renewing the Physical Infrastructure of English Further Education Colleges', describing management information as 'inadequate' and finding that spreadsheets used in the programme were 'not sufficiently robust'. The NAO added that more information was needed on the costs of completed schemes and warned that 'completion of the programme by 2016 will require careful risk management and prioritisation of the capital funds available'. Even so, the tone was generally positive. 'Most new buildings are of a high standard, meeting the needs of colleges and learners, and they have been completed on or close to their budget,' it trumpeted in its press release. Tim Burr, head of the NAO, added:

> The capital building programme for further education is enabling colleges and the Learning and Skills Council to achieve together what neither could have achieved on their own, and is delivering high quality buildings. The sector has taken on a higher level of debt, and therefore of risk, but the cost should be manageable. If the second half of the programme can maintain the success achieved in the first, [then] further education will be well placed to offer enhanced value for money.

The NAO's report covered the period up to March 2008 but it was not published until July. Yet this was precisely the moment at which the LSC started seriously to overcommit its budget. In June alone, the LSC approved total new funding of £555 million, with a further whopping £822 million during July 2008. By December 2008 nearly £2.4 *billion* had been committed. MPs on the innovation and skills committee later argued that the NAO's report did not 'give a sense of the urgency with which a prioritisation mechanism was required' and took the auditors to task:

> Given the seriousness of the mistakes that were made, the NAO report appears in hindsight to be surprisingly positive:

we find it hard to reconcile the fundamental problems that became apparent with LSC's capital management, in particular the lack of national prioritisation and planning for this high-cost, high-profile programme, with the tone of the report. This is all the more surprising given that the NAO had sight of the Capital Affordability Review. We conclude that if the NAO had produced a more hard-hitting report in July the worst of the over-commitment would have been averted.

Given that the overcommitment of the budget only occurred after the NAO's report was published, some may find this criticism unreasonable. However, there were other problems too. The LSC's status as a non-departmental public body or 'quango' was problematic. Its very nature left ministers in the invidious position of being responsible for its actions, while at the same having to treat it as an arm's-length body from government. Although officials at the Department for Innovation, Universities and Skills had regular meetings throughout 2008 with officials from the LSC, it seems that no one thought to mention the colleges' budget concerns with more senior officials. Stephen Marston, the director general for Further Education and Skills at the department, later lamented: 'I deeply regret that it [the review] was not escalated ... I was not aware of the report until November.' This was when the minutes of a meeting of the National Council, attended by Marston, recorded that board members were

concerned about the pressure on the capital budget especially given the added pressures of the unstable economy. It was suggested that a clear steer from ministers was required over whether to continue with capital spend at all costs, or slow down. Marston commented that Treasury's steer was to bring forward capital spend, especially on the public side.

Yet internal minutes from an earlier meeting of the LSC's External Advisory Group on 30 September 2008 suggested the department knew what was going on much earlier. Under the topic 'LSC's Capital Skills prospectus', the minutes stated: 'The prospectus was clear but the proposals were likely to generate a lot of demand, with associated risks. Ministers were currently considering these risks.' When this was raised with John Denham by MPs, he replied: 'I have to say, chairman, I do not know and I have never known what that refers to.' The explanation later given to MPs could have come straight out of the mouth of Sir Humphrey Appleby. Marston explained to the MPs:

> It was a member of my staff who attended the meeting – I think it was in April – that first looked at the February report ... I do not think it was quite right to say it was just ignored. I think a number of things followed from it ... reaction number one to this report was, 'right, we must sort out the short-term position'. The second reaction to it was 'it is right we are going to have to think about prioritisation' ... the bit that we clearly just failed to get right was the speed of understanding that we were at a tipping point, the whole programme was changing and we did not react fast enough.

Rather than escalate the problem to board level, a decision was taken to 'keep it under review' in the belief that 'it is going to be all right', Marston said, adding: 'That is what went wrong.' This *mea culpa* gave ministers the necessary wriggle room to say it was not their fault. Denham said: 'So far as ministers are concerned, none of this reached ministers until November' and even then, 'the thrust of the concerns' was more about how to phase payments and how they would match the planned capital pay-outs than about the actual problem, namely 'the sheer scale of the number of schemes in the pipeline'.

Back at the LSC, members of its capital committee were meeting and agreeing to sign cheques for huge college refurbishment projects. The committee met on 19 September 2008 and recommended projects worth £401 million. It met again on 22 October, and cleared another nine projects worth £530 million. The November meeting agreed to recommend another £500 million worth of projects. Haysom later described how he was 'pretty shocked' when he realised the scale of the LSC's spending commitments, and stated: 'The speed with which the situation changed is one of the most extraordinary things about the whole episode.' The board met on 17 December and finally agreed to take some action by ordering a three-month pause in all further approvals in principle and approvals in detail. This was the cue for pandemonium among the colleges, who had continued to submit ever more grandiose building designs. Even now there was more dither-ing. Ministers urged caution before telling the colleges what was going on. Sir Andrew Foster found that ministers thought 'a full action plan needed to be brought forward about the scale of the problem and how to rectify it, before it should be communicated'. The LSC, to its credit, wanted to be open with the problems. But the department said no. Predictably, chaos ensued, compounding an already difficult situation, with confusion among colleges.

A letter from Mark Haysom to all college principals on 16 January attempted to clear things up.

> I wanted to clarify the situation. There is no freeze on the capital funding programme. However the pace of demand for capital funding has increased as projects and the scale of government funding required becomes increasingly ambitious. On top of this some colleges are finding their ability to raise their own funds curtailed by the economic downturn ... In light of these factors the LSC has taken the decision to look at the proposals for all capital schemes in the pipeline to assess the likely impact on funding support for individual projects.

This meant, he said, that a 'small number of applications that were due for decision' were deferred from December to March. 'The 253 colleges that have been given approval in detail and either have work underway or have previously been given the final go-ahead for works to begin will not be affected...' Yet the final analysis was far crueller: of the 180 projects submitted to the LSC, of which many were given 'approval in principle' status, just thirteen carried onto the next stage. And some of these thirteen were requested to 'substantially reduce the cost and scope of their projects and review other sources of funding'. They were the lucky ones. Others were told there was nothing for them in the current spending round.

So who was to blame for this sorry saga? MPs found evidence of 'very serious failure' in the management of the LSC capital budget during 2008 and neglect of oversight by those in the most senior positions in the LSC, concluding: 'The fact that the situation changed quickly does not excuse the lack of recognition of crucial warning signs.' The MPs also turned their attention to the roles of the management. Haysom quit his £269,000-a-year job on 23 March 2009, taking responsibility for the quango's failures in managing the flagship programme. 'No matter where those mistakes have been made and no matter how many people have been involved in the capital programme, as the chief executive of the LSC I am, of course, finally accountable. That is why I have made my decision to step down at this time.'

But the £51,000-a-year part-time chairman, Chris Banks, a former managing director of Coca-Cola Great Britain, kept hold of his job (he had been reappointed on a three-year contract in February 2008). He told MPs that he and his fellow board members had decided to 'delegate all the day-to-day operations of the organisation to the executive team, if you like, the experts'. This suggested that he had not known about the problems on the capital programme until the end of 2008. He said:

My belief is that, as the day-to-day responsibility for the management of that programme rested with the chief executive and that

he has resigned as a result of this, that is the right thing, and my job is to try to ensure that this organisation delivers all that it possibly can between now and when it is dissolved in the spring.

MPs noted dryly that Cabinet Office guidance says boards of public bodies have

> a collective responsibility for the proper guidance of the body's affairs and for ensuring that staff maintain the strictest standards of financial propriety. As chairman of the LSC Chris Banks had a responsibility to ensure that the executive team had systems in place to manage key programmes ... The chairman and the council clearly failed in their oversight during 2008.

The MPs observed that the department and the LSC

> are jointly liable for not recognising the weak points of a capital programme which suffered from no overall budget and poor management information, but which was heavily marketed by the LSC to colleges. A heinously complicated management structure within the LSC and the approaching Machinery of Government changes bred a lack of responsibility and gave an air of distraction. Everyone wanted this laudable programme to succeed and so failure became unthinkable.

It was down to the managers at the LSC to flag up any problems. And they didn't. The MPs added: 'It is, above all, a sorry story of management within the LSC compounded by failures of government oversight within DIUS which is likely to cost hundreds of millions of pounds.' The MPs concluded: 'As it turns out 2008 was indeed a "once-in-a-generation" opportunity for FE capital expenditure, though not in the way that the LSC and DIUS intended. We are now left with a situation in which funding is scarce and worthy causes cannot be prioritised.'

10

RECRUITMENT OF JUNIOR DOCTORS

It's disgusting. I have secured a job in Australia. I don't want to go, I love the NHS, I want to stay here and I want to work here but if I have to go, I have to go. I've got to pay my mortgage.
Rob Thomas, a doctor from Whipps Cross University Hospital, east London

The hard-working doctors who form the backbone of the National Health Service are not normally a radical bunch. Yet in May 2007, in extraordinary scenes, thousands of them took to the streets to protest. The medics were marching against disastrous new plans by the government to reform the way in which doctors applied for work. The introduction of a new computerised automated system was meant to streamline applications and help promote the best candidates. Instead there was an unalloyed cock-up which saw 33,000 junior doctors chasing just 18,500 posts, even as eight out of ten hospitals were cancelling operations because consultants could not be sure that the right staff would be there to carry them out.

Like so many other Whitehall disasters, the problems started with an attempt to make a bad situation better – how to cut the time it takes to progress from being a junior doctor to a consultant. Medical professionals were well aware that middle-ranking doctors who became senior house officers (SHOs) and staff and associate specialist (SAS) grade doctors could get stuck in 'career limbo'. Many doctors were left stranded for long periods, even up to ten years, unable to progress into more specialised training. For this reason, junior doctors were known colloquially as the 'lost tribe' and the 'workhorses of the NHS'. In August 2002 Sir Liam Donaldson, the Chief Medical Officer, tried to get a grip on the problem by publishing a consultation paper on medical training called 'Unfinished Business'. This document attempted to address the problem head on by reforming the way SHOs and SAS grade doctors worked. Instead of being stuck in a professional *cul de sac*, junior doctors should have access to training and other continuous professional development. The report said that training should be programme based, while also being time limited and flexible to individual needs. Crucially, the report recommended an extra capability: that the new training programmes should address the needs of foreign doctors, too.

In its response to Donaldson's report, the government recognised that something had to be done: training for both SAS and SHO doctors was going to have to change. Added impetus came from the government's decision to commit itself under a new NHS plan in 2000 to deliver health services by fully trained doctors – rather than junior medics still in training.

There was a further complication. The European Union's European Working Time Directive was going to limit junior doctors' work to fifty-eight hours a week by 2004, falling to forty-eight hours a week by 2009; many doctors, particularly the 'workhorse' SHOs, had traditionally worked much longer hours. There was a corresponding jump in medical students after 1999 (up by 60 per cent), as managers realised that limiting the hours worked by doctors would require more staff to do the same work. By October 2003, Donaldson had set up a new strategy working party to oversee the reforms. In April 2004, the NHS unveiled plans for a new two-year Foundation Programme which would be brought in the following year, which would lead medical graduates – via a new computerised applications system – into the safe harbour of more senior, career-oriented jobs within the NHS. It was to be called 'Modernising Medical Careers' or MMC.

In the first year, trainees would be brought up to the standards set by the General Medical Council. The second year, overseen by the Postgraduate Medical Education and Training Board, was designed to give trainee doctors further practical skills. Or, as the Department of Health said in its 'MMC: The Next Steps' report:

Specialist Programmes and the General Practice Programme will,
therefore, be developed to provide a seamless training process
which will see all those emerging from Foundation Programmes
entering a training Programme leading directly to the award of a
Certificate of Completion of Training. Entry will be competitive
but, subject to satisfactory progress, no further competition will
be needed before the completion of training.

The new programmes were piloted by the British Medical
Association in 2004 and began just a year later at England's
twenty-three new foundation schools, a combination of local
medical schools and hospital trusts. The new intake would
complete two-year courses by August 2007 and then sign up
for one of eight different specialty programmes. Yet the pressure from this accelerated timetable meant that there was
no chance to pause and reflect on whether any lessons could
be learned from the pilot process. In 2006, the Department
of Health announced the final piece in this elaborate puzzle,
which involved students applying for the training programmes
using an online application system called the Medical Training
Application Service (MTAS). The idea was that the MTAS
would be built around a website through which trainee
doctors would be able to apply in two consecutive recruitment
rounds. However, during 2006 there were ominous warning
signs about the development of the MTAS. MPs on the health
committee examining the affair later noted: 'The timescale
for developing the MTAS national recruitment system was
short: the development of the new computer software began in
March 2006 and of the new national application form in May
2006, just a few months before recruitment was due to begin.'
It will become apparent to the reader why wags renamed
MTAS as 'Migrating to Australia Soon'. The programme
was given a 'red' risk rating by the Office of Government
Commerce watchdog from May 2006, indicating the need for
serious attention.

Seven months later when the recruitment drive started in

earnest, in January 2007, the OGC's red rating was still in place. Similar concerns had already been raised by junior doctors – the very people who would be expected to use the system. The BMA's own Junior Doctors Committee had published a 'Call for Delay' notice in June 2006 – a month after the red risk rating was issued – and then, in October of that year, the committee argued for a year-long cooling-off period while the emerging problems were ironed out. The BMA was concerned about a 'worryingly short timetable' for selection in the MTAS recruitment process and suggested that 'the application form's questions do not seem to be searching enough'. The training was too inflexible and, for the first time, there were fears that there might be more applicants than training posts. These concerns were also shared privately by the people running MMC and the MTAS programme. Professor Alan Crockard, MMC's national director, later complained that his worries were ignored by officials at the Department of Health: 'We saw the situation unfold from fairly well back.' He said he had made his concerns known both to the senior official in charge of the MMC programme, as well as to the deputy Chief Medical Officer between October and December of that year. He had even taken his concerns far wider in Whitehall: 'I had actually spoken to the regulator, to the people from the Treasury, to the advisers to ministers and to the NAO about my concerns.'

Problems were compounded by an immigration policy which allowed medical students from outside Europe to be trained in Britain whether or not they had a job to go to. The Home Office announced in March 2006 that this 'permit free' training would be coming to an end. Yet this merely moved the problem to another route of entry into the UK for doctors from outside Europe – the Highly Skilled Migrant Programme. Later that year, the Department of Health tried to shut this door too, by issuing guidance to employers that places on the migrant programme could only be offered to people from outside Europe if there was no suitable applicant from within the countries that made up the European Economic Area (EEA). The guidance was challenged in the High Court by the British Association of Physicians of Indian Origin in December 2006, with a decision by the judges to be made in the following February. This delay meant thousands of non-EEA doctors applied for posts under the MTAS system while unsure if they were legally allowed to do so. On 1 February 2007, Lord Warner, the minister in charge, announced that there were 18,000 specialty and GP jobs available for between 16,000 and 17,000 doctors in England who could apply for them. The hope was that only 1,000 would apply for the remaining posts from outside England.

The MTAS computer system was fired up and started to process applications on 22 January 2007. Initially candidates applying under the MTAS system had until 4 February to apply for fifty-nine specialties, sixteen regions and four levels of seniority. The deadline was extended by a day until 5 February after difficulties with the online application system. Consultants ran the short-listing process, and interviews were slated for March and April. Recruitment was to be divided into two distinct rounds: the first was to conclude by the end of April; the second would start in May and finish in August 2007.

Within weeks, the problems which had emerged over the previous nine months finally erupted into a full-scale crisis – an official review later described it as 'the biggest crisis within the medical profession in a generation'. The interview timetable was too short for the consultants to make informed choices. The Royal College of Surgeons said short-listing was 'fundamentally flawed' and the Royal College of Radiologists said the application forms were 'useless'. The BMA dismissed the criteria for short-listing as 'not acceptable to the profession'. Candidate doctors were complaining that the new system was too reliant on open-ended 'white space' questions, rather than analysing actual achievements such as qualifications which were traditionally used on CVs to weigh up the contrasting qualities of candidates. There were even suggestions that some of the answers could be copied or based on model answers available on the internet. The Department of Health itself acknowledged the problems later in evidence to MPs on the health select committee: 'Some consultants' short listing for interview said they found it difficult to differentiate between applicants on the basis of the form. It was also felt that insufficient weight was given to academic achievement in the national short listing scoring.'

The department admitted that there were serious concerns that some of the best applicants were not being short-listed for interview. The MPs commented, with undisguised frustration: 'Department of Health officials did not explain why they pressed ahead with the introduction of the new recruitment system in spite of these inadequacies.' The sheer number of applicants was causing its own problems. The High Court ruled on 9 February that the Department of Health's decision to give preferential treatment to applicants from within the EU was legal. However, the British Association of Physicians of Indian Origin was given leave to appeal, although this appeal was not due to be heard until the following October. While in theory the government could have continued to implement the decision to give preferential treatment to applicants from within the EU at this late stage, it would have caused too much disruption to do so.

As the MPs found:

> The department's decision made it possible for doctors from anywhere in the world who had gained Highly Skilled Migrant Programme status by the time applications opened to compete for UK training on an equal footing with UK and EEA doctors in 2007. This caused an immediate mismatch between the number of applicants and the number of available training posts, raising the prospect of large numbers of UK-educated doctors being unable to continue into specialist training.

Or, put simply, in 2007 there were 40 per cent more applicants than there were training posts. One consultancy hired by the Department of Health to vet applicants had to sift through 28,000 applications for just 20,000 posts. It later told the MPs: 'This inevitably meant that several thousands [of] competent doctors would not be invited to interview, let alone offered a post.' As the MPs noted, the weakness of the whole MTAS system was that it had been designed to match candidates to posts on the assumption that there would be enough training posts for everyone. This was patently not the case, however. Even without the extra 10,000 non-EEA doctors, the system would still have been oversubscribed for applicants for specialty training. Herein lay the twin causes of the crisis that struck doctors' recruitment in 2007: the inadequacy of the short-listing process and the inclusion of non-EEA applicants. The problems were aggravated by the impression among many applicants that the MTAS system was being run on the basis of 'one strike and you're out', with candidates who failed in the first recruitment drive feeling as though they had missed out for the year. This was despite the fact that only half of the posts were due to be offered in the first stage, and the remaining 50 per cent of posts in the second round. The stakes were raised nonetheless because candidates were only allowed to make one main application each year (under the old system doctors had been able to apply for many jobs at once, whenever they liked). In short, as the MPs concluded, 'because of the perceived inadequacy of the short-listing process upon which decisions to offer interviews were based, many candidates felt that they had been unfairly prevented from continuing their careers. This increased the sense of outrage amongst applicants and assessors alike.'

A major crisis was brewing. This started to become clear with reports that excellent candidates were not even getting to the interview stage. On 27 February, on the eve of interviews, the BMA attacked the 'shambolic recruitment system' which had 'descended into pandemonium'. The association asked for the interviewing process to be suspended. Outraged doctors wrote to the *British Medical Journal* suggesting that the profession had been 'torn apart by an Exocet we should have seen coming'. Junior doctors were being 'flung on the scrap heap after a decade of training' while the leaders of the profession were 'hand-maidens to their own apocalypse'. Words turned to action on 5 March when an interview panel in the West Midlands said that they were not going to see any more applicants. The panel said in a statement: 'The MTAS procedure for recruitment to ST3 [Specialty Training] in General Surgery has not been implemented according to agreed guidelines. We have therefore declined to continue with the interviews today.' The group blamed unrealistic deadlines, unexpected numbers of applications, inconsistent marking and problems with the reliability of the computer system, adding: 'We owe it to our patients and the profession that we are able to select and appoint the best candidates to surgical training posts and felt strongly that this was impossible today.' Sir Bernard Ribeiro, the president of the Royal College of Surgeons, later said in a newsletter:

> We owe much to the twelve surgeons in Birmingham who deemed the short listing process not 'fit for purpose' and so did not proceed with interviews on Monday 5 March. I believe this action prompted the urgent review of the MTAS selection process by the secretary of state for health later on the same day.

Health Secretary Patricia Hewitt met later that day with senior figures from the profession. Her officials issued a statement the following day: 'It is clear that there have been a number of problems with MTAS and that the process as a whole has created a high degree of insecurity amongst applicants and indeed more widely in the profession.' Neil Douglas, the vice-chairman of the Academy of Medical Royal Colleges, was asked to find out what had gone wrong with the first round of applications. Hewitt wanted answers within a few weeks. Douglas later told MPs that he had considered pulling the plug on the MTAS system altogether, describing it as a 'very close call on several occasions'. But his mini-review decided to proceed with round two of the recruitment process after Department of Health officials had argued that 'on balance, the benefits of continuing far outweighed the benefits of stopping the process'. Junior doctors

were horrified. Many of those who had spoken out against
the process were now organised into a body called 'Fidelio',
which said in a statement: 'It is incredible that, once the short-
listing arm of MTAS was admitted to be flawed, the Review
Body took more than ten milliseconds to decide whether the
whole process was flawed – and still made the wrong decision!'
Douglas's review also announced ways to improve the system.
CVs would be allowed as part of the process for the first time,
and disappointed candidates who missed out would be allowed
to have their applications reviewed. Applications for more
senior grades would be granted an automatic interview.

Yet this was not enough – it was time for the country's doctors
to take to the streets. On 17 March, days after the publication of the Douglas report, more than 12,000 junior doctors
demonstrated in London, marching from the Royal College of
Physicians in Regent's Park to the Royal College of Surgeons
in Lincoln's Inn Fields. There was another demonstration in
Glasgow. The protests called for the recruitment system to be
scrapped. Some of the placards carried by the doctors, some
wearing theatre gowns and white coats, read: 'Your Health,
Our Training, Their Mistake', 'Training 4 Junior Doctors',
and 'Protect Our Training, Protect Your NHS'. Conservative
leader David Cameron spoke at the demonstration in London,
describing the system as an 'utter shambles' and claiming that
Hewitt was 'the worst Health Secretary in the history of the
NHS'. Richard Sidebottom, a senior house officer at the Central
Middlesex Hospital in north-west London, who was marching
with his brother Paul, a consultant, and father Eric, a retired
Oxford University medical tutor, said he had been unable to
secure an interview for an ophthalmology post. He said: 'My
father taught at Oxford, my brother's a consultant anaesthe-
tist, and I'm going to be a plumber.' Eric Sidebottom said: 'I
have spent my life in medical education and there has not been
anything like this. It just makes us so angry, there is such a
waste.' Rob Thomas, another medic who worked at Whipps
Cross University Hospital in east London, said that despite an

excellent academic record and passing his postgraduate exams first time, he had not been offered any interviews in his chosen speciality of clinical radiology and might have to emigrate.

The Department of Health was seriously worried. More changes to the process were announced. On 22 March, five days after the demonstration, the offer of a guaranteed interview was extended to every applicant. More interviews would take place in May, and the first round would be extended until the end of June, delaying the start of the second part of the recruitment process. The changes to the MTAS – particularly the decision to give every doctor an interview – defused the sense that the short-listing process was unjust. Yet it created a requirement for thousands of extra interviews to take place. By the end of the process, 85 per cent of the jobs – rather than 50 per cent as had been intended – had been filled in the first round of applications. Hewitt announced another review, by Sir John Tooke, chairman of the Medical Schools Council, towards the end of April.

Heads were about to roll. On 31 March 2007, Professor Alan Crockard quit, lamenting in his resignation letter that the programme 'has lacked clear leadership from the top for a very long time'. Within days the programme's national clinical adviser, Professor Shelley Heard, also resigned. Heard said in her resignation letter: 'Some of the core principles which Alan and I had tried hard to embed in taking MMC forward are now lost. I find myself able to support few of the decisions that the review group has taken since they undermine the principles which are at the core of MMC.' And as if there weren't enough chaos already, the MTAS programme was soon beset by breaches of data security. On 25 April, a password protection system failed and candidates' personal details were available to be accessed on the MMC website by anyone. Channel 4 News discovered the lapse. Patricia Hewitt told MPs in the House of Commons: 'There is no evidence that members of the public or other commercial interests apart from staff at ITN and Channel 4 News accessed the site. Nonetheless, it was an extremely

serious breach of security as well as a breach of contract
between the IT provider and the Department of Health.'
The problem was later blamed on human error by a tired
employee who placed the details on an insecure part of the
website. Yet the very next day, 26 April, another (unrelated)
breach occurred, which allowed candidates to access other
applicants' confidential messages, such as interview timings.
The MTAS website was suspended immediately, pending
a full review. When the system was reinstated, Hewitt said
that it would no longer be used for specialty training recruitment. She apologised to MPs, calling the security breaches
'utterly deplorable'.

This had other knock-on effects, notably that rounds one
and two of the recruitment process had to be extended and
delayed once again. MPs later noted the large amount of extra
work which had to be taken on by local postgraduate deaneries. The London Deanery, for example, said that its staff had
worked a total of 7,500 extra hours. The scandal was about to
claim its biggest scalp. James Johnson, chairman of Council at
the British Medical Association, resigned. On 20 May he said:
'It is a matter of regret that I am having to resign because I have
lost the confidence of a very large number of members of the
BMA council. But this is no ordinary political situation. The
medical profession is on the edge.'

On 25 May, the first round of applications was officially
completed, four months after the application process began.
The offers process, run by postgraduate deaneries, ran until 22
June – just a few weeks before candidates were due to take up
their new posts. MPs on the health committee noted gloomily:
'The delayed and drawn-out nature of the process meant many
candidates were forced to decide whether to accept offers in their
second-choice post before knowing the outcome of their first-
choice application.' More changes were announced for round
two. The process would be run entirely by postgraduate deaneries, with 215 extra training posts and a different short-listing
and application system altogether. Ministers told Parliament on

12 July that 85 per cent of the posts in England had been filled, with just 2,320 left available for the next recruitment round. But this high success rate masked large failures, with just 57 per cent of the posts filled in academic medicine for example.

The report from the Commons' health committee was scathing about the failings of the whole MTAS programme:

> The introduction of the new Speciality Training arrangements in 2007 was disastrous. The failure to restrict overseas applicants and the manifest weakness of the national recruitment system made the collapse of confidence in the selection process inevitable. The design of the initial application forms was particularly inappropriate, failing to recognise doctors' key achievements and giving undue weight to 'white space' questions. The short-listing process, which was so critical to the whole future of so many students, had descended into little more than a creative writing exercise. Candidates and assessors alike were justifiably outraged by the sheer inadequacy of MTAS.

The months between February and August 2007 were a period of 'chaos and severe anxiety for thousands of junior doctors', they said: 'The wave of resignations by senior medical leaders and series of emergency ministerial statements which followed were both acutely embarrassing for the government. The reputations of both the Department of Health and the leaders of the profession were severely diminished by the events of 2007.'

Research by the *Daily Telegraph* and Remedy UK in late July 2007 found that more than three quarters of 100 hospital trusts surveyed were cancelling out-patients clinics, and nearly nine in ten had cancelled some operations. Consultants were simply unable to plan operating lists and had no idea which junior doctors would be on their team, or what skills they would have. Junior doctors themselves had also not been told the hours they would be working or what time to arrive, or even at which hospital they would be working. This led to NHS managers having to retain expensive locums or risk shortages as doctors

departed for their new jobs, while some doctors were employed
in roles for which they were overqualified. Dr Ian Wilson,
deputy chairman of the BMA Consultants' Committee, said:
'Any forward planning has been impossible. It's inevitable that
more operations and clinics will have to be postponed.'

It was time to clear up the mess. On 25 July the management of the whole MMC programme was overhauled and a
new team constituted, chaired by the deputy Chief Medical
Officer, with the newly created post of chief operating officer.
The new board was intended to be inclusive, with representatives from the royal colleges, the BMA, NHS bodies and junior
doctors. Patricia Hewitt described this single development
as 'the most important innovation' in the immediate months
after the crisis. The board's most pressing task was to complete
round two of the 2007 recruitment process, which was still
open. They succeeded – just. The interview round was extended
until 31 December, so that the round two process was only
completed a few days before the 2008 selection process began.
And the chaos was not over. The government finally admitted
that the decision not to implement the guidance that foreign
or non-EEA doctors were ineligible for the MTAS programme
had meant that 1,200 British doctors had been left without a
training post. To complicate matters, the government lost the
British Asian and Indian doctors' appeal against the guidance
on 9 November 2007, with the Court of Appeal finding that it
was 'unlawful'. The government appealed further to the Law
Lords, ultimately losing there too, but ensuring that the confusion spilled over into 2008. The Health Select Committee said:

Just as in 2007, non-EEA doctors who had gained Highly
Skilled Migrant Programme status were free to apply on an
equal footing with UK and EEA doctors in 2008. According to
the Department itself, this would mean there would be three
applicants for every training post in 2008, a higher competition
ratio than in 2007 and up to 1,500 UK graduates displaced from
the training system.

The Home Office's new 'points-based' immigration system eased the pressure on places, but only from 2009 onwards. However, this only cut the applicant pool from 8,000 to 5,000 in 2009, while the 10,000 doctors already in the UK and on the Highly Skilled Migrant Programme were not affected. In November 2007, 4,000 British-trained junior doctors had still not found a post.

In September 2007, the Department of Health published a consultation paper detailing how the 2008 programme would be run. The system was substantially overhauled a month later, when the online recruitment system for junior doctors was scrapped. Candidates were also allowed to make as many applications as they wished, on new forms which gave more prominence to CV-based questions. Local timetables were established within a national framework which ran from January to May 2008. There were also two further, smaller recruitment rounds. Sir John Tooke published his findings in early 2008. He found that the policy objectives of MMC were not adequately defined with 'no definitive description of MMC and what it embraced'. The problems were compounded by weak leadership at the Department of Health and the medical profession, while the governance structures at MMC were too complex. Crucially, as the health committee found, 'the implementation of MMC was hit by poor project management, unrealistic timescales, a failure to pilot, poor risk management and the over-ambitious decision to introduce all the changes in the same year'.

In an interview in October 2007, Tooke summed up the chaos from the botched implementation of the online recruitment programme: 'The situation facing the trainees was morale-sapping and damaging,' he said. 'They were faced with a highly complex application process which was rushed in its implementation, and then there were technical glitches which resulted in some really good candidates not getting interviews for posts.' Overall, he said, the problems which hit the online recruitment system had been a 'deeply damaging episode for British medicine'. It seemed, though, that lessons might have been learned after the medical profession's 'annus horribilis' of 2007 – despite reports that junior doctors hoping to become surgeons in 2008 could face competition from at least nineteen other candidates in the most popular specialties. Representatives of postgraduate deaneries offered tentative cause for hope when they spoke to MPs on the health committee in early 2008:

> One might have feared a tidal wave of applications but that has not happened. Obviously people are targeting the post they want ... they are spreading their applications so that across the country people are getting applications in their thousands, though not tens of thousands. Therefore, so far, so good.

The optimism did not last long. Within two years, on 1 June 2010, the BBC was reporting fresh problems with the hiring of new doctors. 'A shortage of junior doctors to start work in hospitals this August is forcing the NHS to try to recruit from India,' it said. 'Tighter immigration rules introduced in recent years meant many overseas medics left Britain and returned home. But the exodus, added to new European regulations limiting the hours of doctors, caused unfilled vacancies.' Four medical schools were found to be trying to fill around 100 posts from overseas, including those for paediatrics, obstetrics, gynaecology and anaesthesia, as well as for accident and emergency. One senior medical professor complained: 'We pulled the plug on overseas recruitment far too quickly. We didn't realise what the implications of that action would be two, three or four years down the line.' A year later in the summer of 2011 there were still significant shortages. A recruitment firm called Medical Locums was merely typical in announcing: 'Currently we are recruiting doctors to the UK from Australia, South Africa, India, Pakistan, Sri Lanka and Middle Eastern countries.' Medical Locums was especially interested in hearing from doctors who had General Medical Council registration and a British passport, and who could therefore work straightaway, telling them: 'We have abundant opportunities in all specialties at very high pay rates. You can work for a duration of weeks to months.' The firm urged doctors: 'Register immediately and we will pour offers at you to come and work in the UK.'

11

NATIONAL PROGRAMME
FOR I.T. IN THE NHS

Redesigning the way care is organised and conducted and supporting those new ways with information science is more important to people's health overall than any new drug we could develop in the next decade, but the engagement of clinicians and managers is not just about telling them what is going to happen.
Dr Anthony Nowlan

The National Programme for IT in the NHS is the largest civilian computer project in the world. It is expected to cost the taxpayer over £12 billion – enough to fund 55,000 nurses for ten years, or the entire cost of Britain's invasion and occupation of Iraq. The foundations of the project were laid in 2001 after Prime Minister Tony Blair met Microsoft founder Bill Gates, who had written a book about the profound impact that information technology could have on economies. Wanting to know more, Blair read the book and, in the words of *Guardian* journalist Michael Cross, 'the Prime Minister, determined to reform Britain's public services, was hooked'.

In February 2002, Tony Blair held a high-powered Downing Street seminar involving ministers, key government officials and representatives of big IT firms such as Microsoft and Cisco. It did not take much for Blair to be persuaded that effective information technology would underpin the future success of the National Health Service, leading to a 'transformation' in people's experience of healthcare. Information could be captured once and used many times, transforming working processes and speeding up communications. Hospital admissions and appointments would be booked online. Electronic drug prescriptions would mean pharmacists would no longer have to struggle with the indecipherable handwriting of GPs. Most important of all, medical records would be computerised, thus transforming the speed and accuracy of patient treatment. The meeting concluded that IT offered 'exciting new opportunities' for new services for both patients and clinicians and was also 'vital' to delivering existing commitments.

As the Department of Health's information director, Sir John Pattison was tasked with delivering this enormous transformation. Blair wanted the vision to become a reality as soon as possible, and the timetable that Pattison first suggested was brushed aside as too slow. Blair's impatience for completion of the project is made clear in the record of the Downing Street meeting, contained in a letter from a No. 10 aide Simon Stevens to the Department of Health. The Prime Minister agreed with the priority areas of work outlined by Pattison 'but asked the Department of Health to look again at its implementation programme and accelerate it where possible'. Under some duress, Pattison was asked to complete his work within two years and nine months from April 2003, so that it would be completed by December 2005.

Pattison and his team set to work, producing a blueprint entitled 'Delivering 21st Century IT Support for the NHS: National Strategic Programme', which was published in June 2002. The aim of this grandly named programme was to 'connect delivery of the NHS Plan with the capabilities of modern information technologies'. This would support the delivery of services 'designed around patients' quickly, conveniently and seamlessly, while also supporting staff through effective electronic communications, better learning, knowledge and management, cutting time to find essential information such as notes, tests and results, and making specialised expertise more widely available. The programme would also improve management and delivery of services by providing good quality data to support clinical audit governance and management information. 'Delivering 21st Century IT' – which was in effect the founding document of what became the National Programme for IT in the NHS – spelt it out clearly: there was to be nothing less than a revolution in the way the NHS used information technology.

There was, however, an odd discrepancy at the outset. In the back of the original version of document were four appendices. Appendix 3, containing the 'project profile model', stated that the project's estimated whole life costs were £5 billion and provided a 'total risk score' of fifty-three out of a maximum possible seventy-two – in other words, the project was very high risk. But when the document was published, the project profile model had been removed and there were only three appendices. Right at the start, the likely costs and the true risks were being concealed.

The published version of 'Delivering 21st Century IT' sounded appealing to many health service professionals. It promised just the combination of local control with national standards which both health IT specialists and clinicians in the NHS had been seeking for many years. There would be choice for local healthcare trusts from a range of acceptable suppliers. And the published timetable was precisely the one which had been exacted from Pattison at the Downing Street meeting – there would be a full national electronic health record by December 2005, two years and nine months from April 2003.

After the launch of 'Delivering 21st Century IT', the Department of Health established a unit, which eventually became an agency called Connecting for Health, to procure and deliver the IT systems. In September 2002, Richard Granger was appointed as director general of NHS Information Technology, at an annual salary of about £250,000. His job was to turn the 'National Strategic Programme', which soon became the National Programme for IT in the NHS, into reality. Granger was a former Deloitte consultant who had successfully overseen the introduction of the London congestion charging scheme. Speaking at a conference in Harrogate some months after his appointment, Granger announced that the cost of the programme would be £2.3 billion, in contrast to the unedited version of Pattison's document a few months earlier, with its much larger estimate of £5 billion.

Granger commissioned a study by a leading consultancy firm,

McKinsey, into the healthcare IT market in Britain, which was then dominated by medium-sized UK firms selling systems to hospitals and GP surgeries. The McKinsey study has never been published but it concluded that no existing company had the capacity to become a prime contractor on a multi-billion-pound programme. Granger soon announced that the procurements for the programme would be structured to attract global IT players to the health service. He divided the NHS in England into what were in effect five regional monopolies. One provider within each region would take responsibility for implementing the key aspects of the programme. The five regions were the northeast, the east, the north-west with West Midlands, the south and London.

Granger had little respect for the skills of most public sector buyers of computing systems, and he knew that IT contractors routinely ran rings round their customers in government. He made it clear that on his watch things would be different. Contractors would not get paid until they delivered; those who were not up to the mark would be replaced. He compared contractors to huskies pulling a sled on a polar expedition:

> When one of the dogs goes lame, and begins to slow the others down, they are shot. They are then chopped up and fed to the other dogs. The survivors work harder, not only because they've had a meal, but also because they have seen what will happen should they themselves go lame.

This bullish approach soon won Granger several admirers in government, including Tony Blair.

Granger started as he meant to go on and hopeful contractors were left in no doubt that the procurement process was to happen very quickly. In May 2003 potential bidders were given a 500-page document called a 'Draft Output-Based Specification' and told to respond within five weeks.

There was little time to find out what was required or to talk to doctors in the NHS to find out what they wanted. The main contracts for the programme were awarded at breakneck speed and by December 2003 they were all in place.

One of the classic failures in many IT projects is the failure to consult adequately those who will actually use the systems once they are delivered. The programme in many respects followed this pattern, but in this case it wasn't by accident. Granger had no patience with what he saw as special pleading by medical staff, who he believed were unwilling to accept the ruthless standardisation which was necessary to deliver the advantages which IT could offer. He believed he knew what the clinicians actually needed better than they did themselves.

Some clinicians fought valiantly to make sure that there was proper clinical input into what was happening. In early 2002 Sir John Pattison had asked Dr Anthony Nowlan, a health informatics expert and executive director of the NHS Information Authority, to secure the involvement of health professionals in the programme. Nowlan began by recruiting senior clinicians to participate in translating healthcare requirements into IT requirements. Nowlan was assisted by a number of senior clinicians including Professor Peter Hutton, then president of the Royal College of Anaesthetists and chairman of the Academy of Medical Royal Colleges. Hutton eventually took on the task of leading a clinical care advisory group linked to the ministerial taskforce that had been formed to oversee the National Programme.

The aim was to obtain a professionally agreed consensus around what was the most valuable information to store and what was achievable in practice. After several months the group had hammered out a consensus. The principles of the group's proposals were accepted in March 2003 on the understanding of continuing close involvement in development. Between them the clinicians had created a working mechanism for delivering clinical input into the National Programme.

However, while this work was fed in at the start of specifying the contracts, it ended up forming only a relatively small part of the overall specification. The large majority of the so-called 'output-based specification', and in particular the crucial major hospital systems, were developed without involvement and scrutiny by the leadership of the health professionals. Nowlan – who had spent his professional life seeking to deliver improved health outcomes by better use of information – fully understood that involvement by users is essential if one wants software that works and which people will use. But as he pointed out, proper consultation in the National Programme could never have been achieved given the determination to complete commercial contracting so rapidly. This meant that all the issues of complexity had to be faced after the letting of contracts. Nowlan began to realise that his efforts were not welcomed. As he added: 'It became increasingly clear to me that efforts to communicate with health professionals and bring them more into the leadership of the programme were effectively obstructed.' Worse still, Nowlan was subsequently asked to provide a list of 'hundreds' of names of people who had been involved in the specification work in order to provide evidence to reviewers that the work was valid. Nowlan regarded this as a 'sham' and refused. Soon afterwards Nowlan was made redundant.

Despite an original request for clinical input into the programme, it turned out that it was not wanted. And despite the best efforts of many senior clinicians to make sure that the programme delivered something that would be of use to them, the programme continued on regardless, without paying attention to the end users.

As Hutton later told MPs:

It was like being in a juggernaut lorry going up the M1 and it did not really matter where you went as long as you arrived somewhere on time. Then, when you had arrived somewhere, you would go out and buy a product, but you were not quite sure what you wanted to buy. To be honest, I do not think the people selling it knew what we needed.

The result was a set of contracts which were signed before either the government had understood properly what it wanted to buy or the suppliers had understood what it was they were expected to supply. The deals were done at great speed and in secret, with contractors bound by the tightest of confidentiality clauses.

When Health Secretary John Reid announced the contract winners in December 2003, the value of the contracts had shot up to £6.2 billion from the original £2.3 billion that Granger had mentioned in Harrogate. The timescale had also tripled in length. Instead of the two years and nine months from April 2003 which had originally been promised – that is, to deliver a full national health record service by December 2005 – the contracts would now run for ten years. Later, one of the most senior officials in the National Programme, Gordon Hextall, even claimed to MPs that 'it was always envisaged it would run for ten years'. Planned costs would eventually reach £12.7 billion, with no end date in clear view.

Four winning bidders were awarded the five prime contracts, worth around £1 billion each: Accenture won two regions, the north-east and the east; Computer Sciences Corporation or CSC was awarded the north-west with West Midlands; Fujitsu won the contract for the south, and British Telecom won the contract for London. BT also picked up two other contracts, to build a broadband network and to install the 'spine' on which the national electronic health records would be stored, while Fujitsu also won the contract for an electronic appointment booking service known as 'Choose and Book'.

These regional prime contractors in the programme were known as 'local service providers' or LSPs. Each LSP was required to pick a specialist software subcontractor to supply the actual software for the electronic health record. BT and Fujitsu – covering London and the south respectively – both picked US software firm IDX, while Accenture and CSC – between them responsible for most of England north of the Severn and the Thames – each picked a British software company called iSoft, which had experience in supplying software to GPs but little track record in software for acute hospitals.

iSoft was a stock market darling which had been spun out of consulting firm KPMG in 1997. The company's flagship product was a software system called 'Lorenzo', which was portrayed enthusiastically in iSoft's 2005 annual report and accounts. iSoft's chairman, Patrick Cryne, told shareholders that Lorenzo had made 'impressive progress', while chief executive Tim Whiston, in describing Lorenzo as 'available from early 2004', stated that it had 'achieved significant acclaim from healthcare providers'. With such promising statements from the company's directors, the stock market was delighted and it was no surprise that iSoft's share price rose sharply. Cryne, Whiston and their fellow directors then sold large tranches of their personal shareholdings in iSoft, making over £90 million in cash. In 2004 Cryne bought Barnsley Football Club.

There was one slight problem. iSoft's flagship Lorenzo product, described in such encouraging terms by iSoft's directors, wasn't actually finished. And this was causing a big headache for Accenture and CSC. Under the Granger rules of engagement, no one was supposed to get paid until something was delivered, but due to iSoft's tardiness in producing a working version of Lorenzo, the brutal reality was that neither Accenture nor CSC had any software they could deploy.

There were still big concerns about the programme's indifference to winning round the users – in this case, clinicians in hospitals – even though numerous studies had pointed to such 'buy-in' as the key ingredient for success in any IT project. Peter Hutton wrote to Sir Nigel Crisp, chief executive of the National Health Service, to express his continuing disquiet. 'I remain concerned,' wrote Hutton,

> that the current arrangements within the programme are 'unsafe' from a variety of angles and, in particular, that the constraints of the contracting process, with its absence of clinical input in the last stages, may have resulted in the purchase of a product that will potentially not fulfil our goals.

Soon after pointing out, politely, that the emperor had no
clothes, Hutton was asked to consider his position and he
tendered his resignation. The IT people running the National
Programme were simply not interested in what clinicians such
as Hutton were telling them.

Belatedly the Department of Health began to realise that
securing the support and cooperation of the clinicians who
would actually have to use the systems might be a good idea.
In March 2004 the deputy Chief Medical Officer, Professor
Aidan Halligan, was appointed alongside Granger as joint
director general of NHS IT and joint 'senior responsible owner'
for the programme – that is, the buck stopped with him in
Whitehall. This was welcomed by clinicians. One delegate
at a healthcare computing conference in Harrogate said that
Halligan's appointment was 'really, really good' because 'he has
the trust of clinicians and can stand up to Granger' although a
GP delegate said it 'spoke volumes' that nobody like him had
been in post earlier. Halligan acknowledged that not enough
had been done to win the support of clinicians, whose buy-in he
said was 'critical to the success of the project'. It appeared that
listening to clinicians was now flavour of the month. However,
there remained one insuperable difficulty. No matter how hard
people listened, and no matter what clinicians said they wanted
in the programme, the contracts had *already* been signed. As
Hutton later explained in a memo to the Public Accounts
Committee: 'It became clear from discussions with suppliers in
early 2004 that what they had been contracted for would not
deliver the NHS Care Record.'

The excessive speed of the procurement was already causing
problems. In May 2004 the leading trade journal *Computer
Weekly* revealed that only five months after the deal was signed
it had 'run into contractual issues'. Quoting from a leaked
BT document, it reported the issues as arising from 'detailed
definition of requirements and practical deployment not envisaged at the Effective Date of the Agreement'.

Aidan Halligan stayed in his post for just six months

before quitting in September 2004, when it was announced he would become head of the Irish health service. A spokesman for the programme said there was 'nothing untoward' about Halligan's departure and that he had been 'made an offer he could not refuse'. Halligan never took up his new post. Instead he remained deputy Chief Medical Officer at the Department of Health until October 2005 before returning to academic appointments in England.

Accenture and CSC struggled on, eventually commissioning a joint study team to examine the prospects for the non-usable Lorenzo. In February 2006 a confidential report was delivered to senior managers which confirmed their worst fears. Lorenzo, the report stated, had 'no mapping of features to release, nor detailed plans. In other words, there is no well-defined scope and therefore *no believable plan* [authors' emphasis] for releases.'

In March 2006 Accenture, which was quoted on the stock exchange in the United States, announced to shareholders that it was making a provision of $450 million (then £270 million) to cover expected losses on the National Programme. These losses were linked to 'significant delays by one of Accenture's major subcontractors in delivering software'. Accenture made repeated offers to the National Programme that it would meet its contractual obligations using software suppliers other than iSoft. But this might have bankrupted iSoft and Granger was having none of it. Accenture started to talk about pulling out altogether.

Granger responded with a threat. Referring to tough penalty clauses contained in the contracts, he said 'if they would like to walk away it's starting at 50 per cent of the total contract value'. Accenture, with two of the billion-a-piece prime contracts, appeared to be facing a cool £1 billion in penalty payments to the government if it abandoned the programme.

But strangely it didn't work out that way. Accenture engaged in some swift negotiating footwork with the health service and by September 2006, after making a penalty payment of just £63 million, the consulting firm had duly exited from the

Accenbur out

programme. It was an eloquent comment on the seriousness of the problems facing the programme that a firm such as Accenture, which undertook so much government work, and thus potentially faced such a risk of reputational damage by leaving the programme, had nonetheless walked away.

Granger's threat that if Accenture left the programme it would face gigantic penalty payments proved to be of little account. There were rumours that if Granger had demanded any more money, he would have faced serious and embarrassing counter-claims from Accenture for failures by the National Programme to stick to its own contractual obligations.

The US firm CSC, with its own £1 billion contract for the north-west with West Midlands region, was of course in no better a position than Accenture to implement the unfinished Lorenzo software. It was also struggling to mop up after having caused the largest computer crash in NHS history. In July 2006 CSC's Maidstone data centre had been hit by a power failure, followed by 'restarting problems'. The backup systems did not work and data held in the centre could not be accessed. This meant that eighty NHS trusts could not use patient administration systems for four days and they had to operate as best they could with paper systems instead.

Another worry was CSC's shareholders. Whereas Accenture had set aside hundreds of millions of pounds against expected losses from the programme and told the stock market accordingly, CSC had not formally declared any losses from the programme at all. In addition to CSC's problems in the UK, the company had troubles back home in the United States, where it faced allegations of boardroom corruption. Two contracts worth around £1 billion each from Britain's NHS might look reassuring to the US stock market. And so as Accenture walked away, CSC quickly took on both the Accenture contracts – despite the fact that there was still no Lorenzo software to install – thereby tripling its involvement in the programme.

Meanwhile, iSoft had been dealing with serious financial accounting problems. Earlier in 2006 the company had delayed announcing its financial results due to 'accounting errors'. In a move which might have made even the most intrepid investors rather queasy, one of iSoft's own advisers, Morgan Stanley, declined to publish profit forecasts while stating: 'We don't feel we have enough visibility to offer a recommendation.' Finally, iSoft was forced to declare a loss of £344 million, which wiped out all the company's past profits. The Financial Services Authority launched an investigation.

To knowledgeable observers in the health IT sector, the position was looking bleak. Three fifths of the programme was now dependent on one troubled local service provider, CSC, which was using a software supplier, iSoft, that was itself under investigation by the Financial Services Authority and whose main software system for acute hospitals, Lorenzo, did not yet exist in a usable form. One regional contractor, Accenture, had been replaced by another, CSC, which had less experience, while the central main problem remained: the software product they had been trying to deploy, iSoft's Lorenzo system, was beset by repeated delays.

Hospitals which had been told to put their own IT plans on hold because of the shiny promise of Lorenzo and the National Programme were now getting desperate, as the replacement dates for their older systems loomed. Unable to install the incomplete Lorenzo, iSoft responded by selling hospitals one of its own older software products that predated the National Programme, known as iPM, which Connecting for Health duly paid for.

Meanwhile, the other two LSPs, British Telecom and Fujitsu, had not seen things go much better with their own chosen software supplier, the American firm IDX. US hospitals work very differently from those in the National Health Service, and the software they use is accordingly very different, too. American hospitals rely on billing for each and every activity, either directly to patients or to their insurance companies, and the software must cope with this. Conversely, US hospitals do not expect software to handle waiting lists, which are largely unknown in the United States, although this feature is sadly essential before such software can be used in hospitals in England.

Both BT and Fujitsu had been awarded contracts on the basis that they would use IDX's hospital system 'Carecast'. But neither BT nor Fujitsu had made significant progress with installing the IDX product and in the limited number of cases where they had tried, it had led to enormous problems. Software which worked well in a US hospital could not simply be uploaded onto the mainframe computer of an acute hospital in England and then switched on. As BT and Fujitsu were finding out, American hospital software needed very significant and costly adaptation and Anglicisation before it could be installed in the NHS. The result was predictable: the programme did not pay the suppliers.

In June 2005 IDX were dropped by Fujitsu. IDX's product had been installed quite successfully by University College Hospitals working directly with the company, and IDX pronounced themselves 'disappointed' by the decision. Yet in truth the firm had other fish to fry. Its new owners, the US firm GE Healthcare – who had been sufficiently impressed with IDX to buy the firm to complement its own offer in the healthcare IT sector – had little appetite for IDX's continuing involvement in the National Programme. After GE's purchase of IDX was completed, IDX pulled out.

With Granger's consent, Fujitsu replaced IDX with another American firm, Cerner, which had a software package for large acute hospitals called 'Millennium'. While the Millennium software had proved itself in hospitals in the United States, there were still the same big problems of Anglicisation to overcome. It was soon plain that, not adapted, Cerner's Millennium product would not be able to produce the management information which the NHS relied on. And once again, under the Granger rules, the LSP suppliers were not supposed to be paid until they had delivered.

BT, meanwhile, some eighteen months after winning its London LSP contract, was still struggling with IDX. By July

2005, BT was facing serious threats from Granger that it could be axed if it didn't start to perform. In an interview with *Computing* magazine Granger said: 'BT had better get me some substantial IDX functionality by the end of [the] summer or some predictable events will occur.' But it wasn't that simple.

As the leading healthcare IT website *E-Health Insider* pointed out, 'replacing BT as LSP would represent a major failure for the programme'. It would raise questions over the whole IT-enabled modernisation of the NHS and lead to even more delays. As *Insider* added: 'Such a move would also potentially raise serious questions about whether the adversarial management style of Connecting for Health is the most likely to deliver new systems that provide clinical benefits to patients in a cost-effective manner.' Instead, BT was allowed to continue as the LSP for London. Eventually, with Granger's consent, BT was permitted to follow Fujitsu's lead and replaced IDX with Cerner. Whatever the quality of a new software system, it will never prove effective without securing real interest from the end users. As LSPs, BT and Fujitsu were failing to persuade hospital trusts and clinical staff to buy into what they were doing.

At a London conference in July 2005, Granger gave a stern warning to suppliers who were lagging behind on delivery: 'We will very soon get to the point where they will either come good with what they've got, or they will get a bullet in the head.' Granger was also showing signs of defensiveness about the programme, stating that 'it might be a policy disaster but it isn't an IT disaster. The system was delivered to spec.' One example Granger gave was the introduction of an electronic staff record which, although it was a necessary pre-requisite for an electronic health record, didn't exist at the time the programme was conceived. He added: 'If some of my colleagues do not think sufficiently through as to what was wanted then it's a specification error.'

Such statements by Granger led to howls of rage from some industry observers, including one who after Granger's speech posted a comment on *E-Health Insider*:

Now and then I check myself from hatred of what Richard Granger stands for and has done to NHS IT, and then the sheer arrogance and ignorance of his public statements brings me back. He set the ridiculously short timescales for decision-making, procured before there was a clear idea of the scope, handed all the 'choice' from NHS clinicians to private contractors. CfH hasn't solved the funding crisis for computerising the NHS, rather landed us with a massively expensive way to do what some of us were achieving already.

The National Audit Office had embarked on a study of the National Programme, due to be published in the summer of 2005, but rumours started emerging of considerable delays. That August the NAO confirmed that the report would not be published until November 2005. The announcement of the delay coincided with a paper published in the *British Medical Journal* which heavily criticised Connecting for Health for poor communication and engagement with clinicians who were to use the systems it was supposed to be deploying.

The factual content of NAO reports must be agreed with government departments before publication. The Permanent Secretary then signs the report, attesting to its accuracy. While the clearance process may involve robust exchanges and differences of interpretation between the NAO and the audited department, it is essentially a sound process with advantages for both auditor and audited. It enables the government department to make sure the auditor is up to date with the most recent developments and it enables the NAO to present agreed facts to Parliament, avoiding fruitless arguments later when the Public Accounts Committee is taking evidence.

But with the National Programme something different happened. It was as if Connecting for Health wanted to use the clearance process to expunge the slightest criticism of its activities. It undertook a war of attrition with the auditors, in a process which the NAO later described as fighting 'street by street, block by block'. The final report was delayed again and again, finally appearing in June 2006, and it was much weaker than seasoned health IT observers had expected. Greg Clark, a member of the PAC, described the report as 'easily the most gushing' he had read, while a BBC correspondent described it as a whitewash. It emerged through Freedom of Information Act requests that earlier drafts had been considerably tougher, but most of the key criticisms were eventually excised as Granger and his team ground down their opponents.

Aside from the battles between the NAO and Connecting for Health, and the changes to the structure of regional LSPs – with the departure of Accenture and its replacement by CSC, and the switching of software suppliers by both BT and Fujitsu – as well as the investigation by the Financial Services Authority into iSoft's accounting practices, one thing remained absolutely constant. Hospitals were not getting the patient administration software they needed to deploy as the essential first step in the creation of electronic health records. This didn't prevent the NHS chief executive, David Nicholson, from telling an invited audience that the National Programme was 'not widely off course'.

People in the health IT sector who wanted the truth about the programme to emerge started to write to the PAC and a small tidal wave of new evidence started to appear. Tom Brooks, a management consultant with years of worldwide experience in healthcare, wrote a devastating submission to the committee in which he questioned the whole rationale of central procurement for the programme. Brooks criticised the 'poor quality of the negotiation of the NPfIT contracts by Mr Granger' and described the view that central procurement would produce systems that met local requirements as 'a fundamental error'. Brooks told the committee that 'MPs are mis-informed if they view the central infrastructure as making reasonable progress'. He pointed out that delivery promises had been missed and that the key central infrastructure item, the patient data repository, was 'doomed from the start'.

Brooks also explained that in relation to the American

software product Cerner Millennium, which BT and Fujitsu were struggling to deploy, the attempted implementations so far 'have demonstrated how difficult it is to "build" and implement Cerner Millennium without very close interaction between Trust clinical staff and the Cerner technicians in Kansas'. Pointedly he added: 'The LSP and Cluster team structure gets in the way of that necessary close interaction.' Brooks dismissed iSoft's Lorenzo, which was 'still not available', as having been 'selected from paper descriptions'. He concluded that 'a full examination of all the procurement facts would illustrate that the procurement and the LSP contractual structure was the root cause of many of the problems that exist today'.

Larry Benjamin, a consultant ophthalmic surgeon at Stoke Mandeville Hospital with an expertise in health IT, told the PAC that the implementation of the programme had been 'backwards' and that 'for a clinical system to be deemed useable by the staff using it, their involvement in its development is vital'. Dr Anthony Nowlan, the informatics expert, also described the programme as 'back to front'. Given that the contracts stating what would be produced *had already been let*, Nowlan pointed out the sheer absurdity of a 'consensus document' produced by the programme which stated: 'Now that the architecture for England has been commissioned, designed and is being built, there is a need for clarity concerning how it will be used.' Robin Guenier, chairman of health IT firm Medix Group, drew attention to a survey which his company had undertaken among clinicians. Doctors had increasing concerns about the costs of the project and how it was being implemented and continuing worries about the confidentiality of patient records. Only 5 per cent of doctors said they had been adequately consulted. Guenier had already warned years previously, in an article penned for *Computer Weekly* in 2002 when the National Programme was first launched, that the government's chosen course was likely to make things worse.

A group of health IT experts then sent the committee a detailed paper which offered a devastating critique of the entire programme. The expert group provided evidence that neither the most important areas of clinical functionality nor the benefits required to justify the business case were likely to be delivered by the programme, and stated quite simply:

> The conclusion here is that the NHS would most likely have been better off without the National Programme in terms of what is likely to be delivered and when. The National Programme has not advanced the NHS IT implementation trajectory at all; in fact, it has set it back from where it was going.

The paper included a background section which offers with admirable clarity one of the best explanations of the whole debate about the National Programme. In view of the frequent misunderstandings about the National Programme by so many journalists, broadcasters, politicians and commentators, it is worth quoting at some length:

> It is useful to begin with the question: 'What is the central point of NPfIT – its chief *raison d'être*? Is it a shared medical record (otherwise known as the "Central Spine" or "Central Summary Care Record Service") across England?'
>
> The answer to this important question is simply: no. In fact, the central point of NPfIT is to provide the local Care Record Service (CRS) systems, namely: Cerner Millennium in the Southern and London Clusters and iSoft Lorenzo in the North East, North West & West Midlands, and Eastern Clusters. Compared with the local CRS, the Central Spine is a much lower priority because it is totally speculative and even if delivered is likely to result in very little clinical benefit. The Central Spine is actually a distraction and anyway cannot happen without the Local Care Record Service (or Local CRS) systems being implemented first.
>
> This is a subtle but critical point. The Local CRS systems, historically always known as 'electronic patient record' (or 'EPR') systems, are a proven technology and typically aimed at the local NHS organisation (acute hospitals, community and

mental health hospitals and GP practices). They are sophis-
ticated software systems and are quite complex because they
need to cater for a range of clinicians and accomplish a wide
range of tasks such as allowing the clinicians to maintain the
clinical history of the patient, to request diagnostic tests, to
prescribe drugs, to schedule theatres, clinics and physiotherapy,
etc. and do so in intelligent ways with a great deal of embedded clinical knowledge to make clinical practice safer and
evidence-based.

These types of software products (Cerner 'Millennium', GE/
IDX 'Carecast', etc.) are well established and proven and earlier
versions of them are successfully operating in several hospitals in the UK. They are what is most needed by hospitals to
support their clinical service delivery. They are what have been
contracted for from the Local Service Providers (LSPs) as specified in Schedule 1.1 of the LSP contracts.

These local CRS systems have always been costly invest-
ments (several million pounds per hospital over several years)
but have been proven in the NHS and elsewhere to deliver
real clinical benefits (such as reducing adverse drug events and
reducing mortality) which are evidenced by sound and extensive
published medical research.

This picture is entirely different for the so-called Central
Spine record, or Central Shared Summary record, which NPfIT
(and the government ministers) would like the public to believe
is the central point of NPfIT. It is not. The Central Spine
record is just a concept, the simple one of having a summary record
about a patient (with his/her key clinical data such as allergies
and latest drugs) which can be shared by all clinicians needing to
have it.

The problem is that clinicians have told us medicine does not
work like this. Clinicians do not just use a summary record to
deliver care. They build and depend upon detailed and specific
medical data that are relevant for each patient.

They do not rely on some other clinicians' definition of

what will be most relevant to put in a summary record. What is relevant clinically will inevitably vary from patient to patient.

The concept of a summary Central Spine record has no scientific basis and no significant clinical support to back it up – just an overly simplistic and naive storyline about a Birmingham patient falling ill in Blackpool. In fact, no one has ever provided any figures on how often this situation is likely to arise to show whether or not the investment in the Central Spine record is worthwhile.

The point here is that the Local Care Record Service is the essential building block for clinically useful health IT to support clinical care in progressive, modern and proven ways. Yes, it is difficult to implement and can take two to three years to roll-out across the whole hospital (or organisation), and yet it is always worthwhile – ask any of the Chief Executives of the few hospital trusts that have implemented these systems in the UK e.g. Guys & [St] Thomas, Chelsea & Westminster, Burton Hospitals Trust, Wirral Hospitals, etc.

These Local Care Record Service systems are the building blocks and are the point of NPfIT, and what NHS Trust Chief Executives want, need and expect. They are not waiting for a Central Spine record to run their hospitals.

However, the Local Care Record Service systems (or the Local Service Providers' newest versions of them) are not likely to be fully deployed now (only the rudimentary patient administration elements of them will be) because NPfIT is putting in old 'legacy' products in place of new modern Local Care Record Service products in its panic to show deployment and because the systems have been so late in being delivered by the LSPs.

What is not reported widely is that the LSPs are late in delivering the new versions largely (though not wholly) because of NPfIT's own delay in providing so-called 'Spine message definitions' to the LSPs during 2004 and 2005. And when they did finally arrive, they were fluid and kept changing.

Thus, the LSPs have been delayed because of the delays and

failures of NPfIT itself, but of course they are afraid to say this for fear of offending their client.

In summary, the Local CRS agenda is the real agenda for NPfIT, not the Central Summary Care Record Service.

The key point of the National Programme for IT is to provide both depth of clinical systems functionality and breadth of integration in terms of delivering the contracted Local CRS functions across organisations and care-settings (acute, primary, mental health, social services). This is the true vision of health IT promised by the National Programme which is embodied in the Local Service Provider contracts and it is what their price reflects.

The trouble is, with all the delays, the LSP schedules are being down-scoped behind the NHS's back and without any accountability to the local NHS Trust chief executives to whom the original vision was promised.

Criticisms of the programme became more widespread and new facts started to emerge. By asking parliamentary questions, Richard Bacon MP established that Connecting for Health was making 'advance payments' to iSoft. The tough talk of not paying contractors until they delivered and of replacing those who were not up to the mark – of shooting the huskies if they failed to perform – appeared not to apply to iSoft, to whom, as the new Health Secretary Patricia Hewitt admitted, advance payments of £82 million had been made. It subsequently emerged that various contractors had benefited from this back-door largesse, with advance payments totalling £443 million.

Robin Guenier published a paper entitled '3 Essentials for Project Success', which spelt out the key ingredients for a successful project: first, 'a hands-on, informed, recognised and sceptical leader with full authority'; second, 'detailed, widespread and regular engagement with key staff and users'; and third (arising from the second), 'brutal realism about the project'.

None of these conditions was met in the case of the National Programme.

In September 2006, Bacon and John Pugh, both members of the PAC, published a paper called 'Information Technology in the NHS: What Next?' The MPs were blunt:

> The government is convincing no one that the situation is under control. The National Programme for IT in the NHS is currently sleepwalking towards disaster. It is far behind schedule. Projected costs have spiralled. Key software systems have little chance of ever working properly. Clinical staff are losing confidence in it. Many local Trusts are considering opting out of the programme altogether. These problems are a consequence of over-centralisation, over-ambition and an obsession with quick political fixes.

The Bacon–Pugh paper analysed 'four fallacies' at the heart of the programme and offered a way forward. The fallacies were that 'patient data needs to be accessible all over the country'; that 'local trusts can't procure systems properly so the centre has to do it for them'; that 'large areas of the NHS need to work on a single massive system'; and that 'the National Programme saves money'. The suggested way forward was to allow hospital chief executives to buy the systems they actually wanted, subject only to common standards, and to partially fund such purchases from the centre while making local chief executives contractually responsible for delivery. The paper also identified that iSoft's Lorenzo system, fundamental to the programme in the Accenture and CSC regions, seemed unlikely to be made fit for purpose at any reasonable cost or in a realistic timeframe.

The Bacon–Pugh paper concluded that

> what is required is to create a proper balance between central standards and central procurement where this offers demonstrable benefits, and local autonomy and responsibility. IT offers enormous potential benefits to the NHS, its staff and above all its patients. It is not too late to make sure that these benefits are properly delivered.

Shortly afterwards, the NHS chief executive, David Nicholson, introduced the National Local Ownership Plan, known as NLOP. But this plan didn't follow the Bacon–Pugh suggestion of giving autonomy to local chief executives in what they bought. Under the NLOP proposals, hospital chief executives would still be required to buy the software which the local service provider was contracted to provide: either the difficult-to-install American system Cerner Millennium or the non-existent Lorenzo. And instead of one 'senior responsible owner' – a central tenet of good project management practice – there would be many dozens of senior responsible owners dispersed among the country's local primary care trusts, strategic health authorities and hospitals. These bodies were given responsibility for implementing and delivering software which was not available or didn't work properly, without a free choice to buy something else. The NLOP was looking more like an attempt to decentralise impending blame than a serious attempt at reform. Tony Collins, a leading computer journalist with *Computer Weekly*, playfully dubbed the NLOP as 'No Longer Our Problem'.

In February 2007 Andrew Rollerson, a senior Fujitsu manager who had assembled and then led the winning Fujitsu team in the original bid process, mentioned at an IT conference that, in his view, the National Programme 'isn't working and it's not going to'. To many informed observers it was a statement of the obvious, yet all manner of metaphorical ordure now descended on his head. The PAC, whose own report had been delayed by the small tidal wave of new evidence, now called a somewhat bashful Rollerson as a witness. Asked if he felt as if he were the one who let the finger out of the dam and allowed a whole collective sigh of relief to go round the health IT sector, Rollerson replied 'I think that is absolutely spot on'. Fujitsu wrote to the committee, stating that Rollerson wasn't a senior executive of the company, that he had not had any involvement with the programme for over a year and that they remained committed to implementing the programme. Given that Rollerson had led Fujitsu's winning bid team, it seemed strange to describe him as 'not senior'. Fujitsu's rather pedantic point was that, in common with almost all employees, Rollerson was not on the company's executive management committee.

By March 2007 another probe had been launched into iSoft by an accounting standards body and the following month the PAC published its report, concluding coolly that 'at the present rate of progress, it is unlikely that significant clinical benefits will be delivered by the end of the contract period'.

By June 2007 Richard Granger had announced that he would be quitting, although he stayed on for another seven months. Shortly afterwards he stated that he was 'ashamed' of some of the systems put in by NHS Connecting for Health suppliers and singled out Cerner for criticism. David Nicholson appointed several new senior executives to join Granger at the top table while continuing to reject calls for a full review. Tony Collins wrote in *Computer Weekly* that the future of the National Programme for IT in the NHS was 'hazy' and that it was becoming 'difficult to delineate success from failure'. Derek Wanless, whose major review for Tony Blair of the future of the health service had identified investment in IT as an area for improvement, publicly questioned whether the programme should continue without a full audit. He stated that 'there is as yet no convincing evidence that the benefits will outweigh the costs of this substantial investment'.

In October 2007 the Department of Health rejected rumours that Matthew Swindells had been appointed as the interim chief executive of Connecting for Health, but admitted that Swindells was advising Nicholson on health informatics, with a wider remit than the National Programme. It transpired that in an industry survey he was named the twelfth most influential person in the NHS, some ten positions above Richard Granger.

The day 31 January 2008 proved to be Granger's last as an employee of the NHS, though it was a week later, on 6 February, before his departure was announced. The interim director of NPfIT and systems delivery, Gordon Hextall, sent a letter to

Connecting for Health staff to tell them that Granger had gone and that there would be two appointments to replace him: a top level chief information officer for the NHS and a director of IT programme and system delivery. Meanwhile the interim chief information officer would be Matthew Swindells.

In February 2008 the Commons health committee published a report on the electronic patient record, in which it was 'dismayed' by the lack of clarity about what information would be included in the summary care record and indeed what the record would be used for. There was 'a stark contrast' between the 'specific and detailed' vision set out for the Integrated Care Records Service in 2003 and the 'vague and shifting' vision set out in 2007. Other trenchant criticisms included the absence of a clear timetable. The committee concluded that there was a 'perplexing lack of clarity about exactly what NPfIT will now deliver'.

Very little was happening on the ground, although there were persistent stories about the government leaning on hospitals to accept immature technology. But the largely autonomous foundation hospitals could not be compelled to take systems they did not want. Meanwhile the non-foundation hospitals – which were being pressurised into taking useless systems in order to help the programme save face – hastened their preparations to become foundation hospitals, and thus obtain relative immunity from Granger's Connecting for Health organisation. At the same time they slowed down on anything to do with the National Programme.

In May 2008 the NAO published a progress update which was much more robust than its earlier report. The NAO concluded that the programme had 'largely failed to deliver on its central objective of detailed care record systems for acute hospital trusts'. However, even before the PAC had had time to take evidence on the new NAO report, the LSP Fujitsu was 'sacked'. Or to put it another way, Fujitsu were willing to continue implementing the *existing* contract but the National Programme was not prepared to see them do this, and wanted Fujitsu to reset the contract. Rumours soon circulated that Fujitsu was preparing a £700 million compensation claim. The foolish decision back in 2002 to allow four service providers and their preferred software suppliers to dominate the programme had led to a shambles, with Fujitsu and Accenture leaving, and the remaining two providers – BT and CSC – facing enormous losses. Meanwhile, neither iSoft nor Cerner were able to deliver software that met the needs of a modern, highly diverse NHS.

In the PAC hearing that followed, Gordon Hextall even said the Lorenzo software had been deployed at Morecambe Bay Hospitals, and only very reluctantly admitted that this was not actually the case. A spokesman for Connecting for Health inadvertently pointed out the scale of the problem in a press announcement:

> Lorenzo is being rigorously tested at early adopter sites with differing care settings and geographies to ensure it meets the necessary quality criteria and is relevant to the needs of diverse healthcare communities prior to going live within a working healthcare environment. Designed to reflect patient journeys and support the modern NHS, the Lorenzo early adopter projects will deliver capability in acute and community services *as a first step* [our emphasis] towards building a truly integrated care record across the entire healthcare delivery system.

In other words, six years into the National Programme, not even 'the first step' to an integrated care record had yet been taken.

In August 2008 the interim manager Swindells was replaced by a new chief information officer for the NHS, Christine Connelly, with Matthew Bellamy appointed her right-hand man as director of IT programme and system delivery. In October, a close follower of the National Programme, Nick Timmins, wrote a front-page story in the *Financial Times*: 'Progress has virtually ground to a halt, raising questions about whether the world's biggest civil information technology project will ever be finished.' He quoted Jon Hoeksma from *E-Health Insider*, who said: 'The key part is stuck.' Hospital chief executives, Hoeksma added, did not want to take the system 'until they had seen it put in flawlessly elsewhere'.

The second PAC report was published in January 2009, concluding that the programme's failures raised questions about the feasibility of the whole project and that 'central contracts are an encumbrance'. The committee recommended that if Connecting for Health and its suppliers could not make the programme work within six months then hospitals should be allowed to do what they wanted. Connelly did not agree but imposed her own somewhat longer deadline of the end of March 2010. This deadline was eventually missed, too, without any immediate consequences for the contractors.

On the ground very little was happening. There was a stalemate between hospitals who refused to be guinea pigs for poor software and suppliers who were in so deep that they didn't know how to find a way out. Only nine months into his job, Matthew Bellamy resigned. Just before Christmas 2009 the Health Secretary, Andy Burnham, gave an interview in which he sang the praises of the National Programme and said that 'parts of the NHS cannot operate without it'. Unfortunately for Burnham, the Chancellor of the Exchequer, Alistair Darling, took a different view – and said so. Darling told a television interviewer that the National Programme was 'not essential for the front line' and announced that he was imposing a £600 million cut in spending on the programme from £12.7 billion to £12.1 billion.

New Year 2010 was not a happy one for the former iSoft directors. The Financial Services Authority, the chief City regulator, announced that it had laid criminal charges against four former directors of iSoft – Patrick Cryne, founder and the former chairman, Timothy Whiston, the former chief executive, and former directors Stephen Graham and John Whelan – who were accused of conspiracy to make misleading statements. All four pleaded not guilty. In the event, their trial collapsed in 2012 when a jury at Southwark Crown Court was unable to return a verdict. The Financial Services Authority has opted for a retrial, which is expected in 2013.

Meanwhile, the Department of Health said it had appointed a senior doctor to 'provide a clinical perspective' on how new technology should be introduced.

In March 2010 iSoft announced that it was 'on track' at Morecambe Bay Hospitals. Bacon wrote to Connelly and asked her to demonstrate that the project was value for money, while asking: 'How can the programme represent value for money when such dramatic reductions in scope and scale are apparently being considered?' As the general election approached, Aidan Halligan, the former deputy Chief Medical Officer for England who had for six months worked on securing clinical engagement, alongside Granger, went public with his continuing concerns about the programme. 'Culture eats strategy for breakfast,' Halligan said. 'And unless any new NHS IT strategy starts from the bottom it will not work.' In August 2011, just over twelve months after the coalition government was formed, the PAC issued a third report, stating bluntly: 'The Department is unable to show what has been achieved for the £2.7 billion spent to date on care records systems.' The following month the Department of Health responded, saying a review had 'concluded that a centralised national approach is no longer required'. Yet to the utter bemusement of the health IT sector, the announcement also stated that 'all existing contracts for the IT programme will be honoured'. The death throes of the world's largest civilian IT programme – which would be very costly and protracted – had only just begun.

12

INTERCITY WEST COAST
RAIL FRANCHISE

Insanity is doing the same thing over and over again and expecting
different results. When will the Department for Transport learn?
Sir Richard Branson, chairman, Virgin Group

It had been a long night and Patrick McLoughlin was abso-
lutely furious. 'I'm very angry about what has happened,' the
Transport Secretary told BBC Radio 4's *Today* programme.
'This is a fault within the department and within the model
and the Permanent Secretary will be making a statement later
today. I want to make it absolutely clear that FirstGroup and
Virgin did nothing wrong, the blame lies squarely with the
Department for Transport.'

Hours earlier on the night of 2 October 2012, McLoughlin,
who had only been running the transport department for a
few weeks, had issued a midnight statement announcing that
the award of a lucrative rail contract to run the InterCity West
Coast franchise between London and Glasgow to a company
called FirstGroup had been abruptly cancelled after flaws were
discovered in the procurement process. McLoughlin also put on
hold the awarding of several other major rail contracts – Essex
Thameside, Great Western and Thameslink – pending an urgent
review of what had gone wrong. The costs of the delays and the
inevitable retendering of the InterCity West Coast franchise and
other affected rail contracts meant that the bill to the government was conservatively estimated at £40 million and rising.

The department's mistake was spectacular. Since the railways
had been privatised in the 1990s, one of the department's most
important jobs was to award franchises to private companies,
whose job was to run Britain's trains in a timely and efficient
manner and not go bust in the process. The appointment of a
new company to run the InterCity West Coast franchise was

the first major decision by the coalition government, which had taken office in 2010 promising change to the way that rail contracts were awarded. The franchise runs from London to Glasgow, connecting on the way some of Britain's biggest cities including Liverpool, Birmingham and Manchester.

Theresa Villiers, the Conservatives' shadow Transport Secretary, had pledged change in 2008 when she said a Tory government would give train operators longer-term franchises, with more flexible contracts lasting up to twenty years. The Coalition Agreement, drawn up by the Conservatives and Liberal Democrats in May 2010, adopted the change: 'We will grant longer rail franchises in order to give operators the incentive to invest in the improvements passengers want – like better services, better stations, longer trains and better rolling stock.'

The new department also brought in a new organisational structure at the Department for Transport among senior civil servants to run the awarding process for new contracts in 2010 so that the responsibilities of the single director general who had been in charge of all aspects of its rail programme were spread across three directors general who were responsible for policy, implementation and the financial advice side of the organisation.

This organisational shake-up came amid a mass exodus of staff from the department, in response to a tough five-year comprehensive spending review which had required departments to cut back radically on their spending. In the Department for Transport's case it meant cutting its £295 million administration budget by 33 per cent by 2014/15, which in turn led to 502 staff leaving in the twelve months to April 2011.

A National Audit Office report charted how the department had haemorrhaged institutional memory, with four permanent secretaries moving on between 2010 and 2012, adding that 'a number of senior staff with a role in rail franchising had left in 2010/11 including the director general previously responsible for rail and the department's head of procurement'.

Many senior officials retired. In all between fifty and seventy members of staff who were working directly in rail – between 20 per cent and 30 per cent of the overall figure – left the department between May 2010 and May 2011, although eighteen staff were drafted in to work on franchising after January 2011.

The NAO was damning about the severe erosion of this 'corporate memory' at such a crucial time for the department. 'It is unfortunate that there have been so many changes of permanent secretary during a period of intense reorganisation,' the NAO said. 'The frequent changes at senior level raise questions about whether there is sufficient continuity to achieve long-term infrastructure projects or service contracts, which is a key part of the department's responsibilities.'

It continued: 'We have the benefit of hindsight but, in our view, the department's restructuring decisions regarding rail franchising increased risk as it was about to embark on a major refranchising programme.'

Specifically, the NAO found that the department's InterCity West Coast project team had 'no senior staff', and added: 'We could not find evidence of effective management oversight. Some bidders also told us they had less access to senior staff compared to previous competitions, and there was a lack of "guiding mind" – someone who had oversight and carried out sense checks on what the system was producing'. Indeed the contract for the InterCity West Coast franchise had no 'senior responsible owner' at all for the first three months of the tendering period, between January and March 2012.

Added to this was a time pressure, with officials trying to let the flagship franchise within fifteen months – an ambitious target which would have to be delivered at a breakneck pace given that the new process was more complicated. Still, the department was fixed on a goal of appointing the winner of the InterCity West Coast franchise contract by the end of the current franchise, 9 December 2012.

The omens were not good in the spring of 2011 when work started in earnest on the letting out of the West Coast contract. In a report dated 20 April 2011, a 'gateway team' from the Office for Government Commerce – now the Major Projects Authority – gave the overall refranchising programme an 'amber' rating and warned of the effects the major restructuring, a loss of expertise at a senior level and a 'very tight timetable' would have on the process.

Under the previous 'cap and collar' funding system, the department reimbursed train operators with 80 per cent of any shortfall if their revenues were lower than the operators had forecast by an agreed year. Officials were concerned that this encouraged train operators to submit overoptimistic bids – knowing that after a few years they would start to get generous payback from taxpayers – and also incentivised them to cut costs in the short term rather than invest. To address this problem, the department developed a complex GDP compensation system which would reimburse train companies if a change in annual GDP growth were less than forecast. Similarly the train operator would pay back the taxpayer if GDP growth were greater than forecast. The department ran a number of scenarios through a 'GDP resilience model' to try to test how rail companies would behave when making losses and to forecast the likelihood of them defaulting on their franchise payments. The department's board investment and commercial subcommittee approved a target default rate of less than 5 per cent of the 500 economic scenarios that were tested.

Crucial to the success of the new GDP model was to ensure that rising and falling passenger numbers – so-called 'elasticity' – was accounted for. But the question the officials had to get right was how to ensure that the government did not overcompensate the rail operator if passenger demand did not fall as much as forecast in an economic downturn. The department's investment and commercial subcommittee agreed the elasticity rate on 15 December 2011 even though it was lower than the demand rate used for long-distance journeys in official guidance. This was vitally important as it impacted on the size of the subordinated loan facility – effectively a 'down payment' from the parent company of the train business bidding for the franchise to guard against its going bust during the contract

– which would have to be paid by the successful bidder. The department intended to ask for a subordinated loan facility that its forecasts showed was large enough to reduce a bidder's risk of default to the rate of fewer than 5 per cent of the different economic scenarios that it had set.

That same month officials on another committee involved in the process – the department's contract award committee and rail refranchising board – approved the letting of the tender, even though a 'hostile review' of the franchise policy in November 2011 had uncovered a number of 'extensive issues' (according to the NAO) which were not all addressed by the time the competition process started the following year. The Treasury also approved the tender in January 2012 but only as a pilot which would help develop policy on franchise retendering and with reservations, notably raising concerns about the risk profile of the franchise programme, and its affordability. A report from accountancy firm Grant Thornton also raised concerns about the way the loan was to be calculated. But these worries only reached the department on 20 March, two months after the invitations to bid were sent out on 20 January. Four short-listed rail companies – the incumbent Virgin Rail, which had run the line since March 1997, its arch rival FirstGroup, and two other companies, Abellio InterCity West Coast and Keolis/SNCF West Coast – stepped forward to develop their bids through the spring of 2012, based on information and assumptions provided by the department, including GDP forecasts and their relationship to passenger demand.

The officials plainly wanted to give the contract to the bidder that offered the best value to taxpayers – essentially the largest premiums which could be paid back to the government. Yet soon a major problem became clear: the tool to calculate the value of each bidder's loan payment was not fit for purpose. Officials had also apparently not thought through how they would provide bidders with enough information to predict the likely size of their subordinated loan facility.

They were told by the department on 24 February that the

crucial value of the subordinated loan facility would be calculated using the 'GDP resilience model' – but officials declined to provide more details because of concerns that disclosing such details would have given too much away about how the department viewed the different bidders. It later emerged that the model was designed for something else altogether – to work out the GDP compensation mechanism and not to calculate the value of the loan facility. Essentially, as Louise Ellman MP, chairman of the Commons transport select committee, was later to say, 'the invitation to tender for the franchise was issued before the department knew how to calculate subordinated loan facilities'.

Instead the department issued a 'ready reckoner' to the bidders containing a generalised set of results from the model. The companies still could not calculate the size of their subordinated loan facility, because they did not know the risk adjustments that the department would apply. This lack of transparency left the whole process wide open to legal challenge, as a later report from leading businessman Sam Laidlaw – who was also a non-executive director in the department – was to find. Laidlaw told MPs later that the lack of clarity about the way the loan was to be calculated was 'at the root of the problems that subsequently emerged'.

Bidders were left having to use clarification questions to try to extract more information from the department about how the size of their individual loan payments would be calculated. The later analysis by the NAO could not prove that all of the enquiries from the bidders received a response or that replies were consistent. The Major Projects Authority gave the refranchising programme an 'amber/red' rating in March 2012, concluding that the programme was highly complex and challenging, adding that it had worries about how the programme was resourced as well as its governance. Despite these problems, bids were submitted by 4 May.

The bids were assessed over the following twelve weeks by a small team at the Department for Transport, supported

by technical and legal support from two firms of advisers, Atkins
and Eversheds. Officials were assessing whether the bids were
compliant and deliverable; the value of the premium payments
– how much each bidder was offering to pay for the right to
take on the franchise; and the size of the loan payment based
on the risk assessments to the cost and revenue projections.

There was a certain element of finger in the wind here. To
calculate the correct value of each bidder's loan, officials used
adjusted costs and revenues which the engineering consultancy
Atkins calculated for individual bidders to work out the level of
risk in the bids the rail companies had made. This had a corresponding impact on the size of the loan. As for the bidders, they
were only told that there was a new policy on how the loan
was calculated but not how it was worked out. Examples put
forward by accountancy firm Grant Thornton showed that if
the department thought that just 2 per cent of a bidder's annual
revenue predictions were undeliverable, then the size of the
loan increased by £296 million.

Further problems emerged. The size of the loan paid by the
winning bidder had to take into account the forecast annual
inflation rate for the period in question. However, the 'ready
reckoner' did not include inflation and only calculated the loan
in 2010 prices. The effect on the size of the facility was stark:
for example, FirstGroup's facility would have had to be £355
million rather than the £252 million produced by the reckoner.
To compound matters, if the department had chosen a higher
elasticity factor the loans required from bidders would have
been much larger.

There was also a puzzling difference between the figures
offered by the two favourite bidders: Virgin and FirstGroup.
The two companies were forecasting that their trains were
going to be taking a similar number of passengers up until
2016/17 whereupon their forecast revenues diverged radically,
with FirstGroup predicting that it would be taking far more
passengers than its rival. Few understood why this was the case.

To forecast its numbers, FirstGroup had taken the decision

to increase its passenger demand levels for 2012/13 and subsequent years, so that they were higher than the department's assumptions. It appeared that they were partially right and Atkins told officials to accept two thirds of FirstGroup's revised forecasts. This had the effect of cutting the size of Virgin's loan, but increasing FirstGroup's.

The contract award committee, chaired by a department director and comprising fourteen officials and lawyers, made its final decision on 27 June 2012. Given the information and 'ready reckoner' the department had given to bidders, it might seem surprising that it used its own discretion to set the size of the loans required, rather than base them on the figures pumped out of its ready reckoner. Crucially the department, denuded of so many senior officials because of spending cuts, could not even provide a director general – and particularly not the director general in charge of the department's refranchising programme – to attend the meeting.

This meeting later took on huge significance for what went wrong. The Laidlaw review, published with sections redacted to protect bidders' commercial confidentiality in the following December, raised serious questions about the conduct of the meeting and asked why there seemed to be such a lack of certainty about what had happened. Astonishingly for such an important meeting, comprehensive minutes were not taken. After interviewing all fourteen officials at the meeting, Laidlaw wrote: 'There remains a significant lack of clarity and a large degree of inconsistency in the evidence as to the discussions and decisions taken at the meeting. This is surprising, not least because it was an important and fairly recent meeting attended by some DfT officials.'

After the meeting, Virgin, which had bid £11 billion for the contract, was asked for a loan of £40 million when none was required, while FirstGroup, which promised to pay £13.3 billion over the life of the deal, saw its facility cut from £252 million to £190 million, after allowing for £10 million of equity in its bid.

The Laidlaw review later described this disparity as 'odd',

given that the risk profiles of both Virgin's and FirstGroup's bids were similar for the first ten years. With hindsight, experts have said the £190 million is about half the sum that FirstGroup should have been required to offer because the department had not included inflation in its calculation.

According to the Laidlaw report, an official, whose name was redacted, 'advised at the meeting that it was open to the DfT to exercise discretion in sizing the SLF [that is, the 'subordinated loan facility'] requirements in respect of the First and Virgin bids'. This proved to be a big problem. While the tender document had indeed stated that it was for the department to 'determine' the size of the subordinated loan facility, the department subsequently issued guidance stating that it would use the GDP resilience model to do this.

The department's external legal advisers, Eversheds, were not present at the crucial meeting, but when they found out later that discretion had been applied, they warned the department that its actions may have been unlawful. This advice was not escalated to members of the board investment and commercial subcommittee, the Permanent Secretary or ministers. Nor were they informed that discretion had been applied. Eversheds' concerns were also not fed back to the contract award committee. The lawyers' concerns were effectively brushed aside. Amazingly, the officials involved were exercising discretion in a way they were not entitled to do while ignoring legal advice that their actions were open to legal challenge and, for good measure, not telling their seniors what they had been doing. The people at the top of the department remained blissfully unaware either that discretion had been used or that doing so was probably unlawful.

These were not the only warnings which were ignored. The Major Projects Authority carried out two critical reviews of the refranchising programme, the first in April 2011 and then again the following year in March 2012. These reviews highlighted that the department lacked project and programme management expertise, that there were inadequate resources, that there were governance issues and that the programme was made more complex because franchise policies had not been finalised. The authority judged that there were significant risks to achieving the programme successfully. However, as the NAO later observed, 'nobody sought to address these issues in relation to this franchise competition'.

Once they were satisfied that the final bids were deliverable, officials were given the more straightforward task of choosing the winning bid based on the value of the bidders' premium payments. FirstGroup was chosen because its bid was higher than Virgin's, even though Virgin was judged to have a 'higher deliverability score'. The information was presented anonymously to the contract award committee, which was to make its decision in July 2012. The Major Projects Authority was asked to carry out a review of the administration of the bids, using a scope agreed with the department. This comprised a document review and interviews, but the authority was not asked to check how the bids were modelled or calculated, or to provide a detailed audit of past decisions. Based on the evidence provided, the authority gave the project a green rating, stating that the department was well placed to award the contract. The NAO later concluded that 'senior managers [in the department] took too much comfort from various assurance processes and reviews with clearly defined but limited scope which are not a substitute for good line management'.

Virgin had smelt a rat. Between 22 June and 23 July the company wrote several letters to the department raising questions about the contract process. On or around 20 July the company was told that it was not the preferred bidder for the contract. On 23 July, Sir Richard Branson, the parent company's chairman, escalated the crisis by writing to Transport Secretary Justine Greening, Prime Minister David Cameron and Chancellor George Osborne, expressing his disappointment that Virgin was going to lose the contract and suggesting detailed and technical arguments about why this decision was wrong. Branson suggested that FirstGroup had overbid to win the franchise. The letter ended with a specific request for Ms Greening to 'look closely at all the facts before making a defini- tive decision'.

Greening waited over a week before replying on 1 August to say that she could not comment because the process of letting the contract was a live competition. As a result of Branson's letter, Greening, following the department's rules which were designed to ensure that a fair decision was made between the bids, also had to pass on responsibility for the process to her ministerial junior, Theresa Villiers, because Branson's letter had compromised the anonymity of the bids. The need for anonym- ity also meant that Virgin's concerns – whether legitimate or not – were not passed on to Villiers, who remained unwittingly in the dark. This in turn seems extraordinary – not least because Villiers would be expected to defend the integrity of the award- ing of the contract in the House of Commons and in media interviews just weeks later.

Virgin's letter writing campaign also meant that senior civil servants in the department, like the Permanent Secretary, who could have stepped in to sort out the problems, and perhaps started the whole process again, had to stand back once they became aware of the identity of the preferred bidder. The NAO noted later:

> The department's use of anonymity had a perverse effect, once Virgin started to raise complaints. Individuals were unable to participate as decision-makers once they knew the identity of the preferred bidder. But we do not consider that this should have prevented them from scrutinising the project processes.

Virgin increased the pressure again. A letter on 30 July asked for more information and raised the prospect of a challenge to the whole process through a judicial review in the High Court. Virgin's campaign had the desired effect, leading to questions being asked by the Prime Minister's office about the whole franchise process, with briefings involving the Cabinet

Secretary and Permanent Secretary and senior officials from the Department for Transport. Despite this high-level scrutiny, not one of the briefings touched on the crucial detail of whether the loans being demanded from Virgin and FirstGroup were set at the right level.

The Department for Transport's board investment and commercial subcommittee discussed Virgin's concerns when it met to agree the franchise award to FirstGroup on 31 July, and asked for more information from the project team. But by now for Virgin, the train had left the station. The subcommittee met again – although only the chairman and one other member from the original meeting could attend, in part because of concerns about preserving the anonymity of the bidders in the process – two days later on 2 August and endorsed the decision to give the thirteen-year contract to run the West Coast Main Line to FirstGroup.

Two contrasting events happened the next day on 3 August. While officials were telling Villiers to award the contract to FirstGroup and asking her to write to Danny Alexander, the Chief Secretary to the Treasury, asking him in turn to rubber-stamp the decision, elsewhere, the official leading the contract project team together with a senior internal lawyer and a part-ner from Eversheds were telling the leading counsel whom the department had appointed – to prepare to defend its decision on the deal in court – that there was 'a potential issue' about the way the loan facility had been determined. The Laidlaw review found that no blame could be attached to Villiers, concluding that 'despite the fact that Department for Transport officials were aware that the [loan facility] sizing was a likely area of challenge in any litigation, the then minister of state was not given an appropriately accurate and full briefing' about the potential problems; moreover, 'inaccurate statements were made to the then minister of state in writing'.

On 14 August, a day before the announcement was due, Sir Richard Branson wrote again to the Prime Minister, stressing that anonymity rules had meant that he could not discuss his concerns with the Cabinet Secretary and urging a delay 'so that an audit can be done to make sure that the right decision is being made'. The letter did no good.

The following day, the Department for Transport announced to the London Stock Exchange that the Secretary of State had stripped the InterCity West Coast franchise from Virgin and given a new thirteen-year deal to FirstGroup. The new franchise holder was offering around 12,000 more train seats a day when a fleet of eleven new six-car trains started running, as well as an additional 106 Pendolino carriages, which would deliver another 28,000 new seats on the service. Journey times between London and Glasgow would be cut.

Villiers said FirstGroup would deliver 'big improvements for passengers, with more seats and plans for more services'. But Branson was incandescent. He pointed out that other operators like GNER and then National Express had run into difficulties trying to run the East Coast Main Line. Virgin started a petition on the 10 Downing Street website with more than 150,000 people signing it in ten days, calling on ministers to reconsider their decision. With the Prime Minister and most of the senior players in the government away on holiday, Branson offered to run the service on a not-for-profit basis until MPs returned to Parliament in September. His offer was not accepted.

Virgin launched legal proceedings against the government on 28 August, the day before ministers were due to sign the new deal with FirstGroup. The contract award was postponed, as officials started to prepare for the court case. FirstGroup said in a statement: 'We have every confidence in the DfT's process which is rigorous, detailed and fair and in which bids are thoroughly tested. There has been no complaint about the process, which was carefully described in advance, until Virgin Rail Group lost commercially.'

PricewaterhouseCoopers was brought in by officials to help the department develop its legal case over the following six weeks and uncover what had gone wrong. On 3 October Patrick McLoughlin, who had replaced Greening as Transport

Secretary in a Cabinet reshuffle, cancelled the contract with FirstGroup – hours before his department was due in court to do battle with Virgin over the application for a judicial review – and halted work on a number of other tenders while lessons were learned.

So who was to blame? Hindsight showed how a number of factors including adopting FirstGroup's revised passenger forecasts, a different choice of elasticity factor and the calculation of the subordinated loan facility had slanted the process in favour of FirstGroup. Lord O'Donnell, a former Cabinet Secretary, blamed a 'brain drain' of top civil service talent from the government, particularly in key areas like procurement, which meant that no single official managed the letting of the contract. MPs hit back. Bernard Jenkin MP, the chairman of the House of Commons Public Administration Select Committee, criticised top mandarins for moving too frequently between departments. Only three of the biggest sixteen departments in Whitehall had the same Permanent Secretary as when the coalition was formed in May 2010. He said: 'With each disaster, finger-pointing and blame become more destructive. Ministers now bad-mouth their officials in public. Even the Prime Minister, who is minister for the Civil Service, has called officials the "enemies of enterprise".'

There were other issues, notably the difficulty of managing an open competition with so few bidders. As soon as one bidder complained, its anonymity was compromised and senior figures who could have intervened to sort out the mess were left out of the picture.

Something had gone very wrong. Experts pointed out that nearly two decades previously it had taken thirteen months to sell off the UK's original twenty-five rail franchises, with the average bid costing just £500,000 each. Now they can easily top £5 million for each one. It appears also that the department was hopelessly outgunned in terms of the level of independent advice it had agreed to pay for. While the bidders were investing an average of £10 million each on a bid, the department did not appoint an external financial adviser for the franchise competition, and costs for advisers and internal staff were just £1.9 million in total. This was less – as it turned out – than the £2.7 million that the department was later forced to spend on preparations to defend its decision in court, until it became clear that its position was indefensible. As Sam Laidlaw later told MPs: 'There is an asymmetry of commercial capability and resource here that probably is not in the best interests of taxpayers ... Rail franchising capability needs to be built up.'

The department's Permanent Secretary, Philip Rutnam – who took over midway through the tendering process in April 2012 – also told the Public Accounts Committee: 'It is a prime example of how one can be penny wise and pound foolish. If we had spent a small amount more on running the competition and had run it properly, we would have got to a result.' He disclosed that the costs of cancelling the competition were £40 million, not including the impact of cancelling other tenders while the process was reviewed. The outcome was 'extremely expensive, very serious, deeply concerning and extremely regrettable', he said.

The NAO's assessment, in its report published on 7 December 2012, was brutal in lambasting the department for its failings. It said there were 'five safeguards against making poor decisions' – 'clarity of objectives' to help decision makers 'form appropriate judgements by being a touchstone to refer back to throughout the decision-making process'; 'strong project and programme management' to co-ordinate work streams; 'senior oversight' to act as a 'sense check'; 'effective engagement with stakeholders' such as suppliers; and 'internal and external assurance'. The NAO added forthrightly: 'It is clear that none of these lines of defence operated effectively in the refranchising of InterCity West Coast.' Or as Louise Ellman said: 'Bidders in relation to the West Coast Main Line were treated inconsistently in a process the department knew to be flawed and was vulnerable to challenge.' Margaret Hodge, the chairman of the PAC, was also forthright, branding the saga a 'first-class fiasco' and adding that the department had 'blundered into this major and complex competition for one of the biggest franchises in the country without even knowing how key parts of its policy were to be implemented'.

Belatedly, the Department for Transport acted, endorsing the recommendations from the Laidlaw review and making it clear that a senior civil servant will be in charge of each rail franchise, from tendering to letting the contract. In the aftermath, Peter Strachan, the department's head of major projects, who was one of the senior officers responsible for the bid, left the department as part of a restructuring just before Christmas 2012. FirstGroup did not take over the InterCity West Coast franchise on 9 December. Instead, Virgin had already been asked to run the route until 9 November 2014 as the process was relet. It was a fitting reminder of one of the most public, embarrassing and costly Whitehall mistakes under the coalition government.

It is worth asking: where were the passengers in all this? Rail privatisation, when it was unveiled by the Conservative government in 1993, was meant to bring an end to inflation busting, costly fare increases. It never happened. And the day before FirstGroup 'won' the franchise, the government announced some train fares would rise by up to 11 per cent in January 2013.

13

THE PUBLIC SECTOR AND I.T.
– A PERMANENT DISASTER?

*Project managers must forever be closing down options early,
while political managers try to keep all options open forever.*
Ross Anderson

Forget about the technology.
Mark Todd

*Everything really interesting that happens on software projects
eventually comes down to people.*
James Bach

It is a commonplace that we learn from our mistakes. One can think of many areas of human activity, from the building of bridges to the manufacturing of aircraft, in which failures have led to improvements. Yet one area of the modern world appears immune. Government IT projects seem to have an endless capacity to go wrong and it seems that we never learn. The same mistakes are repeated over and over again.

Many of the chapters in this book are essentially about IT project failures: the enormous scandal of the Child Support Agency, which simultaneously failed mothers who cared for children and victimised absent fathers; the Inland Revenue tax credits disaster, which produced fear and misery for vulnerable people on low incomes; the chaos at the Passport Office, which ruined the holidays of thousands; the Criminal Records Bureau debacle, which caused such huge problems for nurseries, schools and parents; the bizarre new system for selecting junior doctors, which caused talented medics to emigrate to Australia in an anxious search for work; the catastrophic system for administering single farm payments, which led some farmers to bankruptcy and even suicide; the Individual Learning Account scheme for adult training, which caused respectable training providers to go out of business while allowing unscrupulous operators to make millions because the system was so easy to defraud; and the National Programme for IT in the health service, the largest civilian IT programme in the world, whose design was fundamentally flawed from the beginning. All of these were failures in the planning, procurement and management of government information technology projects.

And there are many more such projects beyond those in the chapters of this book. The Government Communications Headquarters expected to pay £40 million for moving the signals intelligence computer systems into its new building; managers told the GCHQ board it would cost £20 million; actually, it cost £400 million. The Libra Project was a computer system for the magistrates' courts which was originally supposed to cost £146 million for a complete solution including software, although this was soon revised upwards to £184 million. It ended up costing £232 million just for the basic infrastructure of PCs, wiring and a help desk, with more than £250 million of extra costs on top. The Department for Transport and its agencies entered into a shared services agreement which was supposed to save £112 million in return for costs of £55 million; instead, the new arrangements cost £121 million but produced only £40 million of measurable benefits, while the new computer busied itself spitting out messages in German and denying staff annual leave to which they were entitled. A computer system for the probation service which ran hugely over budget had seven programme directors in seven years, five of whom knew nothing about project management. Plans for a new National Offender Management Service Information System known as C-Nomis began in 2004 as a £234 million project intended to allow the prison and probation services to follow offenders 'end to end' through the criminal justice system, but by July 2007 it was two years behind schedule and estimated costs had tripled to £690 million. It subsequently emerged that neither ministers nor senior management at the Home Office, nor even the C-Nomis project board, were aware of problems until May 2007. The original concept for the project was abandoned. Even now, the National Offender Management Service is unable to explain what £161 million spent before October 2007 was used for. The Ministry of Defence's Defence Information Infrastructure, which was supposed to connect up all aspects of the ministry's work from the bureaucrat to the battlefield, saw costs triple from £2.3 billion to £7 billion, while the installation of tens of thousands of the required new computer terminals took place at less than half the speed stated in the contract. The new computer system for HM Revenue and Customs to integrate Pay As You Earn or PAYE with the National Insurance system exposed the fact that the Revenue routinely deducted too much income tax from millions of taxpayers while charging less than it should to millions of others.

Taxpayers are shelling out vast sums on IT systems that do not work properly and that no one wants to use. Worse still, IT failures put lives at risk. In early 2003 before the invasion of Iraq, as army squaddies opened British defence containers in the Kuwait desert just to see what was in them, it became clear the Ministry of Defence could not adequately track equipment deliveries. Notoriously, although there was enough body armour, it was not in the right place. Yet the lack of proper tracking software had been identified twelve years previously in the first Gulf War in 1991.

The problems are not confined to central government. National public sector IT projects do seem more likely to fail than local government ones, partly because they are bigger and more remote, and partly because councils commonly learn by generalising success; if one town hall is known to have made a successful innovation, others will often rapidly follow its example. Nonetheless, local authorities and other bodies have had their share of IT disasters. Avon County Council implemented a new computer programme to pay staff wages without first testing the new system properly. The result was that a janitor was paid £2,600 for a week's work while canteen staff were paid nothing at all for seven weeks; and a deputy headmistress received her year's annual salary once a month, while some people had more tax deducted in a week than they earned all year; within a month 280 council employees were out on strike. The London Ambulance Service spent £7.5 million before abandoning a computerisation project that was originally estimated to cost £1.25 million. The subsequent official report identified a litany of basic problems including an inexperienced procurement team, price put before quality, an overambitious timetable, a superficial analysis of the system requirements, and incomplete software which was not properly tested; for good measure it turned out that a report by Andersen Consulting highlighting problems with the management of the project had been suppressed. Essex Police awarded a £1.5 million contract to GEC-Marconi to supply a new crime handling and police intelligence system before the police had finished specifying the user requirements. The system was to be delivered within two years, but because the specification had been put out to tender before it was complete there had to be further changes; two years later not a single line of program code had been written.

Tony Collins, an investigative journalist who has uncovered many computer scandals, wrote a telling account of the 'life cycle of a public sector IT failure'. First, there is the project design: it accords with best-practice project principles, but there is an expansion of the objectives and the costs as interested parties give their views on what the new systems could do. In the second stage, an invitation to tender is issued: civil servants faithfully reproduce the often unreasonable and, in some cases, simply ignorant demands of ministers that the project be delivered at superhuman speed, when to anyone who knows anything about the subject the timetable looks completely unrealistic; however, the commitment to the time scales and to the project design is too great for heed to be paid to warnings from prospective end users, from trade unions, or indeed from any of the reputable prospective suppliers who are considering bidding for the project, that the timetable is too tight or the scope unrealistically ambitious. The third stage is when contracts are awarded: after that, fuller consultation with potential end users begins, but it is usually inadequate or self-selective. In the fourth stage, the supplier begins to realise that it has overestimated its ability to understand the customer's business, and to convert that into IT systems, and the customer realises that it has overestimated the capability of the supplier. More often than not, the supplier also realises that it has not asked enough questions before signing the contract, and that the customer has not understood its own business sufficiently well to explain its work practices, the complexities of the project, the risks of failure and the real costs to the supplier. In the fifth stage, the timetable begins to lengthen: the projected costs start to increase, but commitment to the project is now far too great for any indecision or U-turn to be allowed, so the government department ploughs on. In the sixth stage the project starts to founder: this is characterised by the beginnings of the cover up, where failure is depicted as success, and MPs do not get well-rounded answers to questions. In the seventh stage, the failure becomes apparent anyway: it is impossible to hide it because the public or officials in the departments are affected by the fact that the contract is being abandoned, changed, rewritten or even reawarded to another supplier. In the eighth stage, often years later, there are sometimes reports from the National Audit Office and the Public Accounts Committee. In the penultimate stage of the cycle, the department says that it has learned from past mistakes, and those who give the assurances that lessons have been learned move on to other jobs, often in different departments. Finally, those people are replaced by new personnel who embark on other projects that repeat the mistakes of the past, and the cycle begins anew.

A major survey by the European Services Strategy Unit, published in December 2007, identified 105 failed or troubled public sector IT projects in the UK, of which eighty-three were either national government or national public sector agency projects. Of the 105 reviewed, the total value of contracts was £29.5 billion, of which the eighty-three national projects accounted for £28.1 billion. Cost overruns totalled £9 billion; 57 per cent of contracts experienced cost overruns; the average percentage cost overrun was 30 per cent; a third of contracts suffered major delays and 30 per cent of contracts were ended.

Why all this failure? For decades now, the words 'government computer project' have led taxpayers to sigh in resignation, while keeping newspaper headline writers in steady employment. It seems there is a repeated litany of failure in government whenever computers are involved. What is it about the public sector which makes it so unbelievably inept in the area of IT?

A common rejoinder to this question is that IT project failure is not only a public sector problem. The private sector too, it is argued, has its share of appalling IT disasters, although businesses, perhaps fearful of shareholder fury or a consumer backlash, are sometimes better at killing off bad projects quickly, as well as minimising the bad publicity. And it turns out that there is truth in these assertions. When new automated warehousing at Sainsbury's supermarket did not work as expected because of poor IT systems, the supermarket's inability to stock the shelves properly hit its business performance; Sainsbury's had to write off £260 million spent on IT and recruit 3,000 additional staff to restock its empty store shelves manually, and then fight off serious speculation about a hostile takeover. Taurus was a multi-million-pound project by the London Stock Exchange to automate share trading, which employed up to 350 technicians for six years before the project was abandoned; it was said to have cost between £75 million and £400 million. In the United States, a consortium of Budget Rent-A-Car, Hilton Hotels, Marriott and AMR, the parent of American Airlines, abandoned a state-of-the-art travel reservation system three and a half years and $165 million into the project, because of project delays and technical difficulties; yet this same group had earlier built the highly effective Sabre reservation system, illustrating that past success is no guarantee of future results.

In another American example, a $5 billion pharmaceuticals wholesaler, FoxMeyer Drug Company, was forced into bankruptcy by malfunctioning computer systems. When in 2010 the Japanese car maker Toyota recalled 1.5 million cars, it was to fix problems with software that controlled the braking systems; Toyota experienced a global PR crisis and spent nearly $2 billion solving the problem. British Gas were submerged in a deluge of complaints when they sent out incorrect bills and disconnection threats; people were disconnected despite paying their bills, while customers paying by direct debit found huge sums of money had been removed from their bank accounts – a doctor from Middlesex had £3,796 deducted from his account even though he had been assured that the real figure was £39. An electricity company, Powergen (now part of E.ON), managed to display the credit card details of 5,000 customers on a public website; it was forced to tell its customers to get new cards and pay them compensation for the inconvenience. In 2013, a series of computer glitches left customers of NatWest and the Royal Bank of Scotland unable to withdraw money from cash machines for long periods and also disrupted online banking services. There are many other such private sector examples.

Observers also note, with some truth, that when IT projects go well in the public sector you just don't hear about it. The London congestion charging scheme, based on vehicle number plate recognition, requires motorists driving into central London to pay a fixed fee if they wish to drive within the central congestion charging zone during the main hours of the business day. People may not like paying the London Congestion Charge but there is little doubt that as a computer system it works well; it is only too efficient at spotting those motorists who have forgotten to pay and sending them hefty fines. The Oyster Card is a successful scheme where travellers on London's tube trains and buses buy a pre-loaded card in advance to obtain cheaper travel than those buying tickets one at a time. It works well. After the publicity surrounding its initial launch, the Oyster Card has attracted scarcely any headlines, except on one occasion when the computer system failed on a Saturday at noon, briefly allowing passengers to travel without deducting a fare from their cards. As if to prove the point, the story was widely covered. And even the fiasco of the Passport Office – which we examined earlier in this book – turned out quite well in the end, albeit after decades of angst and failure; nowadays the UK's passport service is very efficient and will provide a passport to a citizen in less than twenty-four hours if required. While success is what taxpayers generally wish to see, it is not newsworthy. Failure makes better copy.

Computer disasters can indeed be found everywhere, although, as several studies have suggested, there are specific difficulties affecting the public sector. Certainly, such projects are more likely to be reported in newspapers if they go wrong – whereas private sector projects are often not as visible to either the public or to a company's shareholders. There are also other factors at work. Private sector projects are driven by competition, while public sector projects are generally monopolies, providing services people cannot get elsewhere. They are also more likely to focus on measurable financial and service outcomes, whereas public sector projects often have multiple aims which make it harder to measure success. And public sector projects are more likely than private sector ones to be hit by the speed of policy changes and the need to meet politically driven timetables. Nonetheless, a survey of IT projects by Oxford University and *Computer Weekly* reported that a mere 16 per cent of IT projects were considered successful, while finding little difference in the performance of public and private sector.

There is an important caveat about risk, and the poor understanding of risk in the public sector. In his book *Public Sector Auditing* Sir John Bourn observes that the traditional label of the civil service as 'risk averse' is often a misnomer. Bourn agrees that while civil servants are often characterised in this way, the reality is quite different. He points out that government departments sometimes take enormous risks without even being aware of them or their possible consequences, and that this 'risk ignorance' has been a significant factor in explaining policy failure or underperformance. This is particularly relevant in examining failure in IT projects because it is so often the case that changes in government policy require changes in IT systems in order to take effect. And despite a significant shift in the rhetoric of civil servants – who are now able to sound fluent while talking in the language of risk assessments, risk registers and all the rest – it remains broadly true, as Bourn suggests, that

> when a new policy is considered, the three questions most usually asked are
> - Can we get the money?
> - How can we present the new policy?
> - How can we deal with criticism from Parliament, political opponents and the media?

Questions about the other risks on which the policy will depend are rarely asked at this point in the process. Let's accept that some differences between the private and public sectors do make delivering a successful IT project in the public sector even more difficult than it would otherwise be. Even so, the broader question remains: whether we are looking at the public sector or the private, *why* is there so much failure?

Parliamentarians, auditors, journalists, academics in business schools and universities, and government bodies themselves have all devoted considerable attention to answering this question. *Crash: Ten Easy Ways to Avoid a Computer Disaster* by Tony Collins and another leading computer journalist, David Bicknell, remains one of the most illuminating studies of this subject, yet it is only one among many such works. In the United Kingdom the National Audit Office regularly produces value-for-money studies on all aspects of government expenditure and these studies regularly include analysis of the failings of IT projects, which are so often central to the government's activity. Projects which have come under the NAO's spotlight in this way include almost every chapter in this book. In the United States, where according to one estimate the government spends $25 billion per year on computer systems, the General Accountability Office or GAO performs a similar function to the NAO in the United Kingdom. The GAO has issued reports on hundreds of computer projects where billions of dollars have been poorly spent and has for many years issued advice on how to improve the delivery of projects. The House of Commons' Public Accounts Committee published a study which drew out lessons from twenty-five cases from the 1990s where the implementation of IT systems resulted in delay, confusion, inconvenience to citizens and, in many cases, poor value for money to taxpayers. The study highlighted eight key conclusions: the critical importance of commitment from top management; the need to see IT decisions as core business decisions rather than technical ones that could be treated in isolation; the importance of identifying end users; the implications of a project's scale and whether it was too big to undertake in one go; the need for skilled project managers, including greater professionalism in the negotiation and management of IT contracts; the training of staff to maximise the benefit from a project; the importance of contingency planning; and making sure that lessons are learned from a project by undertaking a thorough post-implementation review. There were a further twelve core recommendations with over forty eminently sensible key lessons.

The government does not lack advice.

The truth is that there have been hundreds of attempts over several decades to get to the bottom of why there is so much failure in IT projects and there is now a substantial industry devoted to studying this subject. There are scores of project management techniques, dos and don'ts, core steps, key lessons, check lists and so forth.

One academic study actually identified a risk *created by the process of identifying risks*, specifically the use of project management checklists, on the basis that while checklists would seem to be a useful aid for project managers in assessing what can go wrong, they introduced a further risk that people will assume that a checklist is complete, which may lead project managers to overlook other possible threats to a given project. Academics have even undertaken studies *about the studies* on IT project failure. Malcolm Bronte-Stewart, an academic at the University of Paisley's School of Computing, developed a model from the research on IT project failure to estimate the risk of failure in any given project, using a group of studies which were themselves based on substantial research involving surveys and analysis of experiences of many organisations and IT projects.

It is now simply a statement of fact to say that we now *know* what causes IT projects to go wrong. The shelfloads of studies and reports about IT project failure all say roughly the same thing: if you don't know what you want, or what you want keeps changing; or you can't commit the required money to the project; or you don't have anyone in charge of the project, or you keep changing the person in charge, or the person who is supposed to be in charge doesn't really call the shots; or the person at the top of the business doesn't care about the project; and you don't focus on what the actual benefit to the business is; and you don't regularly talk to the people who will have to use the system; and you don't constantly check progress; or you have an unrealistic timetable and try to run before you can walk; or you fail to test the system properly before you launch it; or if you don't provide enough training; or you don't have a Plan B in case things go wrong; or you try to bite off more than you can chew in one go; or you don't realise that the bigger project the greater the chance of its being overtaken by events or new technology or new legislation; or you don't realise that you may not have the skills you need to manage the project; or you don't realise that some suppliers are quite capable of telling you they can deliver when they can't; then don't be surprised if you end up with a mess that is way behind schedule, damages your organisation, traumatises your staff, costs much more than it is supposed to, and doesn't work.

It is now scarcely ever the case that a mistake is made in an

IT project which someone elsewhere hasn't made before, and which someone elsewhere hadn't previously warned about. Yet this leads to a conundrum. As Martin Cobb of the Treasury Board of Canada Secretariat put it in an address to 'CHAOS University', allied to the Standish Group study, in a now celebrated question which has become known as Cobb's Paradox: 'We know why projects fail, we know how to prevent their failure – so why do they still fail?' A big part of the explanation for this paradox lies in the nature of engineering and, in particular, the nature of software engineering. The other part lies in the nature of people.

Compared with other branches of engineering such as mechanical engineering, structural, civil, electrical or even aeronautical engineering, software engineering is a very young discipline. It may even surprise some people that software writers or computer programmers are known as engineers at all. As Tony Collins and David Bicknell point out in their book *Crash*, when a bridge collapses it is not something that can be covered up, particularly if there are people on it at the time. The lessons from bridge failures are therefore learned as a result of a public or an engineering industry inquiry. Yet, as Collins and Bicknell observe, bridges have collapsed frequently for centuries, and as recently as the 1940s the collapse of the first suspension bridge across the Puget Sound, connecting the Olympic peninsula with mainland Washington state, was regarded as a landmark failure in engineering history. It turned out that the bridge was exposed to aerodynamic forces which were insufficiently understood at the time, and the failure led to more aerodynamic research and important advances. Lessons were still being learned 2,000 years after the Romans believed they had invented the archetypal arched bridge. The computer industry, by contrast, has only had a few decades to learn from its mistakes, and often little or nothing is learned because silence usually follows a computer disaster.

The Royal Academy of Engineering and the British Computer Society established a working group to examine the whole area of project failure and produced a report, 'The Challenges of

Complex IT Projects', which found that only 16 per cent of IT projects are truly successful. It highlighted a series of factors which make software development peculiarly vulnerable to failure compared with other kinds of engineering.

Software is not subject to the laws of physics in the way that, say, a civil engineering project is, and this can easily produce a perception that anything is possible. This is very misleading since software does have constraints, but these tend to be abstract and difficult to communicate. Both customers and suppliers are susceptible to forgetting or simply not understanding the limitations of IT, resulting in unrealistic expectations and overambitious projects – and this tendency is exacerbated because one cannot see software or visualise it. As one of the participants in the working group, Les Hatton, put it:

> If I was a managing director trained in law or accountancy I wouldn't ask an engineer to build a 1,000-metre long concrete beam suspended at one end because I know it can't be done. I have a physical perspective about it. With software, it's never like that. We don't have any underlying feel for whether something is even feasible.

This means that senior managers who are responsible for commissioning IT projects will readily ask for functions that are difficult or impossible to deliver, without the slightest notion that they are doing so.

A related problem, also stemming from the intangible nature of software, is the abuse of software's flexibility. The belief that software is flexible encourages people to flex it, often beyond what is reasonable. People change their minds much more frequently than they might do for solid 'bricks and mortar' engineering projects such as bridges or roads where the constraints are much more obvious. This is made still worse by the fact that in software design there are often many different ways of solving the same problem – all of which would probably work – compared with construction where there tend to be better-defined established processes. People who are quite accustomed to adapting how they have to behave to suit the constraints of a building will request changes to software much sooner than they will adapt how they behave to fit an off-the-shelf proven software package. IT projects are normally undertaken to deliver some kind of change in a process or a business. Sometimes this will be a major transformation, and in other cases it will be to automate an existing process, but even if it is just an automation the people involved will need to alter their practices, so the business will change in some form. This means that IT practitioners need – but do not always have – an understanding of the business or the process concerned if the IT system is to achieve the intended outcome. Worse still, the customer may give to the supplier an inaccurate description of a business process, one which may describe what *should* be done rather than the business process actually employed. In the case of automation, the manual process replaced by IT may be a poor or ineffective one, and automation is unlikely to make a bad process better, even if it performs it more quickly.

Complexity also obstructs successful design. As the working group observed, although major projects in other engineering disciplines also have to contend with complexity, it seems that complexity in software engineering is both harder to detect and less well understood. Complexity may be inherent in delivering what is required but it can also just get in the way, interfering with the efficiency and reliability of the system. In one of the most compelling accounts of the dangers of IT project failure, *Why Software Fails*, Robert Charette, an American risk management consultant, points out that a project's sheer size is a fountainhead of failure and that large-scale projects fail three to five times more often than small ones. As he writes:

> The larger the project, the more complexity there is in both its static elements (the discrete pieces of software, hardware, and so on) and its dynamic elements (the couplings and interactions among hardware, software, and users; connections to other

systems; and so on). Greater complexity increases the possibility of errors, because no one really understands all the interacting parts of the whole or has the ability to test them.

Ideally, a system should contain all of what is required to deliver the objective and none of what is not required. Just as the most beautiful mathematics also has the greatest economy, so the best software engineers solve problems using the fewest lines of code. This recalls the medieval Principle of Parsimony or Law of Succinctness, sometimes known as Ockham's Razor after a Franciscan theologian, William de Ockham. It is known as a 'razor' because it cuts apart and distinguishes two theories from one another. For scientists the most useful statement of the principle is: 'When you have two competing theories that make exactly the same predictions, the simpler one is the better.' To put this in software terms: 'When faced with different ways to write a program all of which would work, go for the simplest one.' While this may sound obvious, the trouble is that the degree of complexity that is actually required in order to solve the problem fully may be difficult to estimate accurately at the outset. There is also no doubt that some people are just attracted to complexity for reasons that vary from curiosity and playfulness to intellectual insecurity. But even where these considerations are absent, it is not easy to identify just how complex something has to be in order to work. As Albert Einstein famously remarked: 'Everything should be made as simple as possible, but not simpler.'

Irwin Owens, a California-based programmer, has observed that software engineers tend to fall into one of two categories: developers who like to program for programming's sake who come up with cool stuff in research and development that is rarely useful; and coders who apply Ockham's Razor to everything, whether they know it or not, and who write concise and clear code because they are always looking for the simplest solution. Owens points out that such developers are highly sought after and command senior positions because they churn out code that is reliable and simple. Spreading this approach would yield enormous dividends. As Owens writes:

> What is really needed here is for many coders to stop being so territorial about their code, and open it up to scrutiny. Allow people to question your use of this framework, or that pattern, and openly consider that perhaps that isn't right for this project, then be willing to change. Lots of the all-night coding marathons which are now the folklore of the dot-com bubble are due to not applying the simplest solution to the problem. Philosophy and programming really go hand in hand, it's just a shame that more programmers don't have literature, philosophy, or sociology backgrounds. In practice, however, I do find that some of the best programmers I've ever met are highly artistic, and many have degrees in English, Philosophy, Science, etc... In fact many hiring managers and headhunters are starting to look for these qualities in their hiring of programmers.

Neat thoughts, even if humans are not famous for opening themselves up to as much criticism as possible, nor for avoiding territorial behaviour, nor for placing a premium in the workplace on elegance, economy, simplicity and beauty.

David Gelernter, a computer scientist at Yale University, thinks beauty should be at the very heart of what computer technologists do, describing beauty as 'the most important quality in the computer world'. Gelernter wrote *The Aesthetics of Computing* to explain how beauty drives the IT revolution, observing that while most technologists are oblivious to beauty 'the best are obsessed with it' and that such differences account for huge variations in productivity.

Gelernter points out that 'beauty is important in engineering terms because software is so complicated. Complexity makes programs hard to build and potentially hard to use; beauty is the ultimate defence against complexity.' The dangers of complexity are exacerbated further by almost continuous improvements in computer processing power and communications technology, which have dramatically escalated the scale of what can be attempted. This means that when someone is tempted to ask for an extra function to be added onto a new system, the computer power to run it is unlikely to be an issue, at least initially. Developments in the design and management of complex IT systems have not kept pace with the potential of hardware, or indeed human ambition.

A further factor is our old friend, Uncertainty. It is common for complex IT systems to seek to undertake or augment tasks previously carried out by people. While the task of implementing a certain system can be relatively straightforward – *once it has been specified* – there can be great difficulty in working out exactly what is required. The Royal Academy of Engineering and British Computer Society working group drew an analogy with building a hospital, where there is clearly much more uncertainty in the specification of the hospital than in the technical risks in building it.

Some uncertainties can be reduced or eliminated but others are there almost by definition, because they are connected with the nature of software design. Because software has no physical parts which degrade through being used, it would seem to follow intuitively that once the designers have got it 'right', it should work correctly, indefinitely. Yet in reality this idealistic state is never achieved. As the computer scientist Manny Lehman put it: 'In every piece of real world software there are embedded an unbounded number of assumptions. Most of the assumptions are not decisions that you have taken, but things that you have not thought about.' Sooner or later, because the number of such assumptions is unbounded, one or more will prove incorrect, potentially causing the software to fail. Even assumptions that were correct to begin with may later become invalid as the project develops. In other words, all complex IT systems have a propensity to fail.

Then there is the question of how one tests software adequately. The US space programme has some of the most rigorous software checking anywhere. Yet as the famous physicist Richard

Feynman, a member of the President's commission into the 19͞͞ space shuttle *Challenger* disaster, observed in an appendix to the main report, though the computer software checking system was of the highest quality, there had, nonetheless, been 'suggestions by management to curtail such elaborate and expensive tests as being unnecessary at this late date in shuttle history'. Feynman's reaction was emphatic: 'This must be resisted for it does not appreciate the mutual subtle influences, and sources of error generated by even small changes of one part of a program on another.' Feynman argued: 'For a successful technology, reality must take precedence over public relations, for nature cannot be fooled.'

Several of the cases we have looked at in this book have involved failure to allow for adequate testing of software before the system went live. With the Rural Payments Agency, a key issue was that as the design of the system progressed, the requirements which that system was to meet changed; so they had to go back in and redesign elements of the system and retest them. The timetable for testing the IT was compressed and there was a limited amount of testing and no end-to-end testing. In the case of the Criminal Records Bureau, the basic problem was a failure to take account of the need for large volumes of paper-based applications, even though this was quite obvious in a system requiring the originals of personal identity documents such as birth certificates, passports and driving licences. The CRB kept pushing back the start date while trying to establish a method for coping with the large paper flow, so that the end-to-end IT system was only put in place for the first time a few days before the final deadline. This meant there was no time left for proper testing, yet calling the whole thing off was not an option, so the CRB launched a system which they knew didn't work properly. With tax credits, the volume testing timetable was compressed from twelve weeks to four weeks and the system was launched while still deeply flawed. Something very similar happened with the Student Loans Company, where there was a failure to apply sufficient volume testing to a scanning system which coped in theory but not with the large volume of documents which would actually be processed in practice.

Volume testing can help minimise problems but it cannot eliminate them. Indeed, one can show mathematically that it is impossible to test completely an IT system of any real size to eliminate every potential problem. In his book *Software Engineering*, Roger Pressman explains why exhaustive testing presents certain basic logistical problems: 'Even a small 100-line program with some nested paths and a single loop executing less than twenty times may require ten to the power of fourteen possible paths to be executed.' Assuming that each path could be evaluated in a millisecond, Pressman calculates that to test all of those 100 trillion paths would take 3,170 years. One writer on software, Jeffrey Voas, suggests that the use of more complicated languages is making it harder to build high-quality software than using older languages that were less feature rich, as well as even more difficult to test, and that making systems harder to test will never lead to higher-quality IT systems.

As well as being difficult to test properly, software can break very easily. Robert Charette from the United States vividly illustrates the problem:

> All IT systems are intrinsically fragile. In a large brick building, you'd have to remove hundreds of strategically placed bricks to make a wall collapse. But in ... 1991, a portion of AT&T's telephone network [American Telephone and Telegraph] went out, leaving 12 million subscribers without service, all because of a single mistyped character in one line of code.

A further danger is the allure of what computers can theoretically do and that some people, understanding the scope of what might be possible, will want to use it. Whether 'ambition' is a good thing or not depends on context. While people might be surprised to meet an ambitious monk – or, at least, one who was ambitious to advance his own material wealth and power – it is still true that by and large the phrase 'lack of ambition' is pejorative; for example, there is still sadly a minority of teachers who have a lack of ambition for the children in their care, telling them that they 'can't' rather than that they 'can'. In most spheres of human activity a degree of healthy ambition for your family and friends, or for your own career, is considered normal. And so in developing an IT project that aims to transform how an organisation goes about its business, one easily sees how 'lack of ambition' could be viewed negatively, and how software writers and IT managers – however deep their understanding of the dangers of taking on too much at once – might wish to avoid being labelled as 'unambitious'. The more one under-stands computing power, the more one sees what is possible; the greater the gap in one's mind between what is possible and what is actually achieved; and the greater the frustration, since the enormous untapped potential is still there. Yale University's David Gelernter expresses his exasperation that 'we are a nation of Ferrari owners with kinked fuel lines'. Of course, Gelernter is right. Even software that has been successfully installed is often underused. Fifty per cent of software sold is not used at all.

Given what we know about software, humility is needed. We know that people tend to forget the constraints around soft-ware because such constraints are abstract and invisible; that people are inclined to flex software too much just because it is possible to flex it; that customers may not be able to describe accurately how their business works, even if they think that they can; that complexity is inherent in developing software but can also interfere and get in the way; that increased processing power can make things worse; that there is inherent uncer-tainty in working out exactly what is required; that there are inherent difficulties because in real life there are necessarily an unbounded number of assumptions; that there is a mathemati-cal impossibility of perfect testing in any human timescale; that software is anyway rather fragile; and that as a result of all this we know that all complex IT systems have a propensity to fail.

All this would, one might think, encourage some humility. It would be prudent and responsible to assume and even build in the likelihood of failure. These inherent features of software should have serious implications for how software is written. As Les Hatton from the Royal Academy of Engineering and British Computer Society group put it:

> There are two engineering obligations with software ... first of all, you design the system in such a way that failure has a minimum effect on the user, and secondly you inject enough into the design to be able to diagnose why it fails so you can correct the failure and incrementally improve the design.

If such precautions are taken, it is perfectly possible for software to fail without the project as a whole being jeopardised.

However, software projects are undertaken by people. And humility is not the most widespread human characteristic. As the Royal Academy of Engineering and British Computer Society group noted, many projects are undertaken on the assumption that the software will be, or can be made to be, 'perfect'. This time it will be different. We know what we are doing, unlike those other people. And so on. This is why an organisation's culture – so often considered to be at the fluffier end of management-speak – is such an important factor in delivering a successful IT project. If an organisation values openness and honest communication it is more likely to correct its mistakes quickly. But in organisations where the culture is driven by arrogance and fear, people keep their heads down when things go wrong and plough on regardless. Mistakes are not corrected and lessons are not learned. To recall from our earlier chapters, there were clear warnings that the web-based Individual Learning Account model was wide open to abuse by fraudulent 'trainers', but no one in the Department for Education would listen until eventually the police were called in after hundreds of millions of pounds had already been spent and the fraud had become too obvious too ignore. The new on-line recruiting process for junior doctors was the subject of widespread concern, but warnings were ignored by officials and ministers from the Department of

Health until there was an eruption later described as 'the biggest crisis within the medical profession in a generation'. In the case of the Rural Payments Agency, officials warned that it would be 'madness' to choose the notorious dynamic hybrid model for calculating farm payments and that if the agency went down that route it would be 'a nightmare', but such warnings were again ignored. In the NHS IT programme, the project profile model containing the very high-risk scoring was removed from the published version of 'Delivering 21st Century IT Support for the NHS' so that the likely costs and true risks were concealed from the outset. Indeed, as Robert Charette puts it, 'if there's a theme running through the tortuous history of bad software, it's a failure to confront reality'.

Technical problems usually have technical solutions but the biggest problems with major IT projects are generally not technical. They are human. As Ian Watmore, a former UK boss of Accenture who became a Whitehall mandarin, told MPs on the Public Accounts Committee:

> It is very rare that the technology is the problem in these so-called IT problems. It is nearly always the case that either the project management has been done incorrectly or the policy ambition was too ambitious. The reason why IT is the place where it gets found out is because that is the place where all the codification of what has been decided finally comes to fruition, and machines are pretty bad at handling ambiguity.

When Mark Todd, quoted at the beginning of this chapter, said 'Forget about the technology', he was really saying: 'Concentrate on the human side and get that right first.' Todd, an MP for thirteen years who served on the PAC, worked as an IT project manager before his career in politics. In a Commons debate on IT projects in the welfare system he told MPs:

> IT project managers are strange people, and they are not comfortable to deal with because they are extremely

detail-oriented if they are doing their job properly. They are highly protective of the discipline of the project, and will constantly remind people who attempt to depart from it of the consequences. It is therefore not easy to deal with a robust project manager, but their approach is valuable, because it is important to resist the desire for change while development is under way. That requires tremendous restraint. We all recognise that human beings make errors, and in the process of designing a major system, people may leave something out or fail to spot something else of importance ... Something is bound to be missed. The project manager's task is to say, 'I am sorry, we will not change this now. It will be changed in a properly planned process in future. The first task is to deliver a stable system that functions according to the original spec.'

Richard Feynman identified one solution in his appendix to the space shuttle report: 'There are perpetual requests for changes as new payloads and new demands and modifications are suggested by the users. Changes are expensive because they require extensive testing. The proper way to save money is to curtail the number of requested changes, not the quality of testing for each.' Many of the senior managers who commission projects fail to understand this, leading to ludicrous numbers of requests for changes. This very significantly increases the risks of ultimate failure and provides suppliers with frequent opportunities to inflate their bills.

The traditional approach to software development is often known as 'waterfall' development: that is, you plan, build, test, review and then deploy, in a relentless cascade. But some IT industry players regard this practice as the chief problem. Tara Hamilton-Whitaker, an expert in digital product development, highlighted the drawbacks on her blog, Agile101:

You don't realise any value until the end of the project ... you leave the testing until the end ... you don't seek approval from the stakeholders until late in the day – their requirements might have changed; you're heavily reliant upon a plan, which you can/will often follow to the detriment of the end result; and you're heavily reliant upon a project manager.

A rather different answer which has emerged in the last ten to fifteen years has been what are called 'Agile Systems', perhaps best described as a philosophical movement in action within the software industry. Its proponents support a 'Manifesto for Agile Software Development' in which they state: 'We are uncovering better ways of developing software by doing it and helping others do it.' Agile is a rather different approach to the conventional 'specify-to-the-Nth-degree' method outlined above and is essentially at odds with it. While apostles of Agile will happily acknowledge the value of following a plan, they have, in the words of the manifesto, 'come to value individuals and interactions over processes and tools, working software over comprehensive documentation, customer collaboration over contract negotiation, and responding to change over following a plan'. The Agile approach contains important insights, particularly in its emphasis on 'working software' as the only really worthwhile criterion of progress. Agile stresses the need to make mistakes early and on a small scale, and to 'deliver early and deliver often'. Remember the £1.5 million Essex Police contract with GEC-Marconi, where after two years not a single line of program code had been written? Using a truly Agile approach, this would not have happened. There is little doubt that Agile has significant possibilities and also growing influence within the software industry, or that it is potentially very threatening to larger, well-established IT suppliers. As Steve Baker, an MP who was formerly an IT entrepreneur, put it: 'Agile systems are what enabled me to run rings around much bigger firms.' Perhaps unsurprisingly, then, one finds controversy and vested interests aplenty when encountering discussion over the appropriate uses of Agile systems, or even whether a project is truly Agile or not. The Department for Work and Pensions has claimed that it is using Agile principles to develop its new Universal Credit – a major reform to the benefits system – but the Major Projects Authority has called the project's Agile credentials 'unproven' and there are concerns from insiders that the project is too large and involves too many separate organisations to be justly called Agile. As *Computer Weekly* mischievously summarised it: 'The Universal Credit project is agile, but not as we know it.'

There is a danger of overstating these issues: 'fast', 'nimble', 'people-focused' and 'responsive' all sound like a Good Thing from the point of view of taxpayers, but no one is suggesting that the need for rigour and consistency has disappeared. As Steve Baker observes: 'You do need specifications and you need to control the way you deliver, but get going and deliver. No one ever won an award for a specification.'

At the heart of any answer to how to improve things must be a deep understanding of what is being done in an IT project and why, and what this implies for the involvement of the customer. Colin Saunders, the IT director of Warburtons, the largest independently owned bakery business in the UK, put this point bluntly when he said: 'There is no such thing as an IT project.' He means that successful projects are about getting benefits and that to do that requires 'ownership' of the project by the business rather than abdicating responsibility and expecting the IT department to sort everything out. The onus for achieving improvement and realising the benefits of an IT investment lie with the business.

Human failure is intrinsic. The situation is then made even worse in government by certain features that are peculiar to the public sector. There is no straightforward answer that will always work but there are many things one can do which will minimise the risks of failure. One of the most insightful observations in the Royal Academy of Engineering and British Computer Society study came from a participant who said 'I always value the ability to walk away from an order or project even though it is very important. If you have a client who is really not prepared to give the leadership, you are better off not taking the business.'

Robert Charette issues a deeply salutary warni̇ ~~244~~
IT projects cost many tens of billions each year; th
the future of many organisations and the people
such failures are mostly predictable and avoidable,
also unprejudiced, happening in every country, to ev type
of organisation, including governments, companies large and
small, and charities, without regard to status or reputation;
most organisations don't see preventing failure as an urgent
matter, even though this view could harm or even destroy them;
software failure can stunt economic growth and quality of life;
and it can imperil national security. As our society comes to rely
on IT systems that are ever larger, more integrated and more
expensive, he warns us that the cost of failure may become
disastrously high: 'Like electricity, water, transportation and
other critical parts of our infrastructure, IT is fast becoming
intrinsic to our daily existence. In a few decades, a large-scale IT
failure will become more than just an expensive inconvenience:
it will put our way of life at risk.' And this is before one considers the sobering fact that cyber warfare is increasingly viewed
as an essential part of the military and strategic landscape and
that, in future, hostile attacks on critical infrastructure may be
better made in cyberspace than by dropping bombs.

The huge risks from poor IT are increasingly understood
in government – and there are some who are determined
to do something about it. In 2011, the coalition set up the
Government Digital Service (GDS) to try to rethink the way
that taxpayers' money has been used to buy IT services and
to see if it could be done more cheaply by more companies;
effectively to break the 'oligopoly' of the twelve big vertically
integrated IT services companies – Capgemini, Accenture and
others – which have supplied the vast majority of the government's IT services for years. By early 2013, the unit had been
able to notch up a number of early wins. It had migrated most
departmental websites onto a single 'gov.uk' internet address
for little more than it costs to run a single large IT procurement
process in Whitehall. It was also digitising online transactional

services, such as a more efficient way to pay for a driving licence, or request a student loan, or apply for an enduring power of attorney.

The GDS's offices are deliberately based away from Whitehall in Holborn, central London. And what it is seeking to do is revolutionary. Mike Bracken, appointed from outside government to run the GDS, believes Whitehall has historically gone about ordering its computer systems in the wrong way. Typically, two years was spent thinking up a policy, working out how it might be put into practice, hiring an IT supplier to deliver it on a long-term contract and then launching the new project onto an unsuspecting and often unwilling public.

In explaining a poorly performing transaction or service, the answer was routinely: 'The department needs are different', but as Bracken noted on his own blog, charting the first eighteen months of his time in government, 'how the needs of a department or an agency can so often trump the needs of the users of public services is beyond me'. Bracken argued that 'delivery is too often the poor relation to policy', pointing to a 2009 Institute for Government report which found that nearly 20,000 civil servants were employed in 'policy delivery' with each government department producing 171 policy or strategy documents on average each year. Bracken quotes one candid civil servant: 'The strategy was flawless but I couldn't get anything done.'

Instead, his unit deploys small teams of a dozen software engineers to research and examine a particular government transaction during a twelve-week 'discovery process'. The teams then run working prototypes known as 'Alpha' tests with users and then, if they get more cash and the green light, more formal 'Beta' tests for several months, before quietly allowing people to use it. There is no big launch, no major hard deadline with its associated risk of delay, overruns and furious end users.

Part of the battle has been to convince people that the government is not as big and unwieldy as they think it is. Bracken had been able to download the entire electronic file containing the COINS database – Whitehall's 'bought ledger' – onto a mobile phone for ease of access. In 2012, central government offered citizens 672 different types of transaction, ranging from the paying of stamp duty during the purchase of a home to obtaining a licence to bury someone at sea. Judged in this way, Bracken told us that departments are 'about the size of an average dating site, they are not that big'. He added: 'It is a very simple point – the government usually services its own departmental and ministerial needs, and we have focused relentlessly on users.' Keeping it small, flexible and manageable meant that big cost overruns were less likely: 'Frankly if something isn't looking like it is going to shape up after three months it is probably going to fail. A three-month failure with a small amount of people and money in the landscape of large IT failures is a rounding error.'

It is probably no accident that this sounds rather like Google, whose co-founder Sergey Brin is quoted in David Vise's book *The Google Story*: 'We run Google a little bit like a university ... we do lots of stuff. The only way you are going to have success is to have lots of failures first.' But the success of Google was to grow the business away from a garage to a multi-billion-pound business. Can the same happen in government? What if people like Bracken were to move on? Or if a very supportive minister like Francis Maude, who has oversight of GDS, were reshuffled?

GDS is potentially an excellent exemplar of how things should be done, but success is by no means guaranteed. The traditional Whitehall departmental fiefdoms have lasted for so long because that is where the accountability sits – and because they control most of the money. And such an approach is scarcely in the interests of the big integrated IT firms, who are very good at persuading themselves – and governments – that what they offer is unique, especially whenever the word 'security' is mentioned. One cannot expect that they will go quietly. Indeed, there are many in government departments who would prefer keeping things as they are. The computer journalist Tony Collins told us:

GDS has made a difference in terms of the attitude to big projects but in terms of savings it is working on the margins. They have made steps towards it with the 'Cloud' but tackling the big procurements, where the tens of billions of pounds are, has not really happened yet. GDS is setting the example. It knows what needs to be done. And at least in theory it has the power to do it. But it can't actually force through the changes because it is not responsible for any failures. The big reforms and standardisation of government administrative processes haven't happened yet.

Even Bracken conceded it will be a long haul before the procurement culture in government is changed. Only time will tell if he and his team are proved right. Our own view is that at least in the UK public sector, *no one* – minister, civil servant, agency chief or local government official – should be allowed anywhere near the spending of public money for IT without a basic understanding of these issues. It is these people who are working on behalf of British taxpayers and spending our money, sometimes in ignorance of the consequences of what they are doing. It is their actions, omissions, decisions and methods of management that have to a considerable extent led to the disastrous failures we have seen. And it is to them that we now turn.

14

WOULD THESE POLICIES WORK BETTER IF KEPT AWAY FROM POLITICIANS?

It is amazing what you can accomplish if you do not care who gets the credit.
Harry S. Truman

Which MP goes into public life hoping bravely to continue the *status quo*? Surely, the purpose of entering public life is to improve things, to change what is wrong, and to make the world a better place. And when an MP becomes a minister, the opportunity finally arrives to put policy into action. So why is it that despite all the best efforts of ministers, the word 'cock-up' runs through the cases we have examined in this book like the lettering through a stick of Blackpool rock? It is not just in the 'ambitious' projects where things go wrong, but also in the unexciting ones – what Kate Jenkins, the former senior Whitehall official whom we cited in the Introduction to this book, calls 'the absolute basics' – where it really ought to be possible to make things work without too much difficulty: issuing passports when they are needed; making student loans on time; counting money before handing it out so that it only gets allocated once; introducing an adult training scheme in which you know something about the trainers before you give them the money. Straightforward matters like these have caused the most intractable difficulties. We can safely assume no one *wants* things to turn out badly – and it would certainly be better for all concerned if there were fewer cock-ups. Ministers are surrounded by impatient and disillusioned voters and naturally want their plans to show quick results, but would things work better if ministers just stopped interfering? We need to start by asking ourselves: what are ministers for? This is sometimes misunderstood, not least because different ministers have varying preferences and skills and can take very different approaches to how they do the job. Yet fundamentally, the role of ministers in a government department is to provide *temporary, political leadership*. Each part of this description is important, and we should examine each in turn.

Ministers are temporary

The first point about ministers is that they are *temporary*. Occasionally a minister occupies the same post for a whole parliament, but far more often he or she will be moved much more quickly. Under the last Labour government there were four Health Secretaries in four years, six Education Secretaries in six years, and eight Work and Pensions Secretaries in eight years. There were five Home Secretaries in less than five years and five Transport Secretaries in three years. And while the post of Defence Secretary had one occupant for five and a half years, this was followed by four Defence Secretaries in three years. Steve Bundred, a local government expert and former head of the Audit Commission, observed in the *Financial Times* that in the six years he had served at the Audit Commission there had been five Cabinet ministers with responsibility for local government. And this isn't a new problem. There were seven ministers of health from 1951 to 1961, seven Education Secretaries from 1964 to 1974 and eight Transport Secretaries from 1979 to 1989. There were five Home Secretaries between 1822 and 1828. On average, ministers hold a job for 1.7 years before being moved on or out. The high level of turnover of ministers is simply a feature of the British system of government.

High ministerial turnover may be a fact of life but it can hardly help good government. Indeed, it has serious and often underrated consequences for the government's operations. Steve Bundred observed that 'in other walks of life a degree of continuity is thought to be not merely desirable but essential', adding that a local authority that had five leaders or chief executives in six years would be worrying those selfsame ministers, and might even find itself on the receiving end of a corporate governance inspection. In a speech in 2008 at the London School of Economics one long-serving former Whitehall mandarin, Sir Richard Mottram, pointed out that the Department for Work and Pensions – where he had been Permanent Secretary – was an employment and financial services organisation of world scale, that over the preceding six years there had been six secretaries of state, and that if it were a regulated financial institution this scale of turnover would surely have attracted the regulator's attention. Yet the regulators never come knocking. There aren't any. While Mottram accepted that ministers move for a variety of reasons, including the impact of 'events', he added that 'the scale of turnover and its impact may be insufficiently appreciated'. Bundred believes that the churn of public offices is probably getting in the way of transformational change in public services, writing:

> This is an issue about the practice of our government that merits more attention. New ministers will always want to promote new initiatives. But policy changes need to follow through if they are to stick. The devil is often in the detail, and ministers need to stay close, for an extended period. How do you learn if you move out and on? If ministers are never around long enough to witness the consequences of their decisions they are unlikely to take the point from either their successes or their mistakes.

Participants can recognise the weakness in the system. Gillian Shephard, now a peer, who held several Cabinet posts in John Major's governments, told the Public Administration Select Committee: 'If you do shift people about every year then you risk governing not very well because you are not getting the best either out of the skills of a minister who wants to make a permanent impact, or indeed out of the Civil Service.' Nick Raynsford, a minister for eight years under Tony Blair, argued in the same inquiry – while acknowledging that political considerations must play a role in appointments – that 'there is not a proper focus on the management aspects and the running of existing departmental programmes when people are appointed'. He added: 'Looking at the constant chopping and changing, with people being moved at, literally, annual intervals ... the expectation that has now grown is that the sign of success as a minister is being moved onwards and upwards quickly.' Raynsford argued that this had a very damaging impact on the process of carrying forward programmes which, by their very nature, take several years to implement. Given that ministers only have eighteen months or so to prove their worth, the pressure is on almost immediately to make a difference now. As Raynsford put it:

> Inevitably, a new minister coming in is going to look at 'What new can we do to make an impact?' because they have their reputation. If there is a culture where they are assumed to have to make their mark within a year or two in order to move on and up, they are going to want to do something quickly. The last thing they are going to want to do is to focus on maintaining a programme that is going to take ten years to produce results when they will not be there to get the benefit and the praise. That, I think, is an insidious culture.

And surely one which is likely to produce sub-optimal results. Any human resources professional would have some questions to answer if senior staff at director level were moved around companies with such frequency.

Ministers are political
This brings us to the second point about ministers, which is that they are *political*. As Gillian Shephard argued, 'the political process and the whole system of reshuffling and preferment and reward for loyalty ... is an HR-free zone. It just is. You cannot be surprised if it does not always work because there are other considerations.' And it is plain enough why this is the case. The Prime Minister has to manage his ministerial and parliamentary

colleagues and retain their support. There will be an expectation that those who have done well will be promoted. Some political balance is needed between different wings of the party so that colleagues feel their views are represented inside government. Sometimes a minister will be forced to resign unexpectedly due to a scandal, or to pay the price of some political failure. Occasionally a duff minister just needs to be weeded out. Sometimes a minister may fail to carry a policy and yet be difficult to sack altogether – for political or personal reasons – and so he or she is moved elsewhere in government. There is also a need to ensure that different regions of the country have some representation in the government. These are all powerful drivers which must influence how ministers are appointed. A coalition government, of course, just complicates the whole balancing act even further. If one adds to this mix the inevitable sense that a 'fresh start' is needed once in a while to improve public perceptions, it is hardly surprising that the turnover is so high. As Shephard put it: 'The political process militates against ideal management.' If the need for a reshuffle arises – for whatever reasons – then political consid-erations will usually trump all others including management, continuity, knowledge, finishing a job and so on. And this is not about to change. It is simply part of politics.

Nor should one be surprised if new ministers seek to make an impact quickly. As Gillian Shephard put it vividly:

> When a new minister takes charge of a piece of department or a new Secretary of State comes in, basically testosterone takes over. I am sorry to put it this way but it is a reality that people come in and say, 'What am I going to do to make my name?' They are entranced to have the opportunity for legislation. It is part of the political process. It is no good saying it should not be like that; it is like that and nothing is going to change the human nature of people engaged in the political process. Senior civil servants ... really should understand that and not be surprised at what they have got caught up in. I would have said that most permanent secretaries should be very clear about that.

It is not merely that a new minister of a different political party, appointed following an election, will have different priorities from his or her predecessor and expect to see those priorities reflected in the department's policies. In truth there is usually a change of emphasis every time the personality at the top changes, and if a minister who is taking a close interest in a particular project is replaced by a minister who is interested in other things, one should not be surprised when the project falls down the list of priorities for the department. And, as with so much else, the fact that ministers will always behave like ministers is not a new problem. Early on in his time as a Cabinet minister after the 1964 Labour election victory, Dick Crossman recorded in his diary what he was beginning to discover about the life of a minister, and the extent to which the job was about public relations and the fight inside the Cabinet for a share of legislation and publicity. A minister needed to sell himself with 'announcements and pronouncements' that gave a sense that he was doing something, even though no new policy was being made. 'And so I see around me in Cabinet all my colleagues … putting up papers in Cabinet committees which really say nothing but which are intended to get the minister on the map.'

In some cases the temptation for a minister to do something just to get media attention may prove irresistible, and this can be seriously disruptive to the work of the department. The former Home Secretary Michael Howard, in defending the role of civil servants while criticising the excesses of the Blair administration, argued that if such disruption occurs it is simply because civil servants are loyally doing what ministers have asked them to do, even if those ministers are misguided:

> I believe that civil servants respond to what they believe to be ministers' priorities, and I am afraid … that if civil servants believe that ministers' priorities are eye-catching initiatives with which they can be personally associated, or they capture tomorrow's headlines, they will concentrate on delivering those ministerial priorities, but it will be at the expense of the grind of

government and the often boring business of making sure that delivery takes place and things get done.

Yet even if one succeeds in avoiding gimmicks created mainly to attract headlines, the need to get re-elected remains ever present. As Sir Richard Mottram put it: 'The issue is how we balance and reconcile the culture and processes of political competition with the needs of management of a large organisation.'

Ministers are leaders, not managers – or are they?

This leads us to the third point about ministers, which is that their primary role is *leadership*, not management or administration. John Reid was very clear about this when he took over as Home Secretary following the exposure of the foreign prisoners scandal and famously declared the Home Office 'not fit for purpose'. He defined his role to MPs on the home affairs select committee as more of a chairman than a chief executive, and certainly not as a hands-on chief operating officer: 'It is not my job to manage this department – it is my job to lead this department, to set a policy, to give the leadership, to give the strategic direction; managers are there to micro-manage it and, as they expect competence from me, I expect competence from them.' And one should not necessarily expect ministers to become general managers of the departments they lead. Most MPs have not run large organisations before entering Parliament and would be ill equipped to take on the overall task of managing a large department of state, with a budget of many billions of pounds, millions of customers, thousands of employees, hundreds of buildings, a panoply of legal obligations and rights, IT systems and the rest. Serving as an MP provides some useful background but by itself it does not offer sufficient insight into the processes of government. As Reid's predecessor as Home Secretary, Charles Clarke, put it:

It is very striking that there is a gulf between those people who

are in government and those who are not, in terms of both access
to an enormous range of different connections and activities and
understanding of what goes on in government. A relatively small
number of Members of Parliament, before going into government, have any idea at all of what it is to be in government.

Kate Jenkins was equally blunt: 'Until you have actually sat at
a minister's desk in a large department and begin to get some
sense of the scale of what is going on, it is very difficult to believe
how different being in government is from being in politics.'
And short of restricting eligibility to become a parliamentary
candidate to those who have run large organisations – which
would be wholly undesirable as well as impractical – this is not
about to change. It is also the case, as one Permanent Secretary
explained, that 'most ministers are uninterested in running
departments; even those that think they run them, in reality
don't – they simply don't have the time'.

So are the civil servants running government departments?
The answer to this question is not as straightforward as one
might think. In her book *Politicians and Public Services*, Kate
Jenkins describes interviews – undertaken for the Next Steps
report that led to the creation of executive agencies – which
uncovered widely differing views from both civil servants and
ministers about who actually ran departments. Speaking about
their ministers, some civil servants told the report's authors
'He leaves me to get on with running the department', while
others reported 'I can't do anything without his meddling, he
thinks he runs the place'. In the discussion with ministers about
their civil servants there was a similar range of views, with
replies ranging from 'Oh, I leave all that to X, it's his job' to
'I can't take my eye off X for a minute. He has no idea how
to run anything.' One minister described permanent secretaries as 'advisers, not managers – they have no experience of
managing'. Most worrying were the departments where both
permanent secretaries and ministers had left the management
to the other – this was found to be the case in at least two major

departments and several smaller ones. Jenkins described how she found

> really quite alarming things about the way in which departments were being managed. On a number of occasions I talked both to the secretaries of state and to permanent secretaries running departments, and on a number of occasions, they said in a rather engaging way 'oh, I don't deal with management. He does it'. But when they both said it in the same department, we became extremely concerned.

The Next Steps report was completed over twenty years ago but the confusion continues. While we were writing this book, one Cabinet minister faced with appointing a new Permanent Secretary told us that his chief consideration had been to find 'a technocrat, rather than someone who thinks they will run the department'. Yet some ministers will indeed expect the Permanent Secretary to run the department even if, like Gillian Shephard, they are very proactive themselves. Shephard was very clear what she looked for:

> What I demanded from the Permanent Secretary was a very good hands-on knowledge of how it worked. It is also true to say that not all permanent secretaries are interested in how things work. You can come across those who are much more interested in the political process. They are the most irritating because they think they are the politicians, so they will say, 'I think, Secretary of State, a really very positive way of doing that would be this' and they practise their amateur politics on you. This is not what I look for in a Permanent Secretary and, indeed, would not tolerate it.

Even if a minister leaves the management job to the civil servants, on the basis that they are the full-time experts, he or she will be making a presumption that those civil servants are capable of it – or interested. And this may be optimistic.

Although there has been considerable change in recent decades, the culture of the civil service has traditionally disdained management as a rather low activity compared with the senior official's 'real job' of providing ministers with policy advice. Michael Heseltine, now in the House of Lords, had already founded and run a successful business when he first entered the Cabinet as Secretary of State for the Environment. He took a huge personal interest in management issues and had the skills and background to intervene effectively. In his autobiography, *Life in the Jungle*, he perfectly illustrated the culture which then prevailed in the higher reaches of the civil service, recalling an early conversation with his Permanent Secretary about the management of the department: 'I asked John Garlick what management information he received on his desk every Monday morning to check whether the department was on track to meet its objectives. On hearing the reply "None", at least I knew where we stood.' As Heseltine explained: 'I wanted to know exactly what the department was doing, who had authorised what objectives, how the objectives met the priorities of the new government and so on.'

Accordingly, Heseltine developed a management information system for ministers – 'MINIS' – so that he could keep track of what the department was doing. The major discipline which drove the 'MINIS' process forward was Heseltine's own personal involvement as Secretary of State but, as he records, his approach was not greeted with universal acclaim. 'One of the most difficult meetings was with an under-secretary ... He explained that in large parts of his command he had no idea what people did and the concept of output measurement had never played a part in his career. I explained that it would from that moment on.'

So there is deep ambiguity at the heart of departments about who is actually running the show. This matters, particularly if things go wrong. It is the minister who has to explain to Parliament and to the public why things aren't working as they should do, not civil servants. It is the minister whose head may be on the chopping block. Ministers may be very reliant on their civil servants to run the department but it does not stop ministers being drawn into the detail of what is happening. John Reid's view that 'it is not my job to manage this department' is not the only one ministers take. In Gillian Shephard's book, *Shephard's Watch*, she writes: 'What is the job of being a minister? Being a minister involves leadership – political, of course, but also managerial – of a large organisation, the department. It therefore involves administration, team leadership, time management, priority identification, meetings, decision and policy-making.'

But where is the boundary line between what ministers do and what civil servants do to run the departments? To what extent should ministers be seen as managers of departments? Quite plainly, regardless of who is Secretary of State for Work and Pensions, the unemployed will still need their out-of-work benefits paid on time and OAPs will still need their pensions. No matter who is Defence Secretary, soldiers will still need their wages. Should the minister have to get involved in every single aspect of the running of the department? Is that not what civil servants are there for? As Shephard told the Public Administration Committee:

> One has to be realistic and to understand that ministers bring different skills to their jobs and not all their skills will have been honed on running large organisations before they become ministers. At the very least they should satisfy themselves that parts of the department are being run properly by examining what is being done, by looking at objectives to see if they are being realised.

Call it micro-management or not, but Shephard said this might even include 'testing help lines to see if there is anybody on the other end' and she was quite emphatic that this type of behaviour by ministers was required:

> You really do have to. The reason you have to is that you are

the one who is accountable. You are the one at the despatch box when somebody says the whole issue is not working. It is you. It is not your Permanent Secretary. It is not anyone else. You are accountable to Parliament, to the electorate, to the public to see to it that it is right.

Shephard acknowledged that she wanted to know things in more detail than other people in her position:

I know I did. When one chatted with colleagues who had also then gone into the Cabinet, saying, 'I have 395 Jobcentres and they are all painted blue' they would look at me as if I were mad. You work according to your own abilities and your own needs and I just felt voracious for information because I felt accountable.

Ministers are responsible

This brings us to what has been the core theme in the debate about ministers and civil servants for decades – the whole issue of ministerial responsibility. Ministers are *responsible* for what happens in their departments. So say all the textbooks on the British constitution, and this is quite simply because of the law. A minister is empowered by law to act in specific ways in particular situations, to hold defined responsibilities and to fulfil precise obligations, due to the powers accumulated through decades of legislation. The legal authority that civil servants wield is the authority of the minister. When civil servants act they are acting on behalf of the minister. Civil servants have no authority of their own – except in very limited cases such as planning inspectors, who are specifically empowered by law to decide certain planning appeals, and tax commissioners, who have statutory powers to assess tax liabilities. So while a minister's job is to set the strategic direction of policy in a department, he or she is also responsible for everything that happens in the department, and is potentially required to answer in Parliament for everything that happens.

It is hard to overstate the importance of this fact for the shape of our political arrangements. It prompts an inevitable concern by any minister who may have to answer in Parliament to know what is being done and, if it is inadequate, to take action to correct the situation. There is a tremendous incentive for ministers to get involved in – or, if you will, to interfere in – the day-to-day management of the work of the department. Some officials take the view that the role of ministers should be 'high level' and far removed from operations. In giving evidence to MPs on the Public Administration Committee, Sir Nick Montagu, former chairman of the Inland Revenue, put the traditional case: 'Ministers set the parameters of policy and permanent secretaries manage and lead departments to implement that policy in the widest sense.' But another witness in the same inquiry, Sir Michael Quinlan, a former Permanent Secretary at the Ministry of Defence, saw things rather differently:

> I do not believe you can, or should attempt to, differentiate ... between policy and administration or organisation, in the sense that one is the minister's business and the other is the Permanent Secretary's. It may be that a particular minister – and, if I may say so, they come in all sorts of shapes and sizes, with different interests, different capabilities – wants to leave administration to the Permanent Secretary; it is still the minister's responsibility. For example, when I was away from the Ministry of Defence, Mr Heseltine did very extensive things ... to the organisation and the administration of the department. It would have been wholly inappropriate for a Permanent Secretary at the time to say, 'Sorry, Secretary of State, that's not your business, it's mine'. *All of it* is the minister's business [our emphasis].

Quinlan underlined his point in a memo sent to the committee afterwards:

> I have to say that I dissent from Sir Nicholas Montagu's view that (as seems clearly implied by his words) Ministers and Permanent

Secretaries have in some sense parallel responsibilities. The Permanent Secretary's responsibilities run to the Minister and are included within his/hers; they do not run separately, aside from the special category of Accounting Officer responsibilities. And these latter are, I believe, narrower than Sir Nicholas conveys; they are not 'for the running of the Department'.

Quinlan added forcefully:

I think it incorrect, unrealistic and undesirable to suppose that Ministers 'should not [in the sense of ought not] get involved in the actual running of Departments', though no doubt for most of the time Ministers may well, and wisely, rely very heavily on their Permanent Secretaries in matters of administration and organisation and concentrate their own energies elsewhere.

The minister, then – even if he or she goes in for some heavy delegation – is ultimately responsible for *running* the department as well as for setting the strategy.

And for many decades, some commentators have said that this is a big problem. It is perfectly obvious that a minister in charge of, say, the Department for Work and Pensions, with 99,000 employees, cannot possibly know every single thing that is going on or be personally to blame for every mistake that occurs. The doctrine of ministerial responsibility supposedly takes account of this; as long ago as 1954 a statement defining ministerial responsibilities by the Home Secretary, David Maxwell Fyfe, made it clear that a minister is not obliged to defend action of which he did not know, or of which he disapproves – but nonetheless the impetus towards greater involvement by ministers in the details of departmental work seems unavoidable. In his magisterial book *Whitehall*, the constitutional expert Peter Hennessy drew attention to one particular submission to the Fulton Inquiry on reforming the civil service in 1966. William Ryrie, an assistant secretary in the Treasury, pinpointed the issue:

A great deal of the cumbersomeness and inefficiency of government can still be traced to the doctrine of a minister's responsibility for all the detailed operations of his department and, in many cases, subordinate organs; and the right of Members of Parliament to enquire into them. It is not just that answering Parliamentary Questions takes up much of the time of the civil service: the possibility of the Parliamentary Question or debate hangs over all public departments as an inhibitor, curbing initiative and stifling the will to take responsibility. Far too many issues are referred to the top not because they are intrinsically important but because they could be brought up in a political encounter in Parliament. A large proportion of the time of ministers is taken up in delving into small issues for this reason, or guarding against this danger. Consequently far too little time and energy is given to the important work of framing basic and long-term policy objectives.

And in more recent years, too, the doctrine of ministerial responsibility has come under attack, with think tanks on both the right and the left identifying it as a fundamental obstacle to improving how government works. Centre-right think tanks such as Reform, which published Rupert Darwall's 'The Reluctant Managers', and the centre-left Institute for Public Policy Research (IPPR), which published 'Whitehall's Black Box' by Guy Lodge and Ben Rogers, each suggest that sorting out a new definition of ministerial responsibility is essential for securing better performance. In 'The Reluctant Managers', Rupert Darwall produced a searing critique of the civil service, describing it as a 'self-selecting' and 'in-bred' system with a 'bias against performance improvement', which promotes people who are 'more comfortable making suggestions than taking responsibility'. Darwall's central charge is that Whitehall is unmanaged; that if you ask the question 'Who manages?' the answer is certainly not ministers, but that neither is it permanent secretaries, who, as Darwall writes, 'lack the fundamental attribute required of a manager – delegated authority for which they are personally accountable'. The current system, says Darwall, produces 'risk-averse patterns of behaviour' that put key objectives of any government beyond reach. Darwall identifies the doctrine of ministerial responsibility as the problem, concluding: 'The pre-requisite for improved performance is to clarify the relationship between ministers and civil servants to define who is responsible for what.' In 'Whitehall's Black Box', Lodge and Rogers also argue that the doctrine impairs Whitehall's operational effectiveness: 'Because decisions drift upwards to the ministers, very often civil servants look to them to lead on operational decisions, but ministers rarely have the time, interest or aptitude for public management. The result is that responsibility for operations falls between the cracks.' As one senior official told Lodge and Rogers:

> You have to wonder where the real accountability is, by which I mean some effective assessment of achievements and failures. This is the accountability that matters and this is what is really missing. The major difficulty in Whitehall is that as soon as you start trying to make civil servants more accountable you very quickly bump into ministers. A major problem in Britain is that we do not have a coherent account of the boundary line between ministers and officials.

Lodge and Rogers argue that 'the priority for Whitehall must now be to reform the way it is governed'. They suggest that ministers should no longer be responsible for day-to-day operations, for which greater responsibility should be given to civil servants, while clarifying the prerogatives and duties of ministers. The key to reform, on this view, lies in ensuring that those at the top of the service 'have clearly defined roles and responsibilities, and the resources to ensure that they can exercise them'. Another Reform paper, 'Fit for Purpose', also suggested abolishing the existing doctrine of ministerial responsibility: 'Ministers should be responsible for the strategic direction of policy and its communication. Officials should be personally responsible for the construction of policy and the use of resources.' In addition, the paper argued that ministers 'should be criticised when they cannot conceptualise and tackle entrenched social problems, not when their departments make individual errors'.

There is an obvious flaw here. The members of the public who elect governments will tend to decide for themselves who to blame when things go wrong, especially if – to take just one example from an earlier chapter – they missed a holiday because the Passport Office couldn't issue a passport on time. And if the public can't decide who to blame, there will usually be someone on hand to remind them. Remember the formidable Ann Widdecombe, as shadow Home Secretary, arriving outside the Passport Office to lend support to customers queuing in the rain, surrounded by television cameras, with worried officials handing out umbrellas and luncheon vouchers until the owner of Harrods, Mohammed Al Fayed, turned up with refreshments from the Harrods food hall? Widdecombe then denounced the government in the Commons, where the Home Secretary, Jack Straw, was forced to make a statement. In that particular case, the passport agency admitted it had been caught unawares by new regulations requiring children under the age of sixteen to get a passport of their own. But just imagine the reaction if the Home Secretary had responded by saying: 'This is nothing to do with me but is due to what *The Times* newspaper has called "managerial incompetence of the highest order".'

There is also a deeper problem. The analysis begs a fundamental question: is it actually possible to draw a sensible line between 'policy' on the one hand and 'operations' on the other? And if one can't draw a clear line between policy and operations, why then should one expect to be able to draw a clear line between the responsibilities of ministers and those of civil servants? Liam Byrne MP, who served as a minister in the Home Office, the Cabinet Office and the Treasury, told MPs:

Sometimes in Whitehall you run into one of the greatest myths, which is that you can somehow separate the business of policy and delivery. In all of my experience that is total nonsense. You cannot formulate policy unless you understand delivery and you cannot get delivery right unless you understand policy.

Some former mandarins also think that the very attempt to split policy and operations is a fundamental mistake. As former Cabinet Office Permanent Secretary Sir David Omand put it:

There has been a gigantic category error of thinking that you could put policy and delivery in separate boxes and then assuming that the policy is a political world and the delivery is just people you hire in to do the delivery. A policy is not something which is confined to a little box in the centre. Good policies are deliverable policies.

Omand added an essential question: 'Who was in the room when the decision was taken? If there was not a key representative of the deliverer in the room when the decision was taken, the chances are it was not a very good decision.' One of the senior non-executive directors in Whitehall told the Reform think tank that 'if you're in business, policy and implementation are the same thing'.

Kate Jenkins told the Public Administration Select Committee:

From working with a large number of extremely well-intentioned ministers all around the world as well as here, I have seen over and over again this deep frustration about why the machine does not respond as they want it to respond, which is based on what I could only describe as a naive innocence of the complexity of running these very big functions.

At this point, Tony Wright, the chairman of the committee, asked Jenkins: 'So it is the fault of the politicians?' Jenkins replied:

No, I have not finished. It is partly the fault of the politicians and I am not sure that 'fault' is a very helpful expression because I think that this is something that has grown up over time, but I think we have reached the stage now ... where the same complaints have been made for forty or fifty years. Fulton described a serious lack of understanding and competence in management and his ire was directed to the old administration, the administrative class of the civil service ... The theory of setting up executive agencies was, in part, to push both ministers and senior officials into a position where they had to do this extremely difficult task, which most of them found very difficult indeed, which is to be specific about what your policies should mean in practice and what it is that is expected of a large government executive operation.

This assumes, of course, that ministers always want to be clear about what their policies mean in practice. And one might assume this should be the case: politicians seeking office set out the policies which they would implement if they had the chance; they seek to persuade the electorate to support them; if successful, they achieve office – and then they have the opportunity to implement those policies. Yet we know that the world does not always work quite like this. Certainly, the political party that can present itself as having a clear and consistent programme is likely to perform better than a party whose programme appears vague and contradictory – after all, political journalists like nothing better than finding mismatches between the stated ambitions of political leaders. But it is not an accident that political parties in opposition are often well advised to keep their public pronouncements at the level of generalities rather than specifics – 'themes not policies', in the words of the author Laurence Rees. And even when politicians succeed in winning an election, the need to allow room for manoeuvre is just as important. Policies often have winners and losers and, while circumstances will vary, one can't expect that anyone seeking votes will always be keen to spell out in grisly detail just how the losers are losing. As Sir Douglas Wass, a former Permanent

Secretary to the Treasury, pointed out in his BBC Reith Lectures
a generation ago:

> Ministers do not always define their political objectives, or if
> they do, they define them in terms which permit quite a lot of
> discretion in their interpretation. On the other hand, administra-
> tive methods are often highly charged political issues. The way
> a tax is administered may greatly affect the political standing of
> the government; and the use of some administrative techniques
> may be anathema to ministers. So in the real world ministers
> and civil servants are inextricably mixed up with each other. And
> they can only function on the basis of a close and harmonious
> partnership in which each has the trust of the other.

Remember Stella Creasy MP's observation at the start of our
book: 'Essentially, implementation is as important as ideology
in politics'? The central conundrum for us is that while this
observation ought to be true – and while in many ways it might
be better for us if it were – it isn't true *for reasons which are
not going to change.* As we said at the outset, governments need
to perform well. Far too often they don't. Indeed, governments
need politics to place a greater premium on implementation –
but ultimately it is only ministers who will get this to happen.
Civil servants won't by themselves – and nor should they be
expected to. They need to know what to implement and it is
only ministers who can tell them.

At the heart of all this is a basic truth that Whitehall is its
own animal. It is not a private company, nor can it simply be run
according to a formal, logical structure with a code of conduct
on how to develop and implement policy. Its very nature means
that it is both administrative and political, and there is bound
to be a tension between politics and management. The idea
that writing down in enormous detail the entire distribution
of responsibilities between ministers on the one hand and civil
servants on the other, defining completely who is responsible
for what – as if the chief problems could all be solved if only

the memo were long enough – misses what is most important. Politics is complex, subtle, messy and ambiguous, and such an approach doesn't begin to get to the heart of the problem. It is true that with more clarity there would be less politics – and sometimes that might be a good thing – but there would also be less democracy, leaving ministers even more circumscribed than they are now, facing civil servants who refused to do as they were asked because it was 'not in the contract'. As Michael Howard told MPs: 'There is no magical structural formula which provides the answer to the complicated, and often difficult, relationships between ministers and civil servants. In the end, in my view, responsibility should be personal.' Howard also provided a suitable definition of how any minister should knuckle down to the job:

> What one needs in any department, including the Home Office, is strong political leadership and a clear expression of determination by the secretary of state as to what he wants to do and a determination to get it done. Then one needs the readiness of the secretary of state to roll up his sleeves and make sure that there is in existence an action plan for doing what he wants to do and to keep in regular contact with those who are responsible for delivering that action plan and to monitor its progress regularly and frequently so that what he wants to get done is actually done. I think that that is pretty much what has to be done in any organisation; it is not rocket science. If you do that the Civil Service will respond and give you what you want.

Howard is simply saying that ministers who are clear about what they want, who are sufficiently determined and focused, avoiding distractions, and who understand that the policy changes they want to see implemented will have management implications for the organisations they lead – and who take the time and trouble to understand what those implications are, while also keeping on top of what is going on – can use the existing system to get what they want. The corollary is also true. As one reader commented in the *Daily Telegraph*: 'The civil service exists to execute the orders of the government of the day. If you get into office on a lot of fine talk but the truth is you haven't got any ideas – actually you haven't got a clue what to do – then the rest follows.'

And as Kate Jenkins wrote: 'There is no simple model that would always work – or we would have found it ... The public sector is far too complicated to be described by a single solution.' She went on: 'What is undervalued by officials as much as by politicians is the scarcest skill of all – making an idea happen.' And once an idea takes root and is adopted as a government policy, there is no substitute for rolling up one's sleeves and getting immersed in the detail of how it is implemented.

The authors of 'Whitehall's Black Box' argue that recent reforms to the way government operates – such as the introduction of a civil service code, a ministerial code, the strengthening of the role of the Civil Service Commissioners and the advent of departmental boards – will only have limited effects because they leave unchanged the fundamental conventions that determine who is responsible for what in Whitehall – and thus the participants 'are all supervising a deeply ambiguous set of relationships'. There is just a touch of unreality about this. The job of ministers involves gaining acceptance for their plans from different groups of people, some of whose aims are diametrically opposed to one another. Perhaps the very last thing one wants to do is to be completely explicit about everything, all the time. As Gillian Shephard put it when she was tasked with developing policy on women's issues after entering the Cabinet in 1992: 'Getting the tone right was essential in order not to alienate all kinds of lobbies, many with opposing aims.' In other words, ambiguity has its uses. As a former No. 10 adviser to Tony Blair, Geoff Mulgan, has observed, all societies are held together in part by accepted ambiguities and silences. Mulgan writes: 'Full revelation is nice in theory but can be deeply destabilising and destructive of self and mutual respect, especially when different groups have diametrically opposed views or interests.'

The politician has to cope with the fact that what may at one moment seem important and pressing may turn out later to be not just undesirable but perhaps even untouchable. Ministers need to be adaptable and agile enough to deal with shifts in opinion and changing circumstances. For sure, this may mean working harder at selling a policy to a sceptical public. It may involve downplaying an objective, or sugar-coating a tough decision, or tacking into a headwind to get to one's destination. But one may also need to change the destination. It follows that having the knack of appearing to know where one is going while also sometimes leaving things in a state of studied ambiguity may be essential for political survival.

Notwithstanding all the calls to clarify the relationship between ministers and senior civil servants, so as 'to define who is responsible for what', the fact remains that greater clarity will only work if ministers are prepared to face up to the consequences of greater clarity. And it is revealing that those who are most insistent in calling for greater clarity are not ministers who have to get re-elected, but former advisers and academics who don't. Rupert Darwall's real ire in 'The Reluctant Managers' – even though it is a sparkling *tour de force* against the current mandarinate – is not chiefly directed against civil servants but rather against politicians for behaving politically, for not being as rational and consistent and brave as he would like them to be. But ministers are not about to stop behaving like ministers. The problem with the view of the relationships between ministers and civil servants described in 'Whitehall's Black Box' and 'The Reluctant Managers' is not that there is no truth in what they say – these works are full of interesting insights – or that they don't identify serious problems; they do. The problem is that they assume what may simply not be the case.

It is one thing to point out that the current system involves supervising a deeply ambiguous set of relationships, but it is another not to acknowledge that they are bound to be deeply ambiguous. This is called politics. As Ross Anderson, professor of computing at Cambridge, put it so neatly: 'Project managers

must forever be closing down options early, while political managers try to keep all options open forever. Project
managers need to work to stable specifications, while political managers need to change the specification every month.'
Anderson was describing an intrinsic problem in fostering
successful public sector IT projects, but he could just as easily
have been writing about the whole world of politics.

The Reform and IPPR view of relations between ministers
and civil servants contains the optimistic assumption that things
would become easier if only there were enough clarity. 'Fit for
Purpose' criticises departments for using 'opaque language
to cloak conflicting objectives, rather than forcing politicians to choose between them'. The solution? 'The National
Audit Office should be empowered to investigate instances of
conflicting governmental objectives, quantify the amount of
public money being wasted, and force those with responsibility
and empowerment to take such decisions (whether ministers
or officials) to decide between them.' But why should it be the
job of an auditor or an unelected official to 'force' a minister
to 'decide between them'? It is the job of elected ministers to
wrestle with the conflicting objectives of government, to handle
them as best they can, and then explain what they have done
to the voters. As the BBC journalist Nick Robinson put it: 'If
we want better politicians to make better decisions, we would
all do well to consider the difficult choices they have to take in
the face of confusing and contradictory advice from those of us
who elect them.'

A government may actually want to pursue conflicting objectives, either to satisfy the demands of opposing groups or to
meet its own opposing interests. An obvious example is the
desire of successive governments to reduce smoking. There are
undoubted health benefits which flow from smoking cessation,
yet the revenue to the government from excise duty on tobacco
substantially exceeds even the highest estimates of the cost of
treating smoking-related diseases. Government makes a big
profit from all those smokers. From a revenue perspective, the

ideal taxpayer would be one who was always in work, smoked sixty a day and then dropped dead just days before becoming eligible to claim an old-age pension, thus contributing the maximum in revenue while costing government the least expenditure in pension payments and other costs. Fortunately, governments do not operate on such a raw calculus, but it is still true that if policy on smoking were wholly successful, the government would have to find many billions of pounds of tax revenue from elsewhere. It is also true that while genuinely wishing to see fewer smokers the government also wants to get the maximum revenue from taxing smokers. The fact that these objectives are directly contrary to one another does not stop the government pursuing both.

A government may wish to pursue a policy without an 'adequate' evidence base. The Advisory Council on the Misuse of Drugs concluded that ecstasy was not as dangerous as other class A drugs such as heroin and cocaine, and should be downgraded to class B. However, the government did not follow the council's advice. In February 2009, the council's chairman, Professor David Nutt, accused the government of making a political decision to reject the scientific advice to downgrade ecstasy, writing a paper in which he stated that in the course of a normal year, more people die from falling off horses than from taking ecstasy. The Home Secretary, Jacqui Smith, insisted that Nutt should apologise, for which she was widely criticised by scientists. In October 2009 after criticising politicians for 'distorting' and 'devaluing' research evidence in the debate over illicit drugs, Nutt was eventually sacked by Smith's successor as Home Secretary, Alan Johnson, who told him: 'It is important that the government's messages on drugs are clear and as an adviser you do nothing to undermine public understanding of them. I cannot have public confusion between scientific advice and policy and have therefore lost confidence in your ability to advise me.' Johnson later explained his decision to fire Nutt: 'He was asked to go because he cannot be both a government adviser and a campaigner against government policy.'

Some may regard this as a Galileo-like clash between truth and power, instinctively siding with the scientists. But this rather misses the point. Johnson was not only acting within his rights to sack an adviser. He was acting *politically*, which was his job. To accuse a politician of taking a political decision is rather like criticising a train driver for driving a train or the Pope for being Catholic. The scientific case for downgrading the classification of ecstasy may well have pointed clearly in one direction. The political case didn't. In defending himself later, Nutt inadvertently made Johnson's point for him, writing:

> I gave a lecture on the assessment of drug harms and how these relate to the legislation controlling drugs. According to Alan Johnson, the Home Secretary, some contents of this lecture meant I had crossed the line from science to policy and so he sacked me. I do not know which comments were beyond the line or, indeed, where the line was.

The episode showed that even if the 'scientific' evidence is apparently clear cut, defining the line – in this case, not just the line between policy and scientific advice but the line between what was politically acceptable and what was not – can still prove very difficult. Johnson was perfectly entitled to consider other issues, including his own opinions and his view of what the public would want. It might not have appeared 'rational' to a scientist. But it wasn't a scientist taking the decision. Do we really think that ministers shouldn't be able to take political decisions? Do we really think that ministers should not be able to ignore advice? There would be no point in having both a minister and an adviser if the minister were merely a cipher for implementing the opinion of the adviser, without any free will in the matter. And of course the ultimate answer to any scientist like Professor Nutt who can't stand the idea of offering 'evidence-based' advice which is ignored is to get elected to Parliament, become Home Secretary and then take the decision himself – and face the wrath of the electorate if they think he has got it wrong.

In *Why Politics Matters*, Gerry Stoker writes: 'Politics is doomed to disappoint because like any centralised collective form of decision making it requires trade-offs between competing interests.' He also points out that 'it was prone to failures in communication which often produce muddled and messy outcomes'. At the heart of it, politics is about the reconciling of differing and sometimes conflicting interests. It is about answering the question 'who gets what, and why'. This is always going to be contested territory. It is never going to be fully settled – and crucially one cannot expect that merely by writing down 'clearly' where the boundaries lie between the responsibilities of civil servants on the one hand and ministers on the other, everything will be just fine. Indeed, the very attempt to be clear may lead to nothing more than a lengthy and fruitless argument about exactly where the line is. As Home Secretary, Michael Howard was in political hot water over a row with the director general of the Prison Service, Derek Lewis. This led to a notorious television interview with the BBC journalist Jeremy Paxman, who was given an award for asking the same question about Lewis fourteen times – although Paxman later explained that he had simply been prolonging the discussion while awaiting a cue for the next item. Howard recounted the tale to MPs on the Public Administration Committee:

Everybody remembers my famous, or infamous, interview with Jeremy Paxman. Most people remember how many times he asked the question. Very few people remember the question. The question was whether I had threatened to overrule Derek Lewis. The man in the street did not give a damn about whether I had threatened to overrule Derek Lewis. The man in the street and I were concerned about whether we were doing all we could to stop dangerous criminals escaping from prison. The only reason the question had any relevance at all was because of the structure of the agency agreement which set up the Prison Service Agency. I am very sceptical about the helpfulness of these structures.

In a profoundly insightful book, *The Silence of Constitutions*, Michael Foley describes what he calls 'abeyances' in constitutional arrangements – tacit agreements to maintain deep and unsettled constitutional issues in a state of genuine ambiguity. Foley argues that these gaps in explicitness are a source of strength rather than weakness, providing the means for continually postponing discussion of anomalies and conflict. As Foley writes: 'It would be no exaggeration to say that the habitual willingness to defer indefinitely consideration of deep constitutional anomalies, for the sake of preserving the constitution from the conflict that would arise from attempts to remove them, represents the core of a constitutional culture.' And, of course, 'constitutional' in the broadest sense might refer to anything from the constitution of a country to what happens at the office, at the factory or at a parish meeting. When in conversation we say jokingly 'don't even go there', we are often referring to something which is highly sensitive, or frustrating, or even absurd, yet which we know can't easily be changed without disproportionate inconvenience or unacceptable damage to the system in which we are operating. Depending on one's view, the 'deeply ambiguous set of relationships' between ministers and civil servants – and in particular the fact that ministers are responsible for everything in theory, even though this seems impossible in practice – is either something to worry about, a serious flaw which needs to be cleared up so that there is much greater clarity at all times about who is responsible for what, or a considerable potential asset. It doesn't seem to have occurred to the think tank commentators that the elasticity of the system could actually be a source of strength. Yet it is plain enough that the system has to be flexible enough to take account of whatever it is that elections offer up. It can deal with a Heseltine or with a management novice. And either may get elected. Who is to tell the people they were wrong? That way lies despotism, as Bertolt Brecht pointed out in a sardonic poem, *The Solution*, about the crushing of the 1953 East Berlin uprising. The poem declared that following the disorder the government had lost faith in the people, who would now have to intensify their efforts to win back the government's approval. Brecht then posed a devastating question: 'Would it not be easier in that case for the government to dissolve the people and elect another?'

If we are to have a democracy, then we need to take it warts and all. If our system of government is to cope with those who happen to get elected and become ministers, a system which maintains a degree of ambiguity might have something to commend it. If we want to have democratic oversight of how we are governed, flexibility is an asset. By all means let us have much better education of all the players in the system – civil servants, ministers and those who may become ministers – so that everyone has a healthier appreciation of the longstanding problems facing any government seeking to deliver policy successfully, but let us not suppose that this will yield a clear answer to every question, or avoid intrinsic difficulties, or allow us to sidestep the truth that in government, as in life, where one stands so often depends on where one sits.

We could of course forget about democracy and leave it to the experts, but there are many reasons for keeping some healthy scepticism about experts and their methods. As the economist Paul Samuelson once observed: 'Wall Street indexes predicted nine out of the last five recessions! And its mistakes were beauties.' The premise of *The Blind Spot* by Gordon Rugg and Joseph D'Agnese is that everyone – including experts – tends to make the same sorts of mistakes, regardless of what field they are in or how clever they are. History is strewn with examples of experts getting things wrong. It was no less a person than Lord Kelvin, President of the Royal Society – Britain's national academy of sciences – who declared that aeroplanes were 'impossible' and that 'X-Rays will prove to be a hoax'. It was advice from experts that prolonged the Vietnam War. And then there is Dr Spock, the best-selling doyen of baby-care advice, whose insistence that babies be laid on their front to reduce the risk of choking and 'flattening the side of their head' is now known to be the exact opposite of best advice and is believed to have led to tens of thousands of avoidable cot deaths. We need not be blinded by unsubstantiated assertions by scientists as if this somehow removes all autonomy we might have in our decisions. In any case, there is no group of people called 'the scientists' who all say one thing. Science proceeds by conjectures and refutations, by arguing about the worth of different hypotheses and then putting them to the test – and it is common for scientists to disagree vehemently with one another in their interpretations of the same data. There is still a lot that science doesn't know – and indeed may never know – because of its intractable complexity. Human beings spend one third of their lives asleep but even after decades of research, scientists still cannot tell us why; nor do scientists know exactly how anaesthesia works as it does; the textbook explanation of why ice is slippery has been found to be wrong after more than a century; and although we have progressed considerably since Lord Kelvin's day, the theory underpinning heavier-than-air flight is still not fully understood. Anything in mathematics involving fluids or turbulence can present enormous theoretical difficulties. The application of very complex techniques from science and mathematics to the financial world was a significant contributing factor to the world banking and financial crisis. This was because some of the world's brainiest people had not appreciated that the probability of something going wrong – across a range of scenarios from very good to very bad – can itself change radically during a crisis, so that assumptions about what a 'worst case scenario' looks like can easily let you down at the very moment when you really need them.

In addition, we cannot take it for granted that the public opinions of experts are objective. Imagine a thought experiment. Let us say you wanted to spend £32 billion on a new high-speed rail link. For convenience, let us call it 'HS2'. Unfortunately, not everyone agrees with your idea. You encounter serious opposition. How would you behave? The obvious answer would be to get 'the truth' on your side. Find some technicians, statisticians and economists who will say, convincingly, what you need to hear. This will help you convince others and also weaken your opponents. Sure enough, this is just how promoters of big transportation schemes behave. In their book *Mega-Projects*, Harvard academics Alan Altshuler and David Luberoff draw attention to interviews that Martin Wachs, a leading urban transportation policy analyst, conducted with a range of public officials, consultants and planners who were involved in forecasting costs and revenues for transport schemes. Following extensive interviews, Wachs was 'absolutely convinced' that cost overruns and overoptimistic passenger numbers were not the result of technical errors, honest mistakes or inadequate methods: 'In case after case, planners, engineers, and economists have told me that they have had to "revise" their forecasts many times because they failed to satisfy their superiors.'

In other words, the forecasts had to be 'cooked' until they produced numbers that were dramatic enough to win support for the projects. Bent Flyvbjerg, a Danish academic, shows in another book in this field, *Megaprojects and Risk*, that both the cost estimates and the cost–benefit analyses which are used in public debates and in decision making about transport infrastructure proposals are 'highly, systematically and significantly deceptive' and that consequently 'megaproject development is currently a field where little can be trusted, not even – some would say especially not – numbers produced by analysts'. It gets worse. Fiona Godlee, editor-in-chief of the *British Medical Journal*, considers that the scientific community is in 'collective denial' about the extent to which there is manipulation of research data in drugs trials, pointing out that most academic papers in the medical field are withdrawn because of fraud rather than error. There is a growing consensus that selective use of data is a deliberate stratagem by pharmaceutical companies to make drugs in clinical trials appear to have greater efficacy than is actually the case, and that pharmaceutical companies consciously control access to the full evidence base so that they cannot easily be contradicted. The author Ben Goldacre wrote *Bad Pharma* to expose the true scale of what he has called 'this murderous disaster' and the extent to which the evidence we use to make decisions in medicine is 'hopelessly and systematically distorted'. Manipulation of data is at last coming to the attention of criminal prosecutors. In April 2013 a man was jailed for three months for altering pre-clinical trial data designed to support applications to perform clinical trials. Steven Eaton was found guilty at Edinburgh Sheriff's Court following a prosecution brought by the Medicines and Healthcare Products Regulatory Agency.

Yet even where experts are honestly seeking to be as objective as possible there is still a problem which Basil Mitchell, an Oxford philosopher, has identified: 'Academic subjects undergo regular revolutions, with the consequence that whatever the experts are saying now they are likely to be unsaying in twenty years' time.' Paul Feyerabend, another philosopher, stated in *Against Method* that 'non-experts often know more than experts and should therefore be consulted'.

It is often the common sense of ordinary people that gets things back on track. As Edmund Burke wrote: 'I have never yet seen any plan which has not been mended by the observations of those who were much inferior in understanding to the person who took the lead in the business.' William F. Buckley's famous quip that 'I should sooner live in a society governed by the first 2,000 names in the Boston telephone directory than in a society governed by the 2,000 faculty members of Harvard University' reflects a deep instinct that the experts don't necessarily always know best, even if we still want access to them and to their expertise.

But how is the intelligent layperson to make decisions? One cannot ignore the experts but neither can one completely trust them. And as John Kay has shown persuasively in his book *Obliquity*, there is no 'science of decision making' which, if done carefully enough, would lead every conscientious person to the same answer. But at the same time, there are choices that must be made. This was the problem which Basil Mitchell addressed in a delightful essay, 'The Layman's Predicament' – and it is of interest to us because at some point this is precisely the conundrum which will face a government minister who has to make crucial decisions involving the expenditure of billions of pounds. Confronted with a jumble of different experts with rival evidence, the minister must discern a path which chooses between competing 'truths'. In our later chapter on the quest for good government we will see that the ability to do this – that is, to weigh in the balance at the highest level 'the expertise of experts' across a very broad range of disciplines and then to analyse its proper relation to policy – is precisely the core professional skill that is supposed to be the unique possession of the administrative civil servant, who can then assist the minister accordingly. But even without any help, the minister still has resources to deploy. As Basil Mitchell pointed out, one of the most important faculties that a layperson has is the ability to assess *people*. Mitchell quotes from Cardinal Newman's *Grammar of Assent*:

> We judge for ourselves by our own lights and on our own princi-
> ples; and our criterion of truth is not so much the manipulation
> of propositions as the intellectual and moral character of the
> persons maintaining them.

In other words, as Sir Douglas Wass reminded us in his Reith Lectures, the real issue is trust. Can ministers trust and rely on the professional expertise of their civil servants? In the InterCity West Coast franchise fiasco it appeared, lethally, that the answer was 'no'. In that particular case, the minister was given information that was simply wrong, while being assured that it was correct. True, ministers had engendered a climate in which using outside consultants was frowned upon, although as the Institute for Government's Peter Riddell observed, 'whatever the pressure, misleading ministers is an extremely serious issue'. And after twenty or more years' experience, should not a senior official be able to say to a minister: 'One simply cannot do this type of franchising competition involving this much money without external financial advice. No one else would. And nor should we'? And furthermore, given the duties of an Accounting Officer, should he or she not have added: 'If you want this, you will have to issue me with a formal Direction'? Shouldn't the officials – anyway – have known that in government it is usually a dreadful idea to try something large and difficult at the same time as undergoing a massive reorganisation? After all, they had made this error at the Rural Payments Agency. And shouldn't they also have known that failing to have project oversight by a 'senior responsible owner' was foolhardy and would lead to trouble? This was exactly the mistake that had been made by the Ministry of Defence in developing the Bowman digital radio system. Bowman is an example from defence procurement, so readers may understandably not be familiar with it. But shouldn't professional administrative civil servants have known about it? And shouldn't they have been deeply familiar with the cardinal nature of this error? Isn't this exactly the sort of accumulation of knowledge that the prized 'breadth' of their career formation is supposed to lead to? Is the civil service incapable of learning or is it just too fragile to stand up to ministers? Fundamentally, are civil servants up to the job?

15

ARE CIVIL SERVANTS
UP TO THE JOB?

Much of the Civil Service was genuinely baffled. At senior levels their job was to discuss major policy issues. The management of resources and the management of government services were dealt with 'elsewhere'. For many of them the 'point' of questions about management was unintelligible.
Kate Jenkins, *Politicians and Public Services*

I cannot stress enough how important this time spent in operational delivery has been for my career. Not only have they been stimulating and challenging experiences in themselves, but they have also made me a more effective policy-maker and strategist. After all, if you want to understand what delivery is really about, you actually have to do it.
Stephen Rimmer, senior Home Office official

When Margaret Thatcher was presented with a progress report on civil service reform she asked: 'Does this mean the civil service is really changing, or have civil servants just learned management jargon?' Thatcher's comment was circulated around Whitehall by mistake and, according to former Cabinet Secretary Lord Wilson, was 'met with the kind of silence which follows a pile of plates being dropped in a restaurant'.

Wilson told the story in an article in the *Daily Telegraph* about rebuilding trust in the civil service which, to the surprise of some, sparked vitriolic comments on the newspaper's website. 'Misleading' was one of the politer words used to describe Wilson's piece, with readers venting their frustration at what they called 'piffle', 'tosh' and 'self-serving claptrap'. All this left one bewildered reader stating: 'I would appear to be alone in finding Lord Wilson's article interesting, perceptive and informative.' And certainly civil servants – or 'bureaucrats' as newspapers often prefer to call them – have in recent years been good for a kicking. While they may not be denounced as villains of popular imagination quite as often as MPs and bankers, there is still a familiar caricature of civil servants finding ways to impose complex regulations on a vexed citizenry, while being personally cosseted with jobs for life and index-linked pensions.

Yet the people who join the civil service include the most able graduates in the country, who have a wide range of choices open to them – and who enter public service because they want to serve the country, no less than the MPs who obtain elected office. As one fast-stream entrant featuring on a civil service recruitment website, Laura Jayawardane, wrote in explaining what attracted her to becoming a civil servant: 'I saw people's profiles who'd been on the fast stream and I saw that they actually work on issues that really matter and it wasn't just something that you'd be working on and making money for someone else. I think you're making an impact on people's lives.'

In this chapter we look at the civil servants whose job is to help elected governments deliver their policies. There is an enormous literature dissecting the British civil service – its attitudes and culture, its recruitment, its structure and performance, and its suitability for the tasks which it faces. And through this analysis a series of themes repeatedly emerges: the outstanding intelligence of senior civil servants as a class; the failure of bureaucracy; the fact that high-quality information – particularly about costs – is so hard to find; that there is weak leadership and that no one wants to manage; that despite their obvious intelligence there is a lack of relevant skills and, now perhaps, a lack of self-confidence; that there has developed a lack of trust between ministers and civil servants; the fact that – far from the cliché of civil servants being 'risk averse' – there is quite often little or no proper appreciation of risks or, if there is, then a widespread inability to explain risks convincingly to ministers; that there is a lack of clarity between the respective roles of the centre of government and of government departments; and above all that there is no accountability.

And of all these aspects one of the most fascinating – one of the enduring paradoxes – is how the civil service manages to take some of the most intellectually gifted people in the whole country and repeatedly make such a hash of things. There is no doubting their fierce intelligence. Many people who have experienced Her Majesty's civil service at close quarters have been dazzled by the brain power on show. Zenna Atkins, former chair of Ofsted, told *The Observer* in June 2008: 'I have never met such bright people who really care about what they are doing.' The former senior Whitehall official Kate Jenkins concurs:

> Many people dealing with senior civil servants speak almost with awe about the quality of intellectual ability which is evident. They are right; there are many highly able people in Whitehall, selected in their extreme youth on the basis of their intellectual capacity as demonstrated in universities, and trained only within the senior civil service.

Colin Talbot of the Manchester Business School also pays a handsome tribute to our civil servants, telling MPs on the Public Administration Select Committee: 'Certainly we have as a cadre probably one of the most intelligent civil services in the world.' So it is rather strange that such people seem able to put up with the sustained mediocrity and industrial-scale cock-ups we have witnessed. How can such clever individuals possibly bear it? Here would seem to be a classic case of the government squandering one of its most valuable resources – its people.

Kate Jenkins tellingly added that 'most' senior civil servants at the start of the twenty-first century were products of a system which had been 'virtually unchanged, except at the margins' for nearly 150 years. Zenna Atkins also said: 'They are working in a machine with a set of customs, cultures, values and practices that are utterly antiquated. A lot of the time the process is more important than the outcome.' And Colin Talbot, in referring to the fast-track recruitment process, which takes the best and the brightest graduates straight from university, also qualified his praise: 'One of the problems about the whole way the fast-stream process has operated is that it has recruited people on the basis of their cognitive abilities, their analytical ability in terms of playing with ideas.' In Talbot's view, the difficulty is the mind set of too many civil servants: 'Do they have what I would call organisational intelligence? The answer in most cases is: no, they do not have a clue about how organisations operate, how they could be made to operate to deliver the things that they want to do. It is not good enough just to recruit the finest minds; it is also necessary to have minds which operate at the level of making things happen.' Indeed, consultants from a leading firm told us that the difference between their staff and top Treasury officials was not primarily to do with levels of intelligence but that if you gave the two groups a problem to solve, 'a week later we would have come up with an answer but the Treasury officials would still be talking about it because it was such an interesting problem'. So is the civil service recruiting brilliant people with cryptic crossword minds, who would excel in Radio 4's *Round Britain Quiz* but have difficulty in running anything? There is plainly an element of caricature in all of this; in truth the civil service probably makes more effort now to be a diverse graduate recruiter than any other large organisation. Yet Helen Goodman, for sixteen years a Treasury official and now a Member of Parliament, wasn't making it up when she wrote that the ivory tower mentality in Whitehall sometimes verged on the Pythonesque: 'I attended a meeting at which senior officials discussed, quite seriously, what was the probability in game theory that the current proportion of women permanent secretaries would occur.'

Meanwhile, a catalogue builds up of spectacular failures such as those we have examined in this book, causing confusion and anxiety for the public who – to add insult to injury – are required to pay for it all through their taxes. Ian Liddell-Grainger, an MP and former member of the Public Administration Select Committee, summed up the recent failings in a memorable exchange with Gill Rider, brought in from Accenture as director general for capability in the Cabinet Office. Liddell-Grainger started by setting out the six core principles of the civil service:

1. People management
2. Financial management
3. Programme and project management
4. Analysis and use of evidence
5. Strategic thinking
6. Communication and marketing.

'They are core fundamentals of a civil service. You are here. They are not working. You have been brought here to sort out a mess.' Rider replied:

I disagree. I do not think they are not working. We are working to improve them. I have not been brought in to sort out a mess; I have been brought in to help everybody do what they want to do, which is to try to make sure we are the best we possibly can be for what we need to do.

Liddell-Grainger replied with a triumphant summary of all that he saw as wrong in the civil service:

Nigel Crisp got fired because he was told the NHS was incompetent. We have a procurement programme which is a disaster. We have IT projects coming out of our ears that have been a shambles. We have the CSA [Child Support Agency] – where do you start with the CSA? We have the Inland Revenue that cannot even fill in its own forms, never mind anybody else's. We have the MoD which cannot even get enough kit for the troops, who are getting killed. We have got tax credits – again, where do you start? We have single farm payments – a catastrophe. We are seeing management failures all the way through the civil service, at the very highest levels, and a lot of people have sat where you have sat to explain why they have made a mess of it ... But you are saying it is all right?

If the chairman had allowed it, there would probably have been loud applause from the public gallery at this point.

So what's going wrong? On this view, it is because civil servants need to be good managers yet for 150 years they have not been hired for their ability to make things happen. The fact is that even in the private sector this ability is rare enough, as well as under-rated. As Lou Gerstner observed in *Who Says Elephants Can't Dance?*, his account of turning around the troubled computer giant IBM: 'Execution – getting the task done, making it happen – is the most unappreciated skill of an effective business leader.' And while senior civil servants are among the cleverest people one could meet, in our experience few of them really want to be managers. There have of course been huge changes in the last 150 years. And some of the most effective performers in the civil service are not fast-streamers but people who have worked their way up from the bottom. Yet, as one minister in the coalition government told us, it is routine to encounter among many officials a marked preference for analysis compared with delivery.

What is worse, this faultline in our civil service is not new. Ministers and their successors have known about it for decades, yet nothing has been done. This has led to suspicions that it is the *politicians* who have found it convenient to continue with an ambiguous relationship where, in reality, the most prized ability of top civil servants is handling and protecting ministers, rather than successfully managing a world-scale department of state. As Sir John Bourn put it: 'The top jobs should go to those who have successfully managed programmes and projects – in health, social welfare and taxation as well as construction and defence. At the moment they are given to those best at helping their ministers get through the political week.'

Then it is little wonder that for some civil servants it is all too much. There is a moment in the *Yes Minister* BBC television series when a talented official called Sarah Harrison resigns to her minister, Jim Hacker, and Permanent Secretary, Sir Humphrey Appleby, to become a director of a merchant bank. She tells Hacker:

> Quite honestly, minister, I want a job where I don't spend endless hours circulating information that isn't relevant about subjects that don't matter to people who aren't interested. I want a job where there is achievement rather than just activity. I am tired of pushing paper. I would like to able to point at something and say 'I did that'.

Sir Humphrey is baffled. 'I don't understand,' he said. Harrison replied: 'I know. That's why I am leaving.' Hacker asked if she was saying that governing Britain was unimportant. 'No,' said Harrison. 'It's very important. It's just that I haven't met anyone who's doing it.'

Unlocking the latent talent of staff is one of the key challenges facing every organisation, large and small, in both the private and public sector. The civil service is hiring some of the brightest people in the country. Should it really be that difficult to release their energies and talents? Lou Gerstner spelt out a similar problem when he became the new chief executive of IBM and met senior staff: 'I will never forget my first impression. It reminded me of a government office – long, quiet corridor after long, quiet corridor of closed offices.' Gerstner told staff how the press had suggested that 'the new CEO has to bring a lot of people in from the outside'. Then he remarked that he hoped this would not be the case, that IBM had always had a rich talent pool, perhaps the best in the world. Later, after touring the firm's operations, Gerstner reflected:

> These were enormously talented people, a team as deeply committed and competent as I had ever seen in any organisation. I reached this conclusion repeatedly over the next few months.

On the flight home I asked myself: 'How could such truly talented people allow themselves to get into such a morass?'

Gerstner could have been writing about the civil service.

However, it is very important to recognise that civil servants face obstacles which are absent in the private sector. We will soon observe that good management is not always good politics and that the need for managers to be 'politically sensitive' may conflict with other expectations. What's more, the state may – for perfectly good public policy reasons – chase a marginal 'customer' at very high cost in a way that a commercial organisation would not do, such as an extremely rural customer of the post office or a young offender who may otherwise turn to a life of crime. There is also the need to be seen to use the resources of the state 'fairly' and to show that procedures have been followed. Indeed, in his book *Public Sector Auditing*, Sir John Bourn identifies a deeper problem about the very nature of bureaucratic institutions: 'Bureaucracy looks inward not outwards, to process rather than outcomes, to hierarchies rather than teams, to rules rather than initiative, and to detachment from, rather than engagement in, human interests.' Bourn suggests that bureaucracies are likely to favour the producer over the consumer, that they will often require the citizen to think and act like a bureaucrat, and that they are poor at learning despite gathering enormous amounts of information. He adds that they create additional problems by enmeshing themselves in complexity, that they are poor at examining their own performance, and that bureaucracies provide little or no incentive to innovate and make better use of resources. Sound familiar? Think about the expectations which the government placed on poor families caught up in the tax credits trap, or the Byzantine complexities of the single farm payment scheme which drove at least one farmer to suicide, or the enormous amount of public money wasted on the NHS IT programme.

Kelvin Hopkins, an MP and formerly a longstanding member

of the Public Administration Select Committee, once said he had 'three golden rules' for good government:

> First of all, have systems that are very well thought out, which work, set them up, establish them and keep them; second, have stable organisational arrangements over a long period; and third, appoint the right people to the right jobs and make sure you get people to do what is necessary. These are elementary things. If you have these things right, everything else will flow from that.

But this is far from the pattern we have seen in recent years. For example, the Department for Innovation, Universities and Skills was actually created and then disbanded in a mere two years – and this, of course, is the fault of the Prime Minister of the day, not of civil servants. As Sir John Bourn observed: 'The machinery of government is in constant turmoil – new departments and authorities being set up and older ones shut down or amalgamated.' The National Audit Office published a study on this 'churning' which identified over ninety central government departments and arm's-length bodies which were subjected to reorganisation between May 2005 and June 2009, over twenty each year on average. The estimated gross cost of reorganisation in the fifty-one organisations which the NAO studied in detail was £780 million, equivalent to £15 million for each reorganisation and just under £200 million each year. As Bourn observed, such churning is largely irrelevant to the programmes and projects that have to be implemented, adding: 'It should be stopped.' The early signs, at least, are that since forming the coalition in 2010 David Cameron and Nick Clegg have resisted the temptation constantly to reshape Whitehall and rebrand its departments.

The failure of the system has vexed both MPs and civil servants for years. As the straight-talking former MP Gordon Prentice put it when quizzing Tim Burr, Bourn's successor as head of the NAO: 'Are we congenitally incapable of learning from mistakes?' Burr said governments had shown 'the ability to repeat the same experience without apparently being able to learn and transmit the lessons'. There was a lively exchange between Whitehall veteran Sir Richard Mottram and Kate Jenkins while they were both giving evidence to MPs on the Public Administration Committee. At times the urbane Mottram came close to suggesting that the public were partly to blame for Whitehall's problems: 'The reason why people are dissatisfied, for example, with public services, is because their expectations keep rising. And it is a very, very good thing that their expectations do keep rising.' Jenkins was having none of it: 'I want to challenge what Richard has said about rising expectations on the part of the public. The public, the group we ought to be thinking about all the time, have two problems: one is they are promised things that are not delivered by organisations that in large measure cannot deliver many of those things. Secondly, the core functions of government, the absolute basics, are constantly failed.' Jenkins argued that if officials focused entirely on the core management of government, delivering a 'tolerable level of service, we will have gone a long way to deal with a lot of these problems'.

The most important of all core functions is simply knowing what is going on. And yet the difficulties in finding good information have been among the hardiest of perennials in the debate about failure in Whitehall. This is nowhere more crucial than in financial management. As Sir John Bourn observed:

> Nearly everyone joining central government from the private sector says how amazed they are that nobody knows exactly what anything costs. Costings are too often moves in the game; figures to argue for or against a predetermined position or course of action instead of the bedrock on which options and alternatives can be reliably considered.

When Jenkins was involved in the Next Steps reforms, she noted that 'the question "what does it cost" was normally met with a blank stare'. As she put it: 'The great gap in the analysis was not ideas – there was never any shortage of key issues – the gap was in basic information.' We saw in Michael Heseltine's early encounters with his Permanent Secretary that *management information* – to enable managers to check whether a government department was on track to meet its objectives – has not been a prized possession in Whitehall. While Heseltine responded by creating a whole management information system to keep track, he really shouldn't have had to do this. As the former Home Secretary Charles Clarke told MPs:

> We have a right as politicians to expect that, as leaders, the permanent secretaries do have ... experience of running large organisations, are equipped to do it ... and their training formation should lead to that. That should be a pre-requisite. It is also helpful if the minister has that experience but it should be a pre-requisite that your Permanent Secretary can run the organisations for which she or he is responsible.

True, Heseltine's first experience as a Cabinet minister was thirty years ago. But how much has changed? Less than one might hope. Oliver Letwin, a Cabinet Office minister in the coalition government, told members of the Public Accounts Committee in 2011 nearly a year after the change of government: 'There is incredibly little good quality information in Whitehall, at the centre of Whitehall, about what is going on in Whitehall.' Letwin was surprised by this, calling it 'the most important fact I have discovered in the last ten months'. And an NAO report on progress in improving financial management in government, also in 2011, concluded that departments 'do not fully understand the costs of their activities' and that good information is 'rare' in some cases. Too often, still, Whitehall simply doesn't have the right information. The reason for this information gap is connected with how people think about organisations and their roles in them. Howard Rolfe, a former senior executive with Marks and Spencer who is now a Department of Health procurement director and a non-executive director of Papworth Hospital, told the PAC: 'A good question for a Trust board would be: what are your top ten non-pay spends and how do those prices compare with the best quartile in your region?' Yet this is just not how most civil servants think or speak, certainly not when giving evidence before the PAC. This way of thinking can be learned soon enough, but it does not come naturally to civil servants because it has not been part of their world. A laser-like focus on costs is simply not what occupies civil servants most of the time – nor does their career formation depend on it. How do you get ahead in Whitehall? Not by delivering programmes. No baby mandarins want to spend their grown-up years organising benefit payments or checking hospitals are cleaned properly. The smart jobs are in advising ministers and crafting policy.

The key skill needed within government to get better outcomes is the ability to marshal a variety of resources – such as money, information, people, technology and time – and handle them very tightly to deliver specific objectives. This is called management. Yet this fundamental skill has never been properly valued in Whitehall. Technical expertise and managerial skills have too often been at a discount. The skill most valued in Whitehall is the ability to help a minister explain why something that looks like a disaster is in fact a triumph or, at least, more than one had any right to expect in the circumstances. Why is this? The reality is that politicians look to their civil servants to help them out of tricky situations which were often created when they failed to pay enough attention or heed warnings from civil servants first time round. So it is hardly surprising if civil servants don't have a relentless focus on management. As the current head of the NAO, Amyas Morse, has put it: 'You can't assume in the public sector that there is an inherent management culture of the kind that you find in the private sector because people don't spend their whole lives in the public sector trying to improve profitability. They would say to you, "That's not my first role."' Morse adds that in the past the ideal skill set for the civil servant has not been one 'primarily focused on being able to control resources very tightly against particular objectives'.

And no one should pretend this is easy. While it is true that aligning the resources with the objectives is done successfully more often in the private sector, it certainly cannot be taken for granted. Lou Gerstner wrote that 'making sure that resources are applied to the most important elements of the strategy is perhaps the hardest thing for companies to do'. And in politics there is the extra snag – for any rationalist – that the way to get more political clout is simply by getting more of the pie. This is not done by having a measured and thoughtful discussion about the strength of a colleague's case. In a BBC radio series in the 1980s, *But Chancellor*, the former Chancellor of the Exchequer Denis Healey reflected somewhat wistfully:

> I tried very hard when I was Chancellor to invent systems of organisation which would enable the Cabinet to decide priorities as between for example, health, education and housing. But somehow or other that never really worked out right. I think the most difficult thing is to get a Cabinet to take a decision on priorities.

More than twenty-five years later, Sir Richard Mottram could be found making a similar point to a House of Lords committee, stating that that one of the real challenges facing the civil service was ensuring 'the capacity of the centre of government to develop a strategy and to link that strategy to the way in which resources are allocated'. And when Sir Michael Barber, the head of Tony Blair's Delivery Unit, asked ministers at a Cabinet meeting if their diaries reflected their priorities, he could tell by the 'nervous laughter' that he had struck a chord.

Tessa Blackstone and William Plowden's study of the Central Policy Review Staff, *Inside the Think Tank* – a central government research body which was voguish in the 1970s – includes a classic description by an official called Richard Wilding of the ideal characteristics of the administrator:

- The belief that the good government of this country is a matter of high importance and the opportunity to contribute to it a privilege;
- The belief that it therefore demands the best you can give it, in all matters and at all times;
- A professional pride in making sure, so far as you can, that the objectives that ministers set themselves are objectives that can in practice be achieved, and that the government then sets about the job in such a way that they are in fact achieved;
- The courage to give unwelcome advice;
- The resilience and humour to accept repeated disappointment and frustration without becoming cynical;
- The willingness to listen to other people, to learn from your own mistakes and to work in collaboration rather than competition;
- Two each of honesty, tenacity and obedience; and one spoonful of humility;
- Season with common sense, a dash of political judgement and a consuming interest in at least one totally different subject and simmer gently for forty years.

Blackstone writes:

Much of this is admirable. But what is instructive about this quotation is not what is in it, but what is missing from it. There is no mention of imagination, creativity, enterprise, interest in change, flexibility and adaptability, or knowledge and expertise in particular subjects. All of these qualities, it could be argued, are needed from departmental civil servants.

But what happens when an official displays initiative? Part of the difficulty is that good management is not always good politics, as former Cabinet Secretary Lord Wilson has pointed out:

Some years ago, an entrepreneurial prison governor with a control problem in his prison contracted for an all-weather football pitch, so that his inmates could exhaust themselves playing football rather than rioting. He was nearly lynched in Parliament for treating criminals softly when the local school had had to sell its playing field.

The need for managers to be 'politically sensitive' may be in direct conflict with expectations that they should be more imaginative, creative and enterprising.

It is tempting to say that civil servants can't win. We criticise civil servants for not being more entrepreneurial. And yet when they show enterprise we criticise them for political insensitivity, or if they go along with ministers' dubious schemes – self-evidently aimed at getting a quick headline – they are criticised for not being vigorous enough nay-sayers in standing up to ministers. True, some of the ideas from ministers who have strayed too near a microphone are plainly so far fetched that they are shot down in flames long before civil servants might have to get to work – such as Tony Blair's proposal that we could solve the problems of anti-social behaviour by marching young hooligans to cash point machines to extract on-the-spot fines. But often ministers are determined and something has to be done. The job of being a civil servant would appear nearly as impossible as that of a minister. It is hardly surprising, then – as we saw in the last chapter – that Rupert Darwall called civil servants 'the reluctant managers'. Jonathan Powell, who was Chief of Staff to Tony Blair in Downing Street, summed up the problem: 'The system is stacked against civil servants who might want to get things done. There is very little upside gain for an individual official who succeeds in resolving a problem and a huge downside risk for permitting something to go wrong.'

Some observers have been surprised by what they found in Whitehall. One former senior official told the authors of 'Whitehall's Black Box': 'The first thing I noticed when I got into Whitehall was just how inaccurate the Rolls-Royce machine label was when it comes to policy. I was confronted by people who had very few specific skills and little understanding of evidence-based policymaking.' And when Lord Sainsbury became science minister he also did not find what he expected, as he explained to the Public Administration Committee:

> I was always brought up to believe that there is a very good policy-making machine in government. I did not find this at all. What I found was that it was very unclear as to what the process was by which a minister actually said what his priorities were or problems were. There was almost a random process by which problems would come to the surface, at which point a team, or individuals, would produce a submission on this and, of course, because it was produced rather rapidly and not as part of an overall process, often it was in no way informed by previous initiatives, let alone experience elsewhere or what had happened in other countries.
>
> It just seemed to me that the basic processes and often the evidence were not there. I remember an example. There was a lot of concern about numbers of people doing science and technology at university and also at A-Level, and there would be various responses from government that it was better than last year, worse than last year, and so on. There came a point when it seemed to me what we were saying was very unclear, it was not clear whether we knew what was happening long-term, so I asked to see the figures over a ten-year period of what was happening. It took three or four months and a lot of harassing of people to get those figures, which at that point showed that actually the number of people doing science and technology at university was going up quite steeply … There was nowhere where that evidence had been collected or asked for and, therefore, statements of initiatives were inappropriate. No one knew what the basic facts were.
>
> We must have proper policy-making processes in which the minister makes clear what his priorities are, and gets proper work done, and it is in a timeframe which enables those policies to be put together in a proper way. Unless you insist that that is a policy across the civil service, that that is the way policy is made and that is what is the responsibility of departments … you will never get good policy-making made.

Such views may be justified but they have taken their toll on civil servants as a breed. As Whitehall observer David Walker told the Public Administration Select Committee: 'The hauteur which senior officials in the fifties had has gone. They simply do not have that self-confidence as a corporate body which existed.' Few will lament the loss of the hauteur but it points to a serious underlying problem. As Walker put it:

> I think there is a loss of nerve in the sense of a realisation from the Cabinet Secretary downwards that there is a skills deficit. The very reason you are having this inquiry is that they lack something. They are told that by ministers; they are told that by us, the media; they are told that by you.

And this is the reason that so many new people have been brought into the civil service at the higher levels, to run things, simply because not enough home-grown officials have the right combination of skills. As Charles Clarke told MPs of his time at the Home Office:

> We appointed three deputy secretaries to the department during the time that I was secretary of state. One of them was a former chief executive in local government; one of them was a former chief executive of a voluntary organisation; one of them was a policy officer originally from central government. None of them were Home Office civil servants who had come through the process. This was after extensive advertising ... the civil service did not have within it individuals to carry out these responsibilities at deputy secretary level.

Whitehall has been prodded into doing something about it. According to Lord Burns, a former Permanent Secretary to the Treasury, the 'glorious amateur' of the past is on the way out. Burns told the House of Lords constitution committee that

> a lot of effort has gone into developing professional skills, hiring

people who have particular specialist skills but also then giving them a career path which enables the professionals also to move through the civil service, which once upon a time was not the case. Frankly, it has been important also to develop a leadership group because quite a lot of the people who came into the civil service many years ago would have come in because they had particular intellectual skills and they were very good at certain types of activity. But they were not necessarily very good managers and were not necessarily very good leaders.

Burns added: 'It is simply having a civil service which is more professional, is better equipped to deal with modern types of complex problems and is able to give better quality advice and better quality execution in terms of delivery of government policies.' David Walker wants to give civil servants a break. As he told MPs: 'The intellectual struggle at the moment is, to be fair to them, to keep the show on the road while reaching for what we might say are partial means of trying to redress the skills imbalance.'

The view of Kate Jenkins is rather more pessimistic. She acknowledges that a number of good things had happened such as the reforms creating executive agencies which, while having detractors, achieved a measure of acceptance and success. The reasons for this success included: the simplicity of the recommendations; the quality and the attention given to implementation; the way practical experience of people working within the system day by day was combined with the longer-term experience of senior management; and the lesson that managing government needs constant attention and simple objectives. But as Jenkins observed, a further lesson was more worrying: *very little was actually done to enhance the skills of people at the critical senior level.* While more managers were introduced, it was by appointing chief executives from outside and inside the civil service – not by changing the people who were in line to be made permanent secretaries. The skills of senior civil servants and ministers remained much the same; the way they work has changed little, the obsession with the short term, the political and the media were as strong if not stronger. As one senior official said privately of the centre of government in 2004, when serious failures in the public services during the Blair administration were becoming evident: *'It hasn't changed at all; underneath it is just the same.'*

Sir Richard Mottram agrees that there is a problem. A report on reforming government from the Better Government Initiative in 2010, led by Mottram and other former mandarins, found that between one fifth and one quarter of the senior civil service were external recruits in the preceding four years. While this may look like a positive development, with plenty of fresh blood coming into top management jobs in the civil service – and bringing serious experience from elsewhere – it is also a sign of internal problems lower down the chain. Many of the world's most successful private sector organisations grow most of their own talent internally and, as the Better Government Initiative commented: 'In any outside organisation, external recruitment on this scale would probably be seen as signifying a serious failure in personnel policy. It risks a weakening of corporate memory where it matters most, in top management.' When former minister Liam Byrne met MPs on the Public Administration Committee he commented:

> I just do not think there is any substitute for people at very senior levels in the civil service having much more delivery strength and capability ... At the moment we are still bringing into senior levels of the civil service a lot of people from outside rather than bringing up more people from the bottom with the right kind of delivery skills.

Likewise, Mottram told MPs that the civil service needed to take professionalism much more seriously. He argues that if it aspires to be managing the process of decision making, including the process of policy development, 'it must have the professional competence to do it properly', adding that:

having the professional competence to do it properly usually means actually people are trained, they have continuous professional development, there are expectations about how they go about managing research, creating networks, understanding what is and is not evidence and all these things ... the civil service finds it very difficult consistently to embed change of that kind and to sustain it, and that is what it needs to do ... it is not great and it requires more professionalism, and we need to think about how it feeds into how we recruit people, educate them, train them and continuously develop them.

Some senior officials will tell you that changes now underway will have a lasting impact, including on recruitment into top posts. As Sir Brian Bender, a former Permanent Secretary, has argued:

You will not get into the senior civil service without operational delivery experience. It does not matter how bright you are, if you do not have practical experience and you do not stand back and plan these things with programme/project management and risk management techniques, you risk screwing up.

The lack of relevant skills leads to one of the biggest issues of all. Do ministers trust civil servants to give them the expert help they need? Do they trust the quality of the advice? Part of the reason for the growth in the use of external consultants and special advisers has been because this trust was missing. As Mottram explains:

You have to have the capacity to go to the minister and say, 'This is a very good idea, but actually it is going to take four years to deliver it and you can't announce it next week, and actually we don't have the money to do it, so we need to do more work on it. We need to bottom out all the risks and we need to do the job properly.' The issue is: do ministers listen to that advice? Do they believe that the people who are giving them that advice are themselves competent and can be relied on?

Many ministers and officials agree about the need for more trust. As Gillian Shephard put it:

> There really needs to be a trust and understanding in both sides of this question, both from politicians and from permanent secretaries ... Our constitution, such as it is, rests on these two pillars: one is the public democracy, the accountability of politicians to the electorate through Parliament, and the other is the existence of an impartial civil service. You have to have mutual trust, otherwise things go wrong.

But, as Mottram adds, because ministers have lost faith that the senior civil service itself knows how to manage things 'they do not believe what they are told about the risks that are being taken' and, as a result, departments take risks that are far too big. And this is always assuming that civil servants themselves have properly understood the risks, although – as Sir John Bourn points out – one cannot take this for granted:

> Public servants are popularly supposed to be risk-averse. The opposite is the case. They take the most colossal risks but without knowing the risks that they are running. For example, tax credits were launched in the knowledge that many recipients would be overpaid but with no clear plan for how to get the money back from some of the poorest people in the community: £6 billion has been overpaid since 2003 and only £2 billion has been recovered.

Bourn believes 'risk ignorant' is a better description of civil servants than risk averse, and that the setting up of the Child Support Agency was a similar example, telling MPs: 'Fathers should bear responsibility for their children, but before you launch a great scheme, you need to think about how you are going to find the fathers who are not doing it now.' This risk, Bourn said, was almost completely ignored.

Part of the problem is that – unlike politicians, who know

their performance will be judged by the electorate every five years at the ballot box – very rarely is anyone in Whitehall held publicly to account for their mistakes. This has created – for better or for worse – what we might describe as 'Teflon civil servants', officials whose career progress through the civil service appears barely dented by spending cock-ups which have cost the taxpayer millions or even billions.

Teflon is a patented polymer material which can withstand high temperatures, which means that it is often used in non-stick cooking pans or as a lubricant. But in everyday conversation it is also used to describe someone who is able to brush off serious criticism with no sign of any lasting effect. US mafia boss John Gotti was dubbed the 'Teflon Don' by American tabloids because charges against him failed to stick.

Civil servants are not like crime bosses who keep evading natural justice. Nor are they immune from feeling shame at presiding over public spending disasters. But there is a clear sense that too few are held to account publicly for when things go wrong. For sure, many of them as departmental accounting officers suffer uncomfortable grillings in front of angry MPs on the Public Accounts Committee. But many more are allowed to slip away and leave the civil service, causing barely a ripple. And even for those who do appear in front of the PAC, it is not all bad, as one Permanent Secretary admitted to the authors of 'Whitehall's Black Box': 'The PAC can be very difficult, but it is not hard-edged accountability ... we are not fired as a result of a bad performance. Indeed, appearing before the PAC doesn't change the price of fish!' The enthusiasm in Whitehall for confidentiality agreements – effectively gagging officials from discussing at a later date what had gone wrong – which are signed as part of financial settlements, means that few civil servants are held publicly accountable for presiding over major misspends. And this just cannot be right.

If civil servants understood risks better, and the penalties for failure were greater, they might be more willing to say no to their ministers. As the political scientist Anthony King has pointed out, two related developments have conspired: 'One is ministers' increasing concern to act and to be seen to be acting, often in response to immediate crises; and the other is civil servants' increasing reluctance to nay-say ministers when ministers feel compelled to act and to be seen to be acting.' As Bourn observes:

> There is an idea that something should be done and there is alto-gether too much of a willingness to say that it can be done next Tuesday. In fact, of course, when there is a programme, when there is a policy to be taken forward, more time should be given to work-ing out, 'How are we going to do this if we're going to succeed?' so you need a project, a programme, a budget, a risk assessment and, above all, you need to know, as Richard [Mottram] and Kate [Jenkins] have mentioned, who down the line is going to imple-ment this, 'Have they been trained? Who is leading them? Who is managing them?', and sometimes to say, 'This is what we're going to do. We're not going to do it next Tuesday. We're going to work out how to do it and make a real success of it.'

One of the classic responses to failure has been more frequent 'meddling' from the centre, as departments would see it. Yet from the centre the scene is all too often one of frustrating inertia, prompting a greater desire to intervene and demand action. There is a lack of clarity between the respective roles of the centre of government and of government departments. Mottram identified the problem:

> It can be argued that the centre has been weak in aspects of the functions only it can perform – ministerial appointments and training and development, government-wide strategy, resource allocation, handling of cross-departmental issues – while over-centralising in other respects – public service reform and micro-management of essentially departmental issues.

Let's recap. Ministers have a nearly impossible job. And for civil servants the outlook might seem just as unpromising. Civil servants need to be good managers to do their job properly but for 150 years they have been recruited on the basis of their cognitive ability, their analytical abilities in terms of playing with ideas, not for their ability to make things happen. Despite being among the most intellectually brilliant people you will find in any workplace, most top civil servants don't want to be managers – they have culturally disdained 'management' – and they also know becoming a top manager will not guarantee their promotion to the top. Far too many top civil servants still don't know how organisations operate or how they could be made to operate to deliver the things that they want to do. There is rhetoric about change but it's the same rhetoric we have heard for fifty years – and although there have of course been changes it is still the case that most government departments do not have all the capabilities they require to do their job. All this leaves us with an obvious question. Will we ever have good government?

16

THE QUEST FOR GOOD GOVERNMENT

It is a delusion to suppose that there is some different kind of structure which will make everything easy and solve the problems.
Michael Howard

Oliver Letwin, a Cabinet Office minister in the coalition government and a major thinker in Conservative politics, has set out an elegant and subtle defence of the professional administrative civil servant. In a speech in September 2012 at the Institute for Government, 'Why Mandarins Matter', he identified a core of four professional skills which the modern administrative civil servant had to possess: the 'accumulation of knowledge', the 'transmission of decisions', the 'provision of advice' and what he called 'guardianship'. Letwin warned that our system of government was not by any means to be taken for granted and cited examples of bad governments from elsewhere that would make most of us blanch. He pointed out how easily it could be forgotten that the functioning of a modern, liberal state depended on due process and that the *maintenance* of due process depended on having administrators to keep track of what the processes were. Someone needed to know the answer to the question 'how does the system work?' Letwin described this accumulation of knowledge of process as 'the first task' of the administrative civil service. He added that the activity of transmission of decisions – which he called 'difficult and complex' – was no less important. It consisted 'not only of recording, but also of translating, enlarging, clarifying, encoding, promulgating, authorising and, often enough, paying and accounting'. The third activity, the provision of advice, required the administrative civil servant 'to perform the extraordinarily difficult task of discerning the nature of the programme or objective sufficiently clearly – and of gauging the effects of both government action and citizen reaction sufficiently certainly – to be able to advise the minister accurately on which specific policy or decision will be most likely to achieve the objective'. And in Letwin's view, this demanded an intellect that was both imaginative and subtle 'because how you do something may have an effect not only on the result but also on the political character of the action, and it is therefore extraordinarily difficult to know where objectives end and implementation begins'.

The first three roles work naturally together, argued Letwin: 'It is only if our administrative civil servants have a great accumulated knowledge of the due process of government that they can be expected to transmit ministerial decisions effectively; and it is only if they have a full understanding of process and of the transmission of decisions that they will be able to advise usefully on the development and implementation of democratically determined policy programmes.' In their capacity as guardians, however, administrative civil servants were servants not of ministers but of the crown, accountable to Parliament, 'above the process of party politics and above whatever is at any given time the present ministerial incumbency'. In this role, the chief concerns were to ensure that the government as a whole acted with propriety and in conformity with the law.

Letwin's description is a classic textbook account of the position of the administrative civil servant, which he called 'a profession in its own right, no less demanding and no less valuable than other professions'. Moreover, Letwin added, there are 'large numbers of people at the apex of the pyramid of today's administrative civil service who have these qualities in abundance'.

Sir Richard Mottram praised Letwin's speech but pointed out that it was an exposition of a concept that had been 'under sustained attack for fifty years' and that a civil servant making such a speech 'would have been held up to ridicule'. Mottram wondered why it was so difficult to sustain the classic ideal of the professional administrative civil servant. Letwin's answer was that the old idea of the 'glorious amateur' had become discredited; that instead, an idea had taken root that if only we were more 'professional' – in the sense of having a technical skill – we would be able to substitute our rather old-fashioned British approach of 'muddling through' with 'modernity' and 'clarity' and that, as a consequence, 'all the problems of the world would quickly evaporate'; and that, in turn, this view was 'overdone' so that people had lost sight of something 'immensely valuable': the importance of the professional skills which were unique to the administrative civil servant. Nonetheless, with Letwin's courtly and donnish manner it was easy to overlook an admission and also a threat. The admission was, in essence, that what Mottram had on an earlier occasion told the Public Administration Committee was correct – the civil service required more professionalism. As Letwin put it: 'The possession of these skills on the part of the best of our administrative civil servants is very precious and the need for them to be possessed by those administrative civil servants who do not currently possess them *is equally great* [our emphasis].'

Letwin's implicit threat came when he described civil servants who 'defeat ministerial objectives, just by ensuring that when the minister has decided to act nothing actually happens' as 'enemies of democracy'. He added that the Civil Service Reform Plan was designed to 'eliminate such failures'.

We believe that a painfully clear answer to the question of why it is so difficult to sustain the classic ideal of the professional administrative civil servant can be found – and rather quickly – by a review of examples from our earlier chapters and elsewhere. These also show the extensive nature of the problem.

Consider Letwin's first activity: 'accumulation of knowledge'. The Passport Agency was caught unawares by new regulations that required children to have separate passports. When the government began to set up the Criminal Records Bureau, ministers found to their alarm that they could not even be sure that convictions in this country were being entered on the police national computer. In the foreign national prisoners scandal, the system simply did not accumulate or retain information on what had happened to prisoners who were asylum seekers; the immigration service did not monitor those liable to deportation; and the promised detailed audit of foreign national prisoners never happened. The head of HM Revenue and Customs, Dave Hartnett, held private talks in order to settle a long-running dispute with the head of tax at Goldman Sachs, an investment bank, yet no one from HMRC even took a note of the meeting. In the case of the further education colleges building fiasco, as John Denham MP grimly put it: 'There was a group of people that we might have expected to know what was going on who did not themselves have a full grasp of it.'

Consider Letwin's second activity: the 'transmission of decisions'. After the Child Support Agency was set up, an official report found that at least four in ten of the maintenance payments that it ordered were wrong. In the National Programme for IT in the NHS, the foolishly rapid and secretive contracting process meant that all the issues of complexity had to be dealt with *after* the contracts had already been signed, so that the programme had no chance whatsoever of achieving its central purpose of a national electronic patient record, even if this aspiration had been a good one, which it wasn't. The Student Loans Company project – in common with so many others – had wholly inadequate testing, while the governance arrangements were so poor that no one seemed to notice the huge emerging risks; and even when serious problems were finally uncovered, the department did not take prompt action to address them. Under the reforms of the Common Agricultural Policy, the government wanted a system that allowed farmers to benefit from 'a reduction in red tape and more efficient and rapid processing of payments' but in the Rural Payments Agency it produced a Kafkaesque nightmare that led some farmers to kill themselves.

Consider Letwin's third activity: the 'provision of advice'. In considering the introduction of Individual Learning Accounts, civil servants did not discuss the vulnerability of the new accounts to systematic fraud and, accordingly – despite plenty

of recent warnings that computer crime was on the increase –
there was no advice at all on what turned out to be the single
most important issue. In the case of the Child Support Agency,
it took successive administrations many years before there was
a belated admission that the problem lay with the way that
the child support system was designed. The proposed use of
call centres by the Criminal Records Bureau ignored the preferences of customers for a paper-based solution – even though it
was inherent in the design of the scheme that a phone-based
call centre would not cope because of the heavy paper flow of
original documents such as birth certificates and passports. In
the InterCity West Coast franchising competition, there were no
senior staff in the project team; even after Virgin raised concerns
about the procurement process, no one in the department independently reviewed it; and officials involved were *unaware* of
advice from external lawyers that their actions were probably
unlawful. And in the case of the Rural Payments Agency, the
choice of the 'dynamic hybrid' method for determining single
farm payments was made, as Dame Helen Ghosh told the PAC,
because 'ministers were being told it was possible when it was
not in fact possible.'

Consider Letwin's fourth activity: 'guardianship'. The issue
of guardianship is – perhaps – the most conspicuous problem.
Guardianship includes ensuring not only that the government
acts in conformity with the law but also that it safeguards
taxpayers' money. The National Programme for IT in the
NHS squandered £2.7 billion in a fruitless attempt to set up
a national electronic patient record, despite numerous early
warnings that the scheme would not work. The tax credits
system has led directly to the overpayment of many *billions*
of pounds and a consequent black mark against HM Revenue
and Customs' financial accounts each year, which – for a highly
developed nation's own tax authority – is as extraordinary as
it is embarrassing. HMRC has also blithely ignored the government's own legal requirements. Where there were new controls
in order to prevent fraud against electronically provided

government services, HMRC did not apply these controls to the tax credit system, even though the new rules were mandatory. In the case of the Individual Learning Accounts, there was a different problem: the rules were so loosely drawn up that there was no need to break them in order to abuse and exploit the scheme ruthlessly, leading to the loss of many tens of millions of pounds. And in relation to the InterCity West Coast franchising competition, the top mandarins running the senior civil service – who jealously guard their own role in shaping the careers of civil servants, largely keeping such decisions at a safe distance from ministers – somehow managed to allow the Department for Transport to have *four* permanent secretaries in two years, which does not say much for their understanding of the word 'permanent'. Indeed, it signifies a dereliction of their duty to secure continuity of management, which in a political system where ministers necessarily change quite frequently must be a central part of the civil service role.

Some government projects seem to have suffered from a 'perfect storm' where almost everything went wrong, in every possible way. In the case of C-Nomis, a computer system for the prison and probation service, a senior official certified in writing that the project did not suffer from any of the 'Eight Common Causes of Project Failure' identified by the Office of Government Commerce, even though – as an analysis by the NAO later found – the project actually suffered from seven out of the eight, either wholly or in part. In the refranchising of InterCity West Coast, the NAO identified 'five safeguards against making poor decisions' but not one of these lines of defence operated effectively. In the fiasco over recruitment of junior doctors, the government created the ludicrous position where medics whose training had been paid for by British taxpayers were forced to search for work abroad, only to be urged to return soon afterwards because of a government-induced shortage of doctors. The extensive catalogue of failures in the junior doctors example – poor project management, unrealistic timetables, a failure to pilot, poor risk management, and an overambitious attempt to introduce a large number of changes all at the same time – uncannily describes almost everything that went wrong with the Rural Payments Agency, which was perhaps the most perfect storm of all.

Whatever we are witnessing here, it is not guardianship, or indeed accurate accumulation of knowledge, or effective transmitting of decisions – and it is certainly not good advice.

Civil servants wondering why the ideal of a professional administrator is at such risk of being held up to ridicule need only look around them. Far too often, in the eyes of the public who have to pay for their government through hard-earned taxes, things just don't work properly. True, many of the screw-ups are the result of poor decisions by ministers who either try to do things too quickly, or who won't listen, or who have stupid ideas. And we also think it would be almost impossible to study this domain intensely without a growing sympathy for what civil servants have to put up with from some ministers including, on occasions, quite vile behaviour. But even if this is a considerable part of the explanation – which it undoubtedly is – it cannot *all* be down to bad ministers. And if it were, it would indicate that the persuasive powers of all our most senior civil servants were drained to the point of exhaustion.

We know there is a danger of painting a picture that is too negative. To sit on the Public Accounts Committee is to look at a wide range of public sector activity through the prism of failure, even though over the years the civil service has notched up some real successes, which are celebrated each year in the Civil Service Awards. There is probably a book to be written about this success. Equally, though, one cannot escape the breathtaking scale of some of the failures we describe, nor can one ignore the numbing ease with which such unbelievable amounts of the British people's money are squandered. And in particular, one has to recognise that there must be a systemic problem of some kind, given the repeated inability of the system to learn from its past mistakes.

For what it is worth, we agree with Letwin. The last thing

we need is government by technicians. It is of the first importance to have politically neutral professional administrative
civil servants of the highest calibre, who have the ability to
marshal a wide variety of different kinds of expertise on an
enormous array of subjects. Our system of government must
indeed ensure that 'the expertise of the expert' is absorbed in
a way that can be rationalised and understood – and that its
proper relationship to policy can be analysed successfully. We
would just like to see it happen rather more often.

•••

Almost all the accounts of the creation of the civil service in the
modern state begin with the Northcote–Trevelyan reforms in
1854. These famous reforms – hastened by the chaos that had
ensued in the Crimean War – were to some extent influenced
by the methods of the Chinese imperial court, which selected
the most talented administrators for its bureaucracy based on
fiercely competitive entrance examinations. For many years
in Whitehall, up until the mid-nineteenth century, ministers'
offices had been habitually used by the ruling classes as a
convenient billet for lazy and inadequate relatives who were
unable to make their own way in the world. Two titans of the
Victorian world, Sir Stafford Northcote, a civil servant who
was private secretary to Gladstone and who later became a
Conservative MP, serving Disraeli as both Chancellor of the
Exchequer and Foreign Secretary, and Sir Charles Trevelyan,
Permanent Secretary to the Treasury, wanted to expunge this
curse of mediocrity, using methods similar to the Chinese.
Competitive examinations were introduced to recruit the ablest
and most ambitious youth of the day, who would be promoted
on merit. The result of applying such principles in Victorian
Britain was to produce an elite cadre of administrators – the
senior ones were soon known colloquially as 'mandarins' –
who assisted ministers in running the apparatus of the state,
although it needs emphasising that apart from the Royal Navy,

the Army and the Post Office, the state itself was by modern standards still very small.

However, the need to mobilise the resources of the state for the First World War inevitably led to considerable changes. As a larger government with the need for executive ministries emerged, in 1918 the Ministry of Reconstruction published the landmark Haldane report. While Viscount Haldane, a former War Minister, resisted contemporary calls for ministerial responsibility to be diluted, his report did recognise that ministers needed more advice and assistance as an integral part of their ministries in order to be effective. The report stated: 'It appears to us that adequate provision has not been made in the past for the organised acquisition of facts and information; and for the systematic application of thought, as preliminary to the settlement of policy and its subsequent administration.' The task of ministries was to be broadened to include 'continuous acquisition of knowledge and the prosecution of research, in order to furnish a proper basis for policy'. The Haldane report strongly influenced the modern shape of the civil service divided into the substantial departments of state that we know today.

While the Second World War was an even bigger logistical undertaking than the First World War, drawing into government all manner of temporary outsiders and irregulars, there was relatively little change to the civil service until more than twenty years afterwards. In February 1966 Lord Fulton, vice-chancellor of Sussex University, was commissioned by Prime Minister Harold Wilson to review the work of the civil service. His terms of reference were simple enough – 'to examine the structure, recruitment and management, including training, of the Home Civil Service and to make recommendations'. His broad conclusion was that government needed to take 'business methods' much more seriously. As the report intoned: 'The principles of accountable management should be applied to the organisation of the work of the departments.' The Fulton review also recommended wider recruitment, professional training for officials, a new civil service department and the restructuring of the administrative class. The report identified a crucial principle which it argued 'applies to any organisation and is simple to the point of banality, but the root of much of our criticism is that it has not been observed. The principle is: look at the job first.' In other words, *make sure that those who are appointed to a job have all the required skills to perform that job.* This meant above all that the senior civil service would need to grapple with the new skills of management, and that in order to do this the most senior levels of the civil service, which for a hundred years had been known as the 'Administrative Class', would have to change radically to meet the new challenges. The nineteenth-century view of an occupation suitable for a gentleman was, as Kate Jenkins has put it, 'hopelessly inadequate for managing modern government'. In essence Fulton proposed the abolition of the career class system which had separated the administrative mandarins from the management and technical classes, into a single grading system. However, Fulton's work was hobbled from the start with Harold Wilson making clear that Fulton would not deal with 'machinery of government' questions. The Fulton committee was steered away from answering the fundamental questions about the adequacy of the Whitehall machine to cope with the increasing workload which it was required to bear. Wilson also told MPs that the government's willingness to contemplate changes in the civil service 'does not imply any intention on their part to alter the basic relationship between ministers and civil servants' – civil servants, however eminent, were to remain the confidential advisers of ministers, who alone would continue to be answerable to Parliament. Fulton was not being allowed to address the most important questions, which critics said needed to be settled before the second-order issues like recruitment, training and management were addressed. His recommendations, when they came, were broadly ignored; the Chancellor of the Exchequer, Roy Jenkins, ruled they were not necessary. Norman Crowther-Hunt, a member of Fulton's committee, said this 'gelding' of Fulton's review was a deliberate, pre-emptive strike from the permanent secretaries' club, displaying once again their genius for damage limitation – and a signal of deep opposition to change.

Indeed, despite Fulton's attempts to make the civil service more meritocratic, his report had little visible effect on the long-standing tendency to appoint young administrators straight into senior policy jobs. Twenty years later when a Commons committee was examining the prospect of establishing the new arm's-length executive agencies, management expert and Labour MP John Garrett was asked whether he agreed that under the new regime people would be able to move from agencies into the policy civil service and vice versa. He replied:

> I think it is much more likely that bright young people in the traditional administrator mould will be shot straight into the policy departments, and the agencies will be run by people who are felt to be rather below the salt: technicians and managers. There is no evidence that the culture has changed one iota in the last twenty years.

Fast forward *another* twenty years and witness bright young thing Laura Jayawardane, who at the start of our last chapter explained why she wanted to work in the public service. Sounding rather thankful that 'there hasn't been one particular job where I've just been doing one thing for a year or anything like that', she added:

> I never expected that within the first few months of my being on the fast stream I'd be briefing an Immigration Minister before he went into Parliament on the Bill, and the provisions within the Bill. I think it's a real buzz to be able to be involved in something so important at such a young age, and so early on in your career. I think that everyone who joined the fast stream shares that view.

Upon taking office Prime Minister Margaret Thatcher asked Sir Derek Rayner of Marks and Spencer to set up an Efficiency Unit in the Cabinet Office, which achieved some success in cutting the civil service payroll, which had been steadily expanding under previous administrations of both parties, and achieved £1 billion of savings. Thatcher also asked Rayner to establish the Financial Management Initiative, which aimed to give managers at all levels a clear view of their objectives, ways to measure performance in relation to those objectives, well-defined responsibilities for making the best use of their resources, for assessing how much it cost to get a task done and whether it was value for money, information about how much things cost, and access to the training and advice which they needed to exercise their responsibilities effectively. The idea was that by identifying the objectives of individual activities and the cost of achieving them, the systems would provide managers at the higher levels with the information they needed to make decisions. For lower levels of management the systems would help managers in their objective of getting the most effective output for the lowest cost. Rayner's successor in the Efficiency Unit was Sir Robin Ibbs from the giant chemical firm ICI. In a report entitled 'Management in Government: The Next Steps', Ibbs proposed to Thatcher that the government should hive off large parts of the civil service into 'executive agencies' which would actually implement the government's policies in many areas. The report's first recommendation had a simple and unequivocal basic purpose: 'Greater priority must be given to organising government so that its service delivery operations function effectively.' As Kate Jenkins, one of the report's authors, observed: 'The aim was not to set up agencies; it was to find the most effective way of providing public services.' The proposals – now widely known simply as 'Next Steps' – emerged during 1987 and became the target of a fierce Whitehall battle, with Nigel Lawson as Chancellor of the Exchequer insisting to Thatcher that the new agencies needed to have stiff financial targets which were agreed in advance by the Treasury and monitored by the Treasury thereafter. With this proviso in place, the creation of executive agencies went ahead at a considerable pace. More than 70 per cent of the home civil service – including bodies as diverse as the National Archives, the Driver Vehicle Licensing Agency and HM Courts Service – was transferred into such bodies.

The purpose of Next Steps was widely understood to be separating 'steerers from rowers'. There would be those who 'constructed' the policy and others who then 'executed' it in a much more business-like way than in the past, through 'executive' agencies, which were to be at arm's length from the controlling department. These agencies were to focus solely on the delivery task, with their own operational boards, with directors and headed up by a chief executive and a chairman. This interpretation was later criticised as not merely an over-simplification but a fundamental misreading of the report. Indeed, the entire reform has been dogged by the most basic misunderstanding. If you were to ask 100 people who were more than averagely knowledgeable about government and politics what the central purpose of the Next Steps reforms was, ninety nine of them would probably tell you that 'separating steerers and rowers' neatly summed it up – the idea of Next Steps, they would tell you, was to separate the development of policy by a small cadre of elite civil servants from its execution and delivery by a much larger group – the bulk of the civil service – who would become expert in managing delivery.

Yet this clear demarcation of roles was emphatically not supposed to be the main point, according to the authors of the Next Steps report. On the contrary, as Sir Peter Kemp – Whitehall's project manager for the Next Steps reforms – stated at the outset: 'All policy work has an element of execution and all executive work has an element of policy.' But as Alan Whitehead, a senior Labour MP, later pointed out, Kemp was saying this at precisely the moment that he was setting up a structure that assumed a 'rigid distinction' between policy and execution. Kate Jenkins has since been emphatic that this division was not the point and that the aim, correctly understood, was to ensure that civil servants had a *balanced* expertise in policy, the political environment and service delivery which too

few civil servants possessed. However, to many observers such
distinctions were sufficiently nuanced to be missed altogether.
It is possible that the need for very careful drafting at the time
may have trumped clarity. Jenkins later wrote a superb book –
Politicians and Public Services – which in part sought to clear
up this confusion. She pointed out that 'the report was clear'
in stating that 'operational effectiveness and clarity need to be
given a higher priority in the interpretation of policy objectives
and the thinking of ministers', but the message that there was no
rigid division between policy and execution was certainly not
hammered out on an anvil at the time. Indeed, the response to
Next Steps had familiar echoes of the earlier reaction to Fulton.
As Jenkins noted: 'The response of the system [to Fulton] was
simply a reflection of the inability of people with the culture and
priorities of the political and administrative elites in Britain to
recognise the need to think about how the policies they devised
might be implemented. Management, except in crisis or war,
was a problem for someone else.'

In the years that followed the introduction of Next Steps
agencies, signs of backpedalling soon emerged. The authors
of Next Steps had repeatedly warned that 'the civil service is
too big and diverse to manage as a single organisation' and
cautioned that such an attitude would throw up serious obstacles to real change. Yet in 1994 John Major's government
published 'Continuity and Change', highlighting precisely this
way of looking at things as an advantage. The report stated:
'The importance of the civil service as a coherent entity, rather
than simply the sum of the staff in individual departments
performing specific roles, has been recognised for more than
150 years.' The government launched the Citizen's Charter – in
a rather laudable attempt to set standards for levels of services
that individual users were entitled to expect – but like so many
sensible reforms this one evaporated soon enough. Increasingly,
the new recipe appeared to be minor tinkering, plus plenty of
White Papers and announcements. 'Continuity and Change' was
followed by 'Taking Forward Continuity and Change', which

was in turn succeeded by 'Modernising Government' after Tony Blair's government took office. The following years saw a steady stream of reports, discussion documents, performance partnership agreements, at least one 'vision', and the setting up of a Delivery Unit (of which more in the next chapter), a Strategy Unit, a Reform Strategy Team, an e-Transformation Unit, a Corporate Development Group, an Office of Public Service Reform – presumably in case anyone doubted that enough was going on – and yet another White Paper, entitled 'Civil Service Reforms: Delivery and Values'. This document sought 'to herald major changes in the way the civil service is managed and organised' according to Martin Stanley, a former senior official turned Whitehall commentator, 'without going into the sort of detail which would create opposition'. Stanley pointed out that the 'Outcomes' section was short and uncontroversial and did not contain a numerical target or date. The document was soon followed by 'Civil Service Reforms: Delivery and Values: One Year On'. There were also major reviews on efficiency and the location of civil servants, as well as programmes for professional skills in government.

Meanwhile Tony Blair declared that 'the world has changed and the civil service must change with it', adding that this required 'politicians as well as civil servants to change'. Blair stated: 'The principal challenge is to shift focus from policy advice to delivery. Delivery means outcomes. It means project management. It means adapting to new situations and altering rules and practice accordingly. It means working not in traditional departmental silos.'

Next in the long caravan of reforms came a set of highly detailed report cards called capability reviews. These were introduced by Sir Gus O'Donnell after he became Cabinet Secretary in 2005. The idea was to allow people to compare the 'capability' of different departments across Whitehall. This was partially a response to criticism that local authorities were being subjected by the centre to a fairly intensive regime of performance review, with a scoring system which affected local authority budgets and autonomy, while central government was avoiding such scrutiny of its own inadequacies. Embarrassingly, the reviews showed that most government departments did not have the right capabilities at the right levels. The findings were 'frankly disturbing', according to Colin Talbot from the Manchester Business School. The reviews looked at ten capabilities in each of seventeen departments – qualities such as leadership, financial management, e-government and human resources among others – and found that in these 170 snapshots, Whitehall departments were 'less than well-placed' in two thirds of the cases. The departments were found particularly wanting in a survey of staff perceptions of the leadership of their departments. Worse, the capability reviews did not examine the *performance* of departments – only their 'capability'– and were thus ignoring one of the most important aspects of a department's work. Colin Talbot said: 'If you have from the capability reviews weak leadership still at the top of the civil service – and that is their own verdict, not mine – poor delivery, and at best "moderately good" on strategy making, I think there are some pretty serious issues that need to be addressed.' And, in perhaps the most astonishing omission, the capability reviews did not even look at departmental *capability* on policy-making. Talbot told MPs: 'I have yet to find anybody who can provide me with any sort of rationale as to why they did not look at that, given that is one of the main things that departments do.' This was particularly surprising because in evidence to the same inquiry O'Donnell had put the provision of policy advice at the top of the skills which civil servants absolutely had to have, if they were to have a rounded skill set. One insider who followed the issue told us he believed that the structure and focus of the capability reviews was 'as much as Gus [O'Donnell] has been able to get past the permanent secretaries'.

In December 2009 Prime Minister Gordon Brown took his turn in publishing a White Paper, 'Putting the Frontline First: Smarter Government', which called for 'smarter not smaller government' with 'open, accountable public services', 'devolved decision making' and a 'renewed focus on value for money'. Rather breathlessly, the document demanded 'a step-change in how government is run for the turbulent times ahead, delivering better public services for lower cost' and identified twelve 'key actions' to 'strengthen the role of citizens and civic society', 'recast the relationship between the centre and the frontline' and 'streamline central government for sharper delivery'. At the launch event, Brown said with typical understatement: 'Our plans will mean some of the most sweeping changes in administration in this country in half a century.' Actually, most of this excitement boiled down to cutting the salary bill for senior civil servants, scrapping or merging some arm's-length bodies, slashing the spending on consultants and moving staff out of London, although there was an intriguing reference to the government's increasing interest in behavioural economics.

After the coalition government was formed in 2010, it was a couple of years before another White Paper emerged, but when Cabinet Office minister Francis Maude launched the Civil Service Reform Plan in June 2012 it contained more 'key actions', including 'more rigorous performance management' and 'strengthening capability'. In an echo of 'Continuity and Change' from nearly twenty years previously, the report emphasised the virtues of a 'unified civil service' although there were also calls for new ways of delivering services, a new presumption in favour of 'open policy making' – with more input from external experts and 'those who will have the task of delivering the policy once announced' – and a review of terms and conditions for hundreds of thousands of civil servants. However, it emerged in March 2013 that this last review would only affect the terms and conditions for new joiners and those who were promoted, perversely penalising strong performers while leaving civil servants who were not good enough to be promoted with the best contractual perks. At the same time, there were other echoes from even further back. Maude emphasised that his plan did not challenge the 'fundamental model' of the civil service, just as at the time of the Fulton report, Harold Wilson had told MPs that the government's willingness to contemplate changes in the civil service did not imply any intention 'to alter the basic relationship between ministers and civil servants'. The Civil Service Reform Plan was the latest chapter in thirty years of apparently incessant reforming activity since the days of Rayner's Efficiency Unit and the Financial Management Initiative, although as ever the commentariat was underwhelmed. Oxford University's Christopher Hood told MPs there was no indication of how the success of the Civil Service Reform Plan would be measured. Peter Hennessy, author of *Whitehall* and now a peer, told MPs on the Public Administration Committee that 'it's only a fragment of the picture'. Martin Stanley thoughtfully suggested that 'it would have done no harm to recognise the tensions and contradictions that are inevitable in any change programme of this nature: "pace" versus the need to consult and think through implementation issues; and a "unified civil service" versus creativity and local flexibility and discretion'. Simon Hoggart noted waspishly in *The Guardian* that Francis Maude 'used enough jargon to stuff a dead grizzly'. Some eight months later, the think tank Reform interviewed civil servants for its paper 'Whitehall Reform: The View from the Inside' and wrote: 'Senior officials reported that the plan had not led to any change in their daily working lives.'

One might be forgiven for thinking that this frenetic reform is like the buzzing of bluebottles in a jam jar. There has been no shortage of proposals for changing things but nothing like as much actual change. So little in return for so much effort. Why is this? Is it perhaps because we are neglecting what is actually done for what should be done? Are we failing to examine closely enough how people actually behave?

17

WHY DO PEOPLE DO WHAT THEY DO?

How do people actually behave?
Frans de Waal, *Peacemaking among Primates*

Outside of the old Warsaw Pact, there has rarely been a more sustained attempt in peacetime to compel a system of government to respond to central diktats than the efforts made by the 'Prime Minister's Delivery Unit' under Tony Blair. The PM was frustrated at the pace of change in the public services and wanted to push his priorities through the system faster. Immediately after the 2001 general election, Blair asked Michael Barber – a former history teacher and professor of education who had previously worked with David Blunkett in the Department for Education – to spearhead a new unit at the centre of government which would oversee the delivery of Blair's top priorities, including literacy and numeracy for eleven-year-olds, hospital waiting times, rail punctuality and street crime. The delicate task confronting Barber – who was later on dubbed 'the most powerful civil servant in the land' – was to become an authoritative source of unvarnished information for the Prime Minister about performance on these key priorities, while at the same time not so irritating the other players in the system – the Treasury, the Prime Minister's Policy Unit, and the great departments of state – that they went out of their way to thwart what he was trying to do.

In his decidedly readable account of four years working for Blair, *Instruction to Deliver*, Barber paints a portrait of how frustrating it is to sit at the centre of government facing a wall of inertia. Barber was highly critical of some Whitehall officials:

> We found that, in a number of cases, the responsible officials had decided in their own minds that because they did not have direct-line management responsibility, they had no influence. In

a phrase I came to hate, they would say: 'We only have rubber levers.' Some officials wallowed in this powerlessness because it enabled them to abdicate responsibility – if results were not delivered, at least it was not their fault.

Barber's conclusion was stark:

> The problem was psychological as much as anything – instead of setting out to decide what they could do and how they might do it, they decided what they couldn't do and how they might explain away the inevitable failure which would result. In short, our effort to promote improved delivery was as much cultural as it was technical.

Curiously, though, Barber does not appear to make the connection that if the problem were chiefly psychological, the solution should also be chiefly psychological. A word with Aidan Halligan from the NHS IT programme might have helped, given Halligan's dictum that 'culture eats strategy for breakfast'. Instead, Barber summarised his plans for delivery in five buzz words: ambition, focus, clarity, urgency and irreversibility. He acknowledged that there are thousands of people in government bureaucracies whose job is to complicate matters and even conceded that this is not necessarily a cause for criticism – 'government is, after all, a complicated thing'. However, as Barber added with a clear and appealing set of questions, 'to get anything done, a countervailing force is required; people who will simplify, keep bringing people back to the fundamentals':

> What are you trying to do?
> How are you trying to do it?
> How do you know you are succeeding?
> If you're not succeeding, how will you change things?
> How can we help you?

These five questions became the essence of the Delivery Unit.

Barber's commitment and good intentions are plain to see. His book offers fascinating insights into how the centre of government operates, especially the incalculable importance of good routines and good relationships, although, as management commentator Simon Caulkin wrote of the book in *The Observer*, 'it's an instructive narrative, if not always in the way Barber intends'. Barber developed and codified what became known as 'Deliverology' – the Treasury's Permanent Secretary Sir Nick Macpherson must take the blame for this hideous word, although whether he was being ironic is not documented – a methodology explaining 'how' to do things rather than 'what' to do, which he said could therefore be used to tackle a wide range of problems. In the appendix of his book, Barber includes a 'delivery manual' spelling out everything a user needs to know before applying the science of Deliverology, even right down to how to format a document.

Barber complains about the British habit of 'muddling through', citing Bill Bryson's classic description of this country, *Notes from a Small Island*, where Bryson says that the British are the only people in the world who, when you ask them how they are, will reply 'Mustn't grumble'. Some might see this as evidence of the traditional British stoicism which has proved quite handy in facing down the Armada, Napoleon and Adolf Hitler, but Barber says this is 'a perfect illustration of the fact that ambition isn't necessarily built into the British psyche'. As he urged on his audience at a Whitehall Delivery Conference in 2002, 'in this era, with this legacy, with this level of investment, muddling through won't suffice. We need bold ideas, boldly executed; we need an expectation of success; and we need success measured by change on the ground, at the frontline.' At the heart of Deliverology – perhaps the very ugliness of the word is a clue to what was wrong with it – was that targets for the frontline, whether in schools, hospitals or elsewhere, would be set out with extreme precision, accompanied by stringent performance management and 'key performance indicators', with each of the links in the 'delivery chain' also given its own list of actions, milestones and timetables. By following all the actions as prescribed, success would follow.

The Delivery Unit ostensibly set about their task with their eyes open. They were aware, 'obviously enough', that if a target is set badly it will cause problems; similarly, that if there are too many targets it can cause confusion; and that there is a risk of unintended and possibly perverse consequences. Yet none of this prevented the team from forging ahead, with Barber calling for an 'irreversible transformation' of structure, culture and results. '*Irreversible*' is an interesting word. The idea of an 'irreversible transformation' most commonly arises in a branch of science concerned with heat, namely thermodynamics, which defines variables such as temperature, pressure and internal energy, and explains how they are related and by what laws they change; an example of such an irreversible transformation is the spontaneous flow of heat from an area of high temperature to a region of lower temperature. The concept of irreversibility in the hard sciences is a predictable affair – notwithstanding the undoubted complexities – because one is dealing with calculable physical phenomena that behave according to certain rules.

In the sphere of human action, the concept of irreversibility is rather less obvious, although this has not stopped politicians of all shades of opinion from running with the idea. The 1974 Labour manifesto pledged to bring about 'a fundamental and irreversible shift in the balance of power and wealth in favour of working people and their families'. Margaret Thatcher teasingly poached the same phrase when, at the height of her powers, she told the 1987 Conservative Party conference that the government's reforms were 'an irreversible shift of power in favour of working people and their families'. The concept has an undeniable appeal. People who believe in their ideas naturally want to implement them and to see them endure. And it was quite clear that Barber believed his approach would deliver. His 'command and control' approach worked on the assumption that so long as one is clear enough, and identifies what is to be measured carefully enough, with unmistakable targets, it would invariably lead to successful delivery of results, almost as if the measurements and targets were all part of one physical system with calculable physical phenomena that would behave according to certain rules.

However, several problems emerged. Barber's target-driven 'command and control' approach led to a situation where details of individual failures – such as an elderly patient waiting for more than four hours in accident and emergency – might literally be chased up from a desk in Whitehall; to have the slightest chance of success, the approach could only be adopted for a very limited number of specific targets, such as literacy attainment for eight-year-olds, say, or falls in recorded knife crime in metropolitan areas, so that other things one cares about were neglected by comparison and untouched by the 'improving ethos'; and most crucially of all, the government inadvertently gave huge creative opportunities to the people working in hospitals, policing and schools to engage in behaviour that would produce the 'right' numbers to report irrespective of what was really going on, otherwise known as gaming the system. For example, when the four-hour maximum waiting time target for accident and emergency units in hospitals was originally introduced, it was measured on specific days. It was easy enough for hospitals to cancel all elective surgery on those days and so free up extra beds. Other ruses included adding a curtain rail around a bed in a corridor so that it was no longer a 'corridor' but an 'admission ward', or ensuring that as soon as a bed was allocated, a patient would be 'transferred' to the bed on the computer system even though it took the hospital porters an hour to actually move the patient, so that the target appeared to have been 'met'. The police also became adept at playing with targets. Their favourite was a domestic dispute between a husband and wife, which offered police the opportunity to book two separate assaults, issue two warnings and allow two crimes to be recorded both as detected and cleared. The Police Federation produced a dossier of ludicrous cases triggered by the chasing of targets, including the arrest of a child in Kent for removing a slice of cucumber from a sandwich and throwing it at another youngster, a man from Cheshire who was cautioned for being 'found in possession of an egg with intent to throw' and a West Midlands woman who was arrested on her wedding day for criminal damage after her foot slipped on her accelerator pedal and her vehicle damaged a car park barrier. Schools, too, had their methods for spicing up the reported exam pass rates, such as choosing easier subjects and less rigorous examination boards, 'teaching to the test', giving disproportionate time and attention to pupils near the threshold between a 'D' and a 'C' grade – at the expense of the worst-performing students – and even encouraging low-performing students to stay at home on the day of an exam. As the professionals became more adept at gaming the targets, the centre would tighten up in response and assume yet more control, resulting in what one Cabinet Office official described to us as 'trench warfare'.

Nonetheless, Barber's zeal in pursuing Deliverology remained undiminished, just as his creed's comic potential still remains underexplored. Another document in the delivery manual within his book is a letter to permanent secretaries, written some three years after the Delivery Unit project had started, which compares the Delivery Unit's journey to the writing of an incomplete thriller:

> Our thriller has had its twists and turns. We've had moments of writer's block and once or twice, like Dostoevsky with *Crime and Punishment*, we have felt like throwing the whole script on the fire and starting again but, especially over the last six months, we've discovered that our text is coming out rather well. The plotlines are sharp, the characters have developed well, the dialogue is rich and the moral of the tale is becoming clear. Now, three-quarters of the way through this, our first book, an insight of stunning importance has occurred to us. With a thriller, however good the beginning and the middle are, it's the end, that final sequence, which decides whether we have a bestseller or

a remainder on our hands. All that work and now everything depends on a few months!

In a presumably unintentional moment of pure slapstick, Barber added: 'The good news is that we've learnt so much that now we know what to do.' In another document in the manual, Barber scolded the naysayers. While not quite scaling the North Korean rhetorical heights, Barber warned that 'extraordinary discipline and persistence are required to defeat the cynics', urging that users of the delivery manual should ask themselves: 'Do you consistently advocate with passion and without compromise the controversial measures that will make a difference, such as school tests, hospital star ratings or publication of police performance data?'

Meanwhile, on the frontline there was growing frustration at the gap between rhetoric and reality. Many people working in hospitals, policing and schools could see for themselves the consequences of the obsession with targets. They railed against the regime with growing frustration that no one would listen – and some of them started to write about it. The mania for targets spawned a whole subgenre of non-fiction by people working on the frontline of public services – often writing under pseudonyms – such as *It's Your Time Wasting* by 'Frank Chalk' about teaching in an inner city school where the senior management team is too busy with pointless paperwork to support its own teachers; *In Stitches* by 'Dr Nick Edwards', who described a target culture in a hospital accident and emergency unit where following the rules made keeping patients safe more difficult; *Screwed* by 'Ronnie Thompson', which opened a fascinating window on the life of a prison officer; *Wasting Police Time* by 'PC David Copperfield', which exposed how thousands of officers were struggling to keep their heads above a sea of paperwork while taxpayers' money was wasted and 'the crime books are cooked in ways that would make Gordon Ramsay proud'; and *Perverting the Course of Justice,* by one 'Inspector Gadget' who wrote: 'I am concerned that our insane obsession with largely irrelevant targets will eventually cost lives', adding sombrely, 'It probably already has.'

An occupational psychologist and management thinker called John Seddon was so vexed by the results of target mania that he devoted a whole chapter of his book *Systems Thinking in the Public Sector* to attacking the Barber approach. Seddon acknowledges his intellectual debts to W. Edwards Deming, an American statistician and consultant – widely regarded as having done more to transform Japanese manufacturing and business than any other non-Japanese – who taught Seddon the importance of understanding and managing organisations as systems, and to Taiichi Ohno, who showed the power and practicality of doing so in manufacturing at Toyota. Deming was largely unrecognised in his US homeland until he was in his eighties and even now, given that he must be considered one of the most important individuals in twentieth-century economic history, it is surprising that Deming is relatively unknown worldwide. Seddon, who studied Deming's work extensively, has built a reputation by translating the Toyota Production System for service organisations, especially in British local government. He relates that when the accident and emergency 'Czar' Dr George Alberti was told about the fiddles reported in Dr Nick Edwards's book *In Stitches*, he simply denied it, saying that if there were any truth in the claims they would have related to teething problems. As Seddon notes: 'Despite all the evidence, the regime maintains that "cheating" or "gaming" is limited and deviant, whereas it is ubiquitous and endemic; it is systemic.' Seddon also tells a story about how Nick Raynsford, when he was local government minister, was puzzled to observe that although targets reported to central government were showing improvement, measures of public satisfaction with services were not. Raynsford apparently rationalised this dissonance by suggesting that citizens took time to change their views; perhaps many of them had not used the services recently and their expectations were, in any event, rising. As Seddon observed dryly: 'The more parsimonious explanation is the obvious one: targets have been making services worse.'

Seddon is interested in how organisations create and then deal with 'failure demand' – that is, demand that produces waste because it shouldn't occur at all. Many organisations assume that all customer demand on the operations of the organisation is 'value work', that is, the work which the organisation exists to perform. For a bank, 'Can I have a loan' or 'Can you help me pay a bill?' are examples of value demand. For the local council 'Can I register to pay my council tax?' would be a similar example. However, a large proportion of the demand on organisations is failure demand – demand that is the side-product of a failure to do something or to do something correctly for the customer. 'I don't understand this cheque' or 'Why haven't you paid my direct debit?' are examples of failure demand. Seddon cites a manager of one of the world's largest banking operations who said if he could reduce the average handling time in his call centres by thirty seconds he could deliver millions more in profits. Seddon studied the manager's bank and others, and concluded that failure demand could be as high as 40 or even 60 per cent – in local authorities it is often as high as 80 per cent – and that the manager's focus on reducing costs would actually drive up costs. It is worth pausing to note that if one is running, say, an outsourcing company which provides telephone call centres to a local council under contract, then such an arrangement might work very well, especially if – as is often the case with such arrangements – the total payments to the company providing the call centre depend on call volumes. Having sold to a local authority, for example, the idea of a shared services call centre which will – in reality – increase failure demand, the contractor not only gets a new revenue stream by being paid as an outsourced supplier to provide what is actually a poorer quality service, but as the increased failure demand – which has been created in the first place by the contractor's bad design – begins to spiral upwards, the contractor also gets the revenue from the extra calls. Seddon highlights the mistake of treating all demand as equal 'units of production': work that has to be done, when actually much of it is valueless, cost-creating work generated by a failure of the organisation to deliver services that work from the customer's point of view. As he puts it: 'Understanding how poor service design creates more demand into the front end is the beginning of understanding the organisation as a system.'

This has profound implications for how managers look upon their staff. Seddon explains that while the current norm assumes 'dumbing-down' service – 'hire cheap people, give them scripts and computer-based diagnostics' – a systems approach can be characterised as 'smartening-up'. People who deliver the service need the expertise required to deliver a variety of customer demand. The command-and-control thinker's first reaction is 'we could never afford it' because they think smarter people mean more cost. But Seddon points out that as the organisation learns to do the value work and *only* the value work (the thing that matters to the customer), the non-value work (the thing that annoys the customer) and its associated cost is driven out of the system. What's more, the second reaction of command and control thinkers to the idea of 'smartening-up', which is 'I will need better people', is also wrong. As Seddon puts it: 'They are always astonished to discover that improvement can be achieved with the same people. They have no idea of the extent to which the current system inhibits their people's contribution.' As the psychologist Frederick Herzberg has put it: 'If you want people to do a good job, give them a good job to do.' Seddon points out that by focusing on the design of the work rather than on issuing arbitrary targets, it is possible to achieve performance improvements vastly greater than any target one might have dared to set. An incomplete list of Seddon's solutions includes: focus on getting knowledge and working continuously to improve your understanding of how the work works; stop worrying about economies of scale and instead seek to improve the 'economy of flow' of the work; scrap targets, because they don't work and people just spend time massaging the statistics; stop coercing managers into doing things that drive cost into the system and worsen the service; and scrap the obsession with sharing back office services in huge call centres because they don't work half as well as front offices where people talk to the public. In fairness, the coalition government has now scrapped many targets amid a general consensus among politicians that they are very problematic. Seddon is acquiring a growing following in local government both among officials and among elected councillors. As a ConservativeHome reviewer of one of Seddon's books wrote: 'The consequences are delighted citizens (they bring you flowers instead of complaints) and cost savings that make Gershon look like a wimp' (Sir Peter Gershon was a businessman who led a major review of efficiency in the public sector for Tony Blair and Gordon Brown). Stephen Greenhalgh of Hammersmith and Fulham council described Seddon as 'a one man army in his battle to dismantle today's command state and inspection industry'.

What is particularly interesting about the traction which Seddon is now getting for his ideas is that while they are indeed attracting support among radical Conservative councillors such as Greenhalgh, the underlying ideas which stem from Seddon's mentor, W. Edwards Deming, are essentially *collaborative* rather than competitive. Deming, who only joined the faculty of Columbia University Business School when he was eighty-eight years old, deplored the emphasis on short-term profits and short-term thinking, and the annual performance appraisal which was a result of management by objective and management by fear. As Deming put it:

It annihilates long-term planning; it annihilates team work; people cannot work together. To get promotion, you have to get ahead. By working with a team, you help other people; you may help yourselves equally but you don't get ahead by being equal; you get ahead by being ahead, produce something more, have more to show, more to count; whereas team work means work together, hear everybody's ideas, fill in for other people's weaknesses, acknowledge their strengths, work together. This is impossible under the merit-rating review of performance. People are afraid. They are in fear. They work in fear. You cannot contribute to the company as they would wish to contribute. This holds at all levels. There is something worse than all of that. When the annual ratings are given out, people are bitter. They cannot understand why they are not rated higher. There is a good reason not to understand, because I could show you with a little time that it is purely a lottery. If it were recognised as a lottery, and called that, then some people would be lucky and some unlucky, they would at least understand the system and some would not feel inferior and others would not feel superior.

Seddon once said that 'my mission in life is to help managers get their thinking right about how to define their problems'. The businessman Gerry Robinson, who made a BBC documentary called *Can Gerry Robinson Fix the NHS?*, said something similar about the state of the National Health Service:

Management is often not about the solution to problems because the solutions are often very, very simple; management is about actually seeing that there is a problem and seeing that something can be done about it. And that's nearly always held at the root of the business, people who really do it at the shop-floor. Now you only manage to garner those ideas, to actually harvest them and to do something worthwhile with them if people feel that they can bring them forward, have them discussed in a useful way and that something might actually happen.

But as Robinson adds:

That absolute sense of 'it doesn't really matter what you say' and you can talk about it and go around the houses on it because actually nobody is going to do any of this stuff, that sense is a killer, because unless people feel that they can get that idea, they can be recognised for it, [and] people can say 'Well done', if they feel that that can't happen, they very quickly stop coming up with anything, and that's what's happened.

Plainly, how people behave matters a very great deal; that is, of course, how people *actually* behave, rather than how they are supposed to behave. No less important is how people feel. Our feelings can alter our appetite for risk, or even whether we want to do anything at all. How people feel affects how they behave. Our behaviour and our feelings shape our success and failure. They determine whether or not things actually get done.

This has not gone unnoticed in the world of economics. Much of modern economics is based on an account of economic behaviour by a Rational Economic Actor – we might call him *Homo economicus* – who has full knowledge of the world and who always acts rationally, in conditions of 'perfect competition', to maximise his or her 'marginal utility'; that is, to maximise the additional satisfaction which can be obtained from spending any extra available money on particular goods and services. In this way, *Homo economicus* achieves the Ideal State in economics: the most nearly perfect allocation which is available between, on the one hand, scarce resources, and on the other, competing and potentially limitless wants. There is a big plus for economists, too – the self-respect which comes with working in a rigorous academic discipline which can not only offer a complete explanation for the behaviour and preferences of *Homo economicus* but also, of course, *predict* them in the future. Economists have always known that *Homo economicus* is an illusion, but it has been such an exceptionally useful starting point for building economic models to help explain the world around us – especially in the absence of anything else – that it has provided the basis for the development of the subject.

Ironically, the earliest economists such as Adam Smith were much more interested in how people really behaved and, indeed, in how they *should* behave – what it was that constituted upright and moral conduct. Seventeen years before Smith wrote his most famous book, *The Wealth of Nations*, he had already written *The Theory of Moral Sentiments*, which laid the behavioural and ethical foundations for his later work. However, as economics began to mature as a discipline it was increasingly anxious to establish itself as a form of predictive science. Meanwhile, psychology was just beginning to emerge, without even a decent veneer of scientific credibility. Worse still, as psychology developed further it affected the voice of impersonal authority while at the same time making colourful but non-testable claims, leaving it wide open to accusations of unbridled quackery. The author Vladimir Nabokov regularly tossed barbs at Sigmund Freud, founder of psychoanalysis, calling him the 'Viennese Witch Doctor'. Psychology was altogether too racy for the economists and certainly not the intellectually respectable company for a rigorous discipline such as economics in an age where science was king. Even so, the expunging of psychology from economics happened slowly. As Colin Camerer and George Lowenstein have observed: 'In the early part of the twentieth century, the writings of economists such as Irving Fisher and Vilfredo Pareto still included rich speculations about how people think and feel about economic choices.' John Maynard Keynes also appealed to psychological insights. Yet by the middle of the twentieth century, economists had shrugged off their behavioural inheritance and many had increasingly found sanctuary in mathematics, seeking the intellectual credibility they hoped would catapult economics among the constellation of the sciences. This was still the case as the IT age dawned. As the Conservative MPs Matthew Hancock and Nadhim Zahawi write in *Masters of Nothing*, their account of the world financial crash: 'The rapid advance of mathematical techniques and computing power were a seductive draw in a profession that had long struggled to justify itself as a science.'

There remained a problem. The purely 'rational' and mathematical approach came under increasing strain as anomalies kept appearing in economists' theoretical models. People were rather more complicated and interesting than any of the economic models had allowed for. It became increasingly obvious that economics needed a better account of why people behaved as they did. And just as economists began to accept that the anomalies were valid counter-examples that could not simply be ignored, there were also promising new developments by psychologists, who turned their attention to neglected topics such as decision making, problem solving and memory. Psychologists started using economic models as a benchmark against which to compare their psychological models. Two psychologists, Amos Tversky and Daniel Kahneman, wrote a paper called 'Judgement under Uncertainty', which questioned two of the basic premises which economics relies on: first, that people are generally rational and that their thinking is normally sound; and second, that emotions such as fear, affection and hatred explain most of the occasions on which people depart from rationality. Their paper attracted widespread attention. Some years later the two authors collaborated again, writing 'Prospect Theory: Decision Making under Risk'. The authors argued that where people face a choice between alternatives where they know the probability of particular outcomes, they make decisions based on the potential value of losses and gains rather than the final outcome, and that an analysis of how they feel – in short, that losses hurt more than gains feel good – offers the most accurate explanation of how and why their decisions depart from what a modern economic theorist would have expected. Published in a leading economic journal, *Econometrica*, it became one of the most highly cited papers ever published in that journal and a founding document of behavioural economics. The collaboration between Kahneman and Tversky on judgement and on decision making was the reason for the Nobel Prize awarded to Kahneman in 2002, which Tversky would have shared had he not sadly died in 1996. Kahneman later wrote an international bestseller, *Thinking, Fast and Slow*, which explains their ideas. The

underlying truth that *Homo economicus* had never really
been a very accurate portrayal of how people actually conduct
themselves was now becoming part of the mainstream. Over a
25-year period, economics had recovered some of its earliest
insights about how people actually behave, and the topic of
behaviour – from having been something of a fringe field – had
returned to the centre stage. What we now call 'behavioural
economics' had arrived.

There has now been a stream of books, such as the highly
entertaining *Freakonomics* by Steven Levitt and Stephen
Dubner, which was so successful that rather like a Hollywood
film they produced a sequel, *Superfreakonomics*. Two Chicago
academics, a behavioural economist called Richard Thaler
and a legal scholar, Cass Sunstein, wrote *Nudge*, which
showed how to use the insights of behavioural economics for
'improving decisions about health, wealth and happiness'. Not
surprisingly, governments began to take notice. The 2009 White
Paper 'Putting the Frontline First' stated:

> Learning from the latest advances in behavioural economics,
> government can help people to help themselves, for example by
> using people's knowledge of what works for them to manage a
> chronic health condition, or by supporting them to get involved
> with their children's education or by providing them with infor-
> mation on lifestyle choices. Small changes in behaviour can have
> a valuable impact on the quality of life of individuals, families
> and communities, as well as leading to valuable savings in
> public expenditure.

The government launched a Behavioural Insights Team in the
Cabinet Office – known colloquially as the 'Nudge Unit' – to
assist government departments in taking advantage of this
new knowledge. An early example of its work was a project
to improve the speed at which some recalcitrant taxpayers
paid their income tax bill. Tax demands from HM Revenue
and Customs were redrafted in light of behavioural insights,

refracting them, as it were, through a 'behavioural prism'; so that instead of sending threatening letters that ended with 'see you in court', HMRC sent taxpayers a polite 'nudge' letter pointing out that '89 per cent of people in your part of Devon have already paid their income tax'. The results were startling. In return for merely the cost of postage, taxpayers who had relentlessly put off paying their taxes suddenly forked out, adding many millions to the Exchequer's coffers.

This raises a very big question. If it is correct – which it certainly seems to be – that *actual* behaviour is so important in economics, and that for many years the most significant part of our understanding of economics has been missing because we didn't properly understand behaviour, then of what else could this also be true? Could *actual* behaviour be having important effects elsewhere that we don't understand properly, if at all? How about in government and politics? It is one thing to use behavioural insights as a searchlight helping us to see how we can encourage people to pay their tax bills. But what if we used behavioural insights to examine relations between ministers and civil servants, or relations among civil servants – or among ministers? What if we used our understanding of how people behave to reform the inside of government itself? Or Parliament? Let's not forget that the people who brought the study of behaviour back into economics after an absence of 100 years were not economists, but psychologists. There are many kinds of behaviour in government which have nothing to do with economics, of course, and this is true in business, too; the desire to own football clubs and newspapers – and sometimes airlines – is an obvious example. Perhaps there is a deeper reason why the efforts at civil service 'reform' over the last thirty, or forty, or fifty years sound so much like a scratched record? Is there a reason why the effects of attempted reform have always seemed to be at the margin? Why is it that the same old problems – very high staff turnover, lack of information, lack of key skills, lack of financial management, lack of good project management, lack of capability in procurement, a lack of coherence at the centre of government even though it is full of bright people, and an approach to risk that swings wildly between risk aversion and jaw-dropping risk ignorance – keep cropping up again and *again*? Might the causes have something to do with behaviour?

Curiously, political scientists who study government and politics for a living have devoted little attention to this area. The studies whose chief focus is human relationships and how participants in the system actually behave – such as *The Private Government of Public Money* by Hugh Heclo and Aaron Wildavsky, and the much more recent *Everyday Life in British Government* by R. A. W. Rhodes – stand out as much for the rarity of their approach as for their considerable merit. It might seem obvious that if one wishes to change a culture one must first change behaviour. But how does one change behaviour? One can use a big stick – but the moment you turn your back, there is a good chance that people will start making faces at you while writing books under pseudonyms about why your big stick doesn't really work. What is required is *really* to change behaviour. And how do you do that? First you must understand behaviour.

And where does our behaviour come from? Schmoozing, scheming, consensus building, mediating conflicts, developing trust, abusing trust, mutual fear, total domination, reconciliation under the pressure of circumstances, the development of rivalries, the repairing of ruling coalitions – which of these behaviours do you recognise? All of them, we would guess, even though they are all well-observed behaviours of chimpanzees.

Primatologists such as Frans de Waal remind us that the roots of politics are older than humanity. In *Peacemaking among Primates*, de Waal told the story of how he asked a world-renowned psychologist who specialised in human aggression if he knew anything about *reconciliation*. The psychologist had no information on the subject, de Waal explained, adding: 'He looked at me as if the word were new to him.' The psychologist's interest turned to irritation when de Waal suggested that conflicts were 'inevitable' among people and that aggression had such a long evolutionary history that it would be logical to expect powerful coping mechanisms. The psychologist could not see what evolution had to do with it. On the contrary, the important task was to understand and then remove the causes of aggressive behaviour. However, de Waal believed that the wish for antagonism to disappear was both forlorn and misguided. One of the central arguments he has made is that aggression is one of a large number of human behavioural characteristics that cross the boundaries of language, culture, race, even species – and that it cannot be fully understood without taking the biological component into account.

The same applied to strategies for reconciliation. Anyone who watches chimpanzees or other higher primates will experience the dawning recognition of behaviours that are deeply familiar, not just screaming and fighting but also a range of conciliatory gestures such grooming, stretching out a hand, smiling, kissing and embracing – and given that we share more than 98 per cent of our genetic material with them, no one should be surprised. As de Waal wrote: 'The fact that monkeys, apes and humans all engage in reconciliation behaviour means that it is over thirty million years old, preceding the evolutionary divergence of these primates.' He also wrote that 'it is time we learned how people use aggressive behaviour to reach their goals, and how they subsequently deal with the consequences.'

In his book *The Righteous Mind*, the American psychologist Jonathan Haidt relates how it is now much less risky than in the past for a scientist to claim that there are 'innate' human behaviours. Haidt explained that previously to back up such claims 'you had to show that the trait was hard-wired, unchangeable by experience, and found in all cultures'. With such a definition, not much is innate. Anyone who tried to propose that something was innate would be told: 'There's a tribe somewhere on Earth that didn't show the trait, so therefore it's not innate.' Neuroscientists now understand that traits can be innate without being either 'hard wired' in the sense of being wholly fixed, or universal. Our brains are best understood as *pre-wired* – flexible and subject to change – rather than *hard wired*, fixed and immutable. Haidt draws attention to the work of the neuroscientist Gary Marcus, who suggests that the brain is like a book, the first draft of which is written by the genes during foetal development. And although no chapters are complete at birth, there are also no 'blank pages' on which one could just write any conceivable thing. Rather, as Marcus writes: 'Nature provides a first draft, which experience then revises ... "built-in" does not mean unmalleable; it means "organised in advance of experience".'

Given that the range of behaviours we exhibit is so important for our future and is already circumscribed, shouldn't we know more about what those behaviours are? We are very interested to note that the subtitle of Hancock and Zahawi's *Masters of Nothing* is *How the Crash Will Happen Again Unless We Understand Human Nature*. A former Wall Street trader called John Coates has shown that we think with our bodies as well as with our brains. Coates, who worked for Goldman Sachs and ran a trading desk for Deutsche Bank, was convinced that there is a basis in biochemistry for the feelings of euphoria and fear which traders experience while they are taking enormous risks. He returned to Cambridge to retrain as a neuroscientist and then wrote *The Hour between Dog and Wolf: Risk Taking, Gut Feelings and The Biology of Boom and Bust*. As Coates observes: 'Financial risk-taking is as much a biological activity, with as many medical consequences, as facing down a grizzly bear.'

Isn't this stuff we should know more about? Could it affect the way we treat each other in Parliament and in government? Could it affect other kinds of risk? How on earth did we manage to squander several billion pounds on a non-existent electronic patient care record in the National Programme for IT in the NHS? In the InterCity West Coast franchise competition, how did the top people in the Department for Transport not know that lawyers had warned the department its actions were probably unlawful? Did by any chance the *behaviour* of the participants have something to do with it?

How would unqualified people at the top of enormous banks behave if they wanted to become even richer by selling products they didn't actually understand but which plainly led to enormous personal bonuses? The obvious starting point would be to exploit the fear that others have of looking stupid. And for many years, some bankers managed to get away with behaving in just this way, while the rest of us are now paying the price after they inadvertently crashed the whole Western world.

How would you behave if you wanted the United Kingdom to invade another country but you knew most people were opposed? Especially if your intelligence agencies told you that the evidence of weapons of mass destruction – the reason you gave for wanting war – was actually rather 'limited, sporadic and patchy'? Would it not be much easier if you described the evidence as 'extensive, detailed and authoritative'? And sure enough, this was exactly how Tony Blair behaved over Iraq.

Understanding behaviour will matter just as much in future, too. The foreign policy analyst Trita Parsi suggests in *A Single Roll of the Dice* that the catastrophe that has been US–Iranian relations over the last thirty years is not merely an antagonistic relationship but has become 'institutionalised enmity' – a set of behaviours so entrenched on both sides that the participants cannot find a way out.

One London-based risk consultant, Anthony Fitzsimmons, believes that in analysing risk within organisations, 'behavioural risk' is among the most important as well as the least understood. Such risks include everything from the dangers of charismatic corporate leaders to inappropriate performance incentives for top managers. But studying this is an infant science – particularly in the public sector – precisely because of the dangers involved for those who draw attention to the wrong types of behaviour. The '360 degree' staff review is still seldom used.

In discussing the behaviour of US government employees, Clay Johnson, a former senior official in the US Office of Management and Budget, told us: 'You don't get 1.8 million federal employees to do something they don't want to do.' Allan Leighton made a similar point about employee behaviour when he became chairman of Royal Mail: 'Fundamental change is not something you do *to* people. It is something you do *with* people.'

If Clausewitz's dictum is true that 'war is merely the continuation of politics by other means', then it follows that politics is the continuation of war by other means. Politics is about mediating between and seeking to *reconcile* differing and sometimes conflicting points of view. This is something we have been learning how to do for hundreds of thousands of years but if we were more actively aware of what is going on, might we not get better results, both at home and in our international diplomacy? Greater understanding of how people actually behave in government and politics – and why – will not eliminate the difficulties we face, or remove the need for tough choices, but if we had a richer awareness, noticing and understanding more of what is actually happening, it would help us frame our choices better.

Economics has now rediscovered its earliest roots in the study of human behaviour. We urgently need a similar shift in how we seek to understand the way government and politics actually work. Without this fuller understanding of how human behaviour affects us, our attempts to deliver change in government and politics will always be impoverished and at much greater risk of failure. Instead of buzzing around like bluebottles in a jar – with incessant exhortations that there must be improvements and with ever longer lists of proposed reforms – we should devote more time to answering Frans de Waal's question: 'How do people actually behave?' It will not be easy. Nothing worthwhile is. But we will learn things which will help us in navigating our way through the problems we face. Sir Ken Robinson, a teacher renowned worldwide in the development of creativity, wrote that 'human resources, like natural resources, are often buried deep. In every organisation there are all sorts of untapped talents and abilities.' Don't we need every hand on deck in order to get out of the mess we have landed ourselves in? It is always sensible to make the most of what you have. The answer is to look more closely at ourselves and our nature – and to act on what we find.

SELECT BIBLIOGRAPHY

Reports and Papers

Since the work of the House of Commons Public Accounts Committee (PAC) involves taking evidence on reports from the National Audit Office (NAO), the subsequent PAC reports often have identical titles to their corresponding NAO reports. Rather than mention the identical title twice, where we have consulted both reports we name the title of the report only once below, and then note separately the House of Commons papers reference number for both the NAO report and its corresponding PAC report.

Other abbreviations:

Cm/Cmnd	HM Government Command Papers
HC	House of Commons Papers
HLCC	House of Lords Constitution Committee
PASC	Public Administration Select Committee

This book has no footnotes, which may vex some and please others. We draw heavily on a rich seam of parliamentary and government papers and also other sources. In addition to PAC and NAO reports that are fundamental to most case study chapters, we salute the Public Administration Select Committee under the chairmanship of Tony Wright and now Bernard Jenkin, whose work we found indispensable. The Royal Academy of Engineering and British Computer Society working group on complex IT projects was one of the most helpful sources on that subject among hundreds we consulted. We also highlight the superiority of John Seddon's book *Systems Thinking in the Public Sector*; Martin Stanley's website, http://www.civilservant.org.uk; Kate Jenkins's book *Politicians and Public Services: Implementing Change in a Clash of Cultures* – which we found unrivalled for analytical depth of the underlying issues – and highly insightful speeches by Oliver Letwin and Sir Richard Mottram. All are listed below. Readers wishing to look up specific quotations from anywhere will find Google most helpful.

Child Support Agency

Child Support Agency – Implementation of the Child Support Reforms, NAO Report: Session 2005–06, HC 1174; and PAC 37th Report of Session 2006–07, HC 812

Child Maintenance and Enforcement: Commission Cost Reduction NAO Report: Session 2010–12, HC 1793; and PAC 83rd Report of Session 2010–12, HC 1874

House of Commons Work and Pensions Committee: *The Child Maintenance and Enforcement Commission and the CSA's Operational Improvement Plan*, 3rd Report of Session 2009–10, HC 118; and *Child Support Reform*, 4th Report of Session 2006–07, HC 219 Volumes i and ii; and *The Performance of the Child Support Agency*, HC 44 Volumes i and ii, 19 April 2004

Child Support Agency, *Child Support Agency Report on Handover to the Child Maintenance and Enforcement Commission*, December 2008

Treasury Minutes: *Child Support Agency: Implementation of the Child Support Reforms*, Cm 7216

Passport Agency

Manpower Planning in the Home Office: The Passport Agency and the Nationality Division, NAO Report: Session 1992–93, HC 585

The Passport Delays of Summer 1999, NAO Report: Session 1998–99, HC 812; and PAC 24th Report of Session 1999–2000, HC 208

Tax Credits

Comptroller and Auditor General's Standard Reports on the Accounts of the Inland Revenue; and HM Revenue & Customs; *passim*

Tax Credits and Income Tax, PAC 14th Report of Session 2008–09, HC 311

Tax Credits and PAYE, PAC 8th Report of Session 2007–08, HC 300

Tax Credits, PAC 22nd Report of Session 2006–07, HC 487

New Tax Credits, PAC 37th Report of Session 2005–06, HC 782

Tax Credits, PAC 14th Report of Session 2003–04, HC 89

Tax Credits, PAC 67th Report of Session 2001–02, HC 866

Treasury Committee: *The Administration of Tax Credits*, 6th Report of Session 2005–06, HC 811 Volumes i and ii

Parliamentary and Health Service Ombudsman: *Tax Credits: Putting Things Right*, 3rd Report, Session 2005–06, HC 124; and *Tax Credits: Getting It Wrong?*, 5th Report, Session 2006–07, HC 1010

Individual Learning Accounts

Individual Learning Accounts, NAO Report: Session 1998–99, HC 357; and PAC 10th Report of Session 2002–03, HC 544

House of Commons Education and Skills Committee: *Individual Learning Accounts*, 3rd Report of Session 2001–02, HC 561 Volumes i and ii; and *Individual Learning Accounts: Government's Response to the Committee's Third Report of Session 2001–2002*, Third Special Report of Session 2001–02, HC 987

Ghost in the Machine: An Analysis of IT Fraud and Abuse, Audit Commission for Local Authorities in England and Wales, London 1998

Criminal Records Bureau

Criminal Records Bureau: Delivering Safer Recruitment?, NAO Report: Session 2003–04, HC 266; and PAC 45th Report of Session 2003–04, HC 453

House of Commons Home Affairs Committee: *Criminal Records Bureau*, 2nd Second Report of Session 2000–01, HC 227; and 5th Special Report of Session 2000–01, HC 467

The Bichard Inquiry Report – *A Public Inquiry Report on Child Protection Procedures in Humberside Police and Cambridgeshire Constabulary, Particularly the Effectiveness of Relevant Intelligence-based Record Keeping, Vetting Practices since 1995 and Information Sharing with Other Agencies*, June 2004, HC 653

Rural Payments Agency

The Delays in Administering the 2005 Single Payment Scheme in England, NAO Report: Session 2005–06, HC 163; and PAC 55th Report of Session 2006–07, HC 893

A Progress Update in Resolving the Difficulties in Administering the Single Payment Scheme in England, NAO Report: Session 2007–08, HC 10; and PAC 29th Report of Session 2007–08, HC 285

A *Second Progress Update on the Administration of the Single Payment Scheme by the Rural Payments Agency*, NAO Report: Session 2008–09, HC 880; and PAC 1st Report of Session 2009–10, HC 98

House of Commons Environment, Food and Rural Affairs Committee: *Rural Payments Agency*, 6th Report of Session 2002–03, HC 382; and *The Rural Payments Agency and the implementation of the Single Payment Scheme*, 3rd Report of Session 2006–07, HC 107 Volumes i and ii

Foreign National Prisoners

Returning Failed Asylum Applicants, NAO Report: Session 2005–06, HC 76; and PAC 34th Report of Session 2005–06, HC 620

Management of Asylum Applications by the UK Border Agency, NAO Report: Session 2008–09, HC 124; and PAC 28th Report of Session 2008–09, HC 325

Home Affairs Committee: *The Work of the UK Border Agency*, quarterly reports, *passim*

Vine, John CBE QPM, Independent Chief Inspector of the UK Border Agency, *A Thematic Inspection of How the UK Border Agency Manages Foreign National Prisoners*, February–May 2011.

Student Loans Company

The Customer First Programme: Delivery of Student Finance, NAO Report: Session 2009–10, HC 296; and PAC 8th Report of Session 2010–11 (*sic*), HC 424

PricewaterhouseCoopers, *Independent Health Check Review of Student Finance England*, 22 April 2010

The Hopkin Review – *Review of the Delivery of Financial Support to Students in England by the Student Loans Company for the Academic Year 2009/10 and Plans for Academic Year 2010/11*, by Professor Sir Deian Hopkin, December 2009

FE Colleges Building Programme

Renewing the Physical Infrastructure of English Further Education Colleges, NAO Report: Session 2007–08, HC 924; and PAC 48th Report of Session 2008–09, HC 924

Innovation, Universities, Science and Skills Committee: *Spend, Spend, Spend? The Mismanagement of the Learning and Skills Council's Capital Programme in Further Education Colleges*, 7th Report of Session 2008–09, HC 530

The Foster Review – *A Review of the Capital Programme in Further Education*, by Sir Andrew Foster, March 2009

Recruitment of Junior Doctors

The Tooke Inquiry – *Aspiring to Excellence: Finding and Final Recommendations of the Independent Inquiry into Modernising Medical Careers led by Professor Sir John Tooke*, January 2008

Health Committee: *Modernising Medical Careers*, 3rd Report of Session 2007–08, HC 25 Volumes i, ii and iii; and *Workforce Planning*, 4th Report of Session 2006–07, HC 171 Volumes i, ii and iii.

National Programme for IT in the NHS

National Programme for IT in the NHS, NAO Report: Session 2005–06, HC 1173; and PAC 20th Report of Session 2006–07, HC 390

National Programme for IT in the NHS: Progress since 2006, NAO Report: Session 2007–08, HC 484-i and *Project Progress Reports*, HC 484-ii; and PAC 2nd Report of Session 2008–09, HC 153

National Programme for IT in the NHS: an Update on the Delivery of Detailed Care Records Systems, NAO Report: Session 2010–2012, HC 888; and PAC 45th Report of Session 2010–12, HC 1070

House of Commons Health Committee: *The Electronic Patient Record*, 6th Report of Session 2006–07, HC 422 Volumes i, ii and iii

Richard Bacon MP and John Pugh MP, *Information Technology in the NHS: What Next?* http://www.richardbacon.org.uk/parl/npfit/default.htm

InterCity West Coast Franchising Competition

Lessons from cancelling the West Coast InterCity West Coast Franchise Competition, NAO Report: Session 2012–13, HC 796; and PAC 31st Report of Session 2012–13, HC 813

House of Commons Transport Committee: *Cancellation of the InterCity West Coast Franchise Competition*, 8th Report of Session 2012–13, HC 537

The Laidlaw Inquiry: *Initial Findings Report*, only available on the Department for Transport website: http://assets.dft.gov.uk/publications/laidlaw-report/laidlaw-report.pdf

Final Report of the Laidlaw Inquiry – *Inquiry into the Lessons for the Department for Transport from the InterCity West Coast Competition*, December 2012, Session 2012–13, HC 809

The Brown Review of the Rail Franchising Programme, January 2013, Cm 8526

Information Technology Projects

Royal Academy of Engineering, *The Challenges of Complex IT Projects: The Report of a Working Group from the Royal Academy of Engineering and the British Computer Society*, April 2004

Government and IT – 'a Recipe for Rip-offs': Time for a New Approach, PASC 12th Report of Session 2010–12, HC 715 Volumes i, ii and iii

Charette, Robert N., *Why Software Fails*, Institute of Electrical and Electronics Engineers, September 2005, http://spectrum.ieee.org/computing/software/why-software-fails

R. P. Feynman, *Report of the Presidential Commission on the Space Shuttle Challenger Accident: Volume 2, Appendix F – Personal Observations on Reliability of Shuttle*, http://history.nasa.gov/rogersrep/v2appf.htm

Work and Pensions Committee: *Department for Work and Pensions Management of Information Technology Projects: Making IT Deliver for DWP Customers*, 3rd Report of Session 2003–04, HC 311 Volumes i and ii.

Further Parliamentary Reports and Papers

Assessment of the Capability Review Programme, NAO Report: Session 2008–09, HC 123; and PAC 45th Report of Session 2008–09, HC 618

Assurance for Major Projects, NAO Report: Session 2010–12, HC 1698; and PAC 14th Report of Session 2012–13, HC 384

Accountability for Public Money, PAC 28th Report of Session 2010–11, HC 740

The State of Government, PASC Oral Evidence, Thursday 11 March 2010, HC 458

On Target? Government by Measurement, PASC 5th Report of Session 2002–03, HC 62 Volumes i and ii

Politics and Administration: Ministers and Civil Servants, PASC 3rd Report of Session 2006–07, HC 122 Volumes i and ii

Governing the Future, PASC 2nd Report of Session 2006–07, HC 123 Volumes i and ii

Skills for Government, PASC 9th of Session 2006–07, HC 93 Volumes i and ii

Good Government, PASC 8th Report of Session 2008–09, HC 97 Volumes i and ii

The Cabinet Office and the Centre of Government, HLCC 4th Report of Session 2009–10, HL Paper 30

The Accountability of Civil Servants, HLCC Volume of Oral and Written Evidence; and HLCC 6th Report of Session 2012–13, HL Paper 61

Reforming NHS Dentistry: Ensuring Effective Management of Risks, NAO Report: Session 2004–05, HC 25; and PAC 30th Report of Session 2004–05, HC 167

Policy and Delivery: The National Curriculum Tests Delivery Failure in 2008, House of Commons Children, Schools and Families Committee 6th Report of Session 2008–09, HC 205; and *Government Response*: House of Commons Children, Schools and Families Committee, 6th Special Report of Session 2008–09, HC 1037

The Sutherland Inquiry: An Independent Inquiry into the Delivery of National Curriculum Tests in 2008, The Stationery Office, 16 December 2008, HC 62

Opra: Tackling the Risks to Pension Scheme Members, NAO Report: Session 2001–02, HC 1262; and PAC 15th Report of Session 2002–03, HC 589

The Thames Gateway: Laying the Foundations, NAO Report: Session 2006–07, HC 526; and PAC 62nd Report of Session 2006–07, HC 693

Delivering Digital Tactical Communications Through the Bowman CIP Programme, NAO Report: Session 2005–06, HC 1050; and PAC 14th Report of Session 2006–07, HC 358

The Implementation of the National Probation Service Information Systems Strategy, NAO Report: Session 2000–01, HC 401; and PAC 32nd Report of Session 2001–02, HC 357

Further Government Reports and Papers

Managing Public Money, HM Treasury, October 2007

The Fulton Report – *The Report of the Committee on the Civil Service*, Cmnd 3638, June 1968

Efficiency and Effectiveness in the Civil Service, Treasury and Civil Service Committee, 3rd Report of Session 1981–82, HC 236

Efficiency and Effectiveness in the Civil Service: Government Observations on the Third Report from the Treasury and Civil

Service Committee, Session 1981–82 HC 236, Cmnd 8616, September 1982.

Improving Management in Government: The Next Steps – Report to the Prime Minister by Kate Jenkins, Karen Caines and Andrew Jackson; Efficiency Unit, HMSO 1988

Civil Service Management Reform: The Next Steps, Treasury and Civil Service Committee, 8th Report, Session 1987–88, HC 494 Volumes i and ii

The Civil Service: Continuity and Change, Cm 2627, July 1994

The Civil Service: Taking Forward Continuity and Change, Cm 2748, January 1995

Modernising Government, Cm 4310, March 1999

Civil Service Reforms: Delivery and Values, Cabinet Office, 2004

Civil Service Reforms: Delivery and Values: One Year On, Cabinet Office, 2005

Putting the Frontline First: Smarter Government, Cm 7753, December 2009

The Civil Service Reform Plan, HM Government, June 2012

Civil Service Fast Streamer profiles: http://faststream.civilservice.gov.uk/ Fast-Streamer-Profiles/Laura-Jayawardane/; and http://faststream. civilservice.gov.uk/Fast-Streamer-Profiles/Stephen-Rimmer/

Reports and Papers from Commentators and Think Tanks

Atkins, Derek; Fitzsimmons, Anthony; Parsons, Chris; and Punter, Alan, *Roads to Ruin: A Study of Major Risk Events – Their Origins, Impact and Implications*, Cass Business School and Airmic (Association of Insurance and Risk Managers in Industry and Commerce), London, 2011

Darwall, Rupert, *The Reluctant Managers: Report on Reforming Whitehall*, Reform, London, December 2005

Deming, Dr W. Edwards, *Management's Five Deadly Diseases: A conversation with Dr W. Edwards Deming*, Encyclopaedia Britannica Educational Corporation (EBE), 1984, http://www.youtube.com/watch?v=ehMAwIHGN0Y

Douglas, Sir Roger; Richardson, Ruth; and Robson; Sir Steve, *Spending without Reform: Interim Report of the Commission on the Reform of Public Services*, Reform, London, June 2002

Fang, Ferric C.; Steen, R. Grant; and Casadevall, Arturo, *Misconduct Accounts for the Majority of Retracted Scientific Publications*, in

Proceedings of the National Academy of Sciences of the United States of America, vol. 109 no. 42, 17028–17033 http://www.pnas.org/content/109/42/17028.short

Haldenby, Andrew; Majumdar, Tara; and Rosen, Greg, *Whitehall Reform: The View from the Inside*, Reform, London, February 2013

Haldenby, Andrew; Parsons, Lucy; Rosen, Greg; and Truss, Elizabeth, *Fit for Purpose*, Reform, London, March 2009

Letwin MP, Rt Hon. Oliver, 'Why Mandarins Matter', keynote speech at Institute for Government, 17 September 2012

Lodge, Guy and Rogers, Ben, *Whitehall's Black Box: Accountability and Performance in the Senior Civil Service*, Institute for Public Policy Research, London, August 2006

Macpherson, Sir Nick, 'The Origins of Treasury Control', lecture at Queen Mary, University of London, 16 January 2013

Mottram, Sir Richard, 'Fifteen Years at the Top in the UK Civil Service – Some Reflections', MPA Capstone Speech at the London School of Economics, 6 May 2008

Parker, Simon; Paun, Akash; and McClory, Jonathan, *The State of the Service: A Review of Whitehall's Performance and Prospects for Improvement*, Institute for Government, London, July 2009

Parker, Simon; Paun, Akash; McClory, Jonathan; and Blatchford, Kate, *Shaping Up: A Whitehall for the Future*, Institute for Government and The Constitution Unit, London, January 2010

Stanley, Martin, *How to be a Civil Servant*, http://www.civilservant.org.uk

Straw, Ed, *The Dead Generalist: Reforming the Civil Service and Public Services*, Demos, London, September 2004

Books

Altshuler, Alan and Luberoff, David, *Mega-Projects: The Changing Politics of Urban Public Investment*, Brookings Institution Press, Washington DC 2003

Barber, Michael, *Instruction to Deliver: Tony Blair, Public Services and the Challenge of Achieving Targets*, Politico's, London 2007

Bentley, Alex; Earls, Mark; and O'Brian, Michael, *I'll Have What She's Having: Mapping Social Behavior*, MIT Press, Cambridge MA 2011

Blackstone, Tessa and Plowden, William, *Inside the Think Tank: Advising the Cabinet 1971–1983*, William Heinemann, London 1988

Bloggs, WPC E. E., *Diary of an On-Call Girl: True Stories from the Frontline*, Monday, Cheltenham 2007

Boles, Nick, *Which Way's Up?: The Future for Coalition Britain and How to Get There*, Biteback, London 2010

Bourn, Sir John, *Public Sector Auditing: Is It Value for Money?*, John Wiley and Sons, Chichester 2007

Bovens, Mark and 't Hart, Paul, *Understanding Policy Fiascoes*, Transaction, New Brunswick NJ 1996

Brecht, Bertolt, *Poems 1913–1956*, edited by John Willett and Ralph Manheim, Methuen, London 1987

Brittan, Samuel, *The Treasury under the Tories 1951–1964*, Pelican, London 1964

Bruce-Gardyne, Jock and Lawson, Nigel, *The Power Game: An Examination of Decision Making in Government*, Macmillan, London and Basingstoke 1976

Burke, Edmund, *Reflections on the Revolution in France*, Penguin Classics, London [1790] 1986

Camerer, Colin F. and Loewenstein, George, 'Behavioral Economics: Past, Present, Future' in *Advances in Behavioral Economics*, edited by Colin F. Camerer, George Loewenstein and Matthew Rabin, Princeton University Press, Princeton 2004

Chalk, Frank, *It's Your Time You're Wasting: A Teacher's Tales of Classroom Hell*, Monday, Cheltenham 2006

Chambers, Robert, *Whose Reality Counts?: Putting the First Last*, Intermediate Technology Publications, London 1997

von Clausewitz, Carl, *On War*, Everyman, London 1993

Coates, John, *The Hour between Dog and Wolf: Risk-Taking, Gut Feelings and the Biology of Boom and Bust*, Fourth Estate, London 2012

Collins, Tony and Bicknell, David, *Crash: Ten Easy Ways to Avoid a Computer Disaster*, Simon and Schuster, London 1997

Copperfield, PC David, *Wasting Police Time: The Crazy World of the War on Crime*, Monday, Cheltenham 2006

Craig, David and Brooks, Richard, *Plundering the Public Sector: How New Labour are Letting Consultants Run Off with £70 Billion of Our Money*, Constable, London 2006

Crossman, Richard, *The Diaries of a Cabinet Minister*, Hamish Hamilton & Jonathan Cape, London 1975

Deming, W. Edwards, *Out of the Crisis*, MIT Press, Cambridge MA 1982

Diamond, Jared, *The Rise and Fall of the Third Chimpanzee*, Hutchinson Radius, London 1991

Duhigg, Charles, *The Power of Habit: Why We Do What We Do in Life and Business*, Random House, New York 2012

Edwards, Dr Nick, *In Stitches: The Highs and Lows of Life as an A&E Doctor*, Friday, London 2007

Fernandez-Armesto, Felipe, *So You Think You're Human?: A Brief History of Humankind*, Oxford University Press, Oxford 2004

Feyerabend, Paul, *Against Method* (Third Edition), Verso, London 1993

Flyvbjerg, Bent, *Rationality and Power: Democracy in Practice*, University of Chicago Press, Chicago 1998

Flyvbjerg, Bent; Bruzelius, Nils; and Rothengatter, Werner, *Megaprojects and Risk: An Anatomy of Ambition*, Cambridge University Press, Cambridge 2003

Foley, Michael, *The Silence of Constitutions: Gaps, 'Abeyances' and Political Temperament in the Maintenance of Government*, Routledge, London 1989

Fry, Geoffrey, *The Changing Civil Service*, George Allen and Unwin, London 1985

Gadget, Inspector, *Perverting the Course of Justice: The Hilarious and Shocking Story of British Policing*, Monday, Cheltenham 2008

Garrett, John, *Managing the Civil Service*, William Heinemann, London 1980

Gawande, Atul, *Better: A Surgeon's Notes on Performance*, Metropolitan, New York 2007

Gelernter, David, *The Aesthetics of Computing*, Weidenfeld and Nicolson, London 1998

Gerstner, Louis, *Who Says Elephants Can't Dance?: Inside IBM's Turnaround*, HarperCollins, New York 2002

Goldacre, Ben, *Bad Pharma: How Drug Companies Mislead Doctors and Harm Patients*, Fourth Estate, London 2012

Goodman, Helen, 'Whitehall and the Civil Service' in *Towards a New Constitutional Settlement*, edited by Chris Bryant, Smith Institute, London 2007

Haidt, Jonathan, *The Righteous Mind: Why Good People Are Divided by Politics and Religion*, Pantheon, New York 2012

Hancock, Matthew and Zahawi, Nadhim, *Masters of Nothing: How The Crash Will Happen Again Unless We Understand Human Nature*, Biteback, London 2011

Heclo, Hugh and Wildavsky, Aaron, *The Private Government of Public Money: Community and Policy inside British Politics* (Second Edition), Macmillan, London 1981

Henderson, Mark, *The Geek Manifesto: Why Science Matters*, Bantam Press, London 2012

Hennessy, Peter, *Whitehall*, Secker and Warburg, London 1989

Hennessy, Peter; Morrison, Susan; and Townsend, Richard, *Routine Punctuated by Orgies: The Central Policy Review Staff 1970–1983*, University of Strathclyde, Glasgow 1985

Heseltine, Michael, *Life in the Jungle*, Hodder and Stoughton, London 2000

Jenkins, Kate, *Politicians and Public Services: Implementing Change in a Clash of Cultures*, Edward Elgar, Cheltenham 2008

Kahneman, Daniel, *Thinking, Fast and Slow*, Penguin, London 2012

Kay, John, *Obliquity: Why Our Goals Are Best Achieved Indirectly*, Profile, London 2010

Kellner, Peter and Crowther-Hunt, Lord, *The Civil Servants: An Inquiry into Britain's Ruling Class*, Macdonald, London 1980

King, Anthony, *The British Constitution*, Oxford University Press, Oxford 2007

Kuhn, Thomas S., *The Structure of Scientific Revolutions* (Third Edition), University of Chicago Press, Chicago and London 1996

Lawson, Nigel, *The View from No 11: Memoirs of a Tory Radical*, Bantam Press, London 1992

Leahy, Terry, *Management in 10 Words*, Random House Business, London 2012

Lopp, Michael, *Managing Humans: Biting and Humorous Tales of a Software Engineering Manager*, Apress, Berkeley CA 2007

Machiavelli, Niccolo, *The Prince*, translated by George Bull, Penguin, London 1999

Mandelbrot, Benoit B. and Hudson, Richard L., *The (Mis)Behaviour of Markets: A Fractal View of Risk, Ruin and Reward*, Profile, London 2004

Marmor, Theodore, *Understanding Healthcare Reform*, Yale University Press, New Haven CT 1994

Marr, Andrew, 'Foreword' in Duncan Campbell-Smith, *Follow the Money: The Audit Commission, Public Money and the Management of Public Services 1983–2008*, Allen Lane, London 2008

Mitchell, Basil, 'The Layman's Predicament' in *How to Play*

Theological Ping-Pong: Collected Essays in Faith and Reason, Hodder and Stoughton, London 1990

Mulgan, Geoff, *The Art of Public Strategy: Mobilizing Power and Knowledge for the Common Good*, Oxford University Press, Oxford 2009

Myddelton, D. R., *They Meant Well: Government Project Disasters*, Institute of Economic Affairs, London 2007

Norman, Jesse, *The Big Society: The Anatomy of the New Politics*, University of Buckingham Press, Buckingham 2010

Nutt, David, *Drugs without the Hot Air*, UIT Cambridge, Cambridge 2012

Page, Lewis, *Lions, Donkeys and Dinosaurs: Waste and Blundering in the Armed Forces*, William Heinemann, London 2006

Parkinson, C. Northcote, *Parkinson's Law or The Pursuit of Progress*, Penguin, London [1957] 1985

Parsi, Trita, *A Single Roll of the Dice: Obama's Diplomacy with Iran*, Yale University Press, New Haven CT 2012

Pinker, Steven, *The Blank Slate: The Modern Denial of Human Nature*, Allen Lane, London 2002

Popper, Karl, *Conjectures and Refutations: The Growth of Scientific Knowledge*, Routledge & Kegan Paul, London 1963

Powell, Jonathan, *The New Machiavelli: How to Wield Power in the Modern World*, Bodley Head, London 2010

Pressman, Jeffrey L. and Wildavsky, Aaron, *Implementation: How Great Expectations in Washington are Dashed in Oakland; Or, Why It's Amazing that Federal Programs Work at All*, University of California Press, Berkeley 1974

Pressman, Roger S., *Software Engineering: A Practitioner's Approach* (Seventh Edition), McGraw-Hill Higher Education, New York 2010

Rees, Laurence, *Selling Politics*, BBC Books, London 1992

Rhodes, R. A. W., *Everyday Life in British Government*, Oxford University Press, Oxford 2011

Robinson, Ken, *Out of Our Minds: Learning to Be Creative* (Revised Edition), Capstone, Chichester 2011

Ross, John F., *The Polar Bear Strategy: Reflections on Risk in Modern Life*, Perseus, Reading MA 1999

Seddon, John, *Systems Thinking in the Public Sector: The Failure of the Reform Regime ... and a Manifesto for a Better Way*, Triarchy Press, Axminster 2008

Shephard, Gillian, *Shephard's Watch: Illusions of Power in British Politics*, Politico's, London 2000

Stoker Gerry, *Why Politics Matters: Making Democracy Work*, Palgrave Macmillan, Basingstoke 2006

Thaler, Richard and Sunstein, Cass, *Nudge: Improving Decisions about Health, Wealth, and Happiness*, Yale University Press, New Haven CT 2008

Thompson, Ronnie, *Screwed: The Truth about Life as a Prison Officer*, Headline Review, London 2007

Tyrie, Andrew, *The Prospects for Public Spending*, Social Market Foundation, London 1996

Vise, David, *The Google Story*, Macmillan, London 2005

de Waal, Frans, *Chimpanzee Politics: Power and Sex among Apes* (25th Anniversary Edition), Johns Hopkins University Press, Baltimore 2007

de Waal, Frans, *Our Inner Ape: The Best and Worst of Human Nature*, Granta, London 2005

de Waal, Frans, *Peacemaking Among Primates*, Harvard University Press, Cambridge MA 1990

de Waal, Frans, *The Age of Empathy: Nature's Lessons for a Kinder Society*, Souvenir Press, London 2011

Wass, Sir Douglas, *Government and the Governed*, Routledge and Kegan Paul, London 1984

Young, Hugo, *The Hugo Young Papers: Thirty Years of British Politics – Off the Record*, Allen Lane, London 2008

Young, Hugo and Sloman, Anne, *But Chancellor: An Inquiry into the Treasury*, British Broadcasting Corporation, London 1984

Young, Hugo and Sloman, Anne, *No, Minister: An Inquiry into the Civil Service*, British Broadcasting Corporation, London 1982

Yourdon, Edward, *Death March*, Prentice Hall, Upper Saddle River NJ 2004

INDEX